PELICAN BOOKS

ENGLISH SOCIETY IN THE EARLY MIDDLE AGES
(1066–1307)

Lady Stenton was the wife of Sir Frank Stenton, sometime Vice-Chancellor of the University of Reading. She was educated at the Abbey School, Reading, and the University of Reading, where until 1959 she held the post of Reader. From 1923 to 1961 she was Honorary Secretary and General Editor of the Pipe Roll Society. She was an Honorary D.Litt. of Oxford University, LL.D. of Glasgow University and a Fellow of the British Academy. In 1957 she published *The English Woman in History* and in 1963 was the Jayne Lecturer for the American Philosophical Society at Philadelphia. These lectures have been printed as *English Justice from the Norman Conquest to the Great Charter*, Philadelphia 1964 and London 1965. Lady Stenton died in 1971.

DORIS MARY STENTON

ENGLISH SOCIETY IN
THE EARLY
MIDDLE AGES

‹ 1066–1307 ›

PENGUIN BOOKS

Penguin Books Ltd, Harmondsworth, Middlesex, England
Penguin Books, 625 Madison Avenue, New York, New York 10022, U.S.A.
Penguin Books Australia Ltd, Ringwood, Victoria, Australia
Penguin Books Canada Ltd, 2801 John Street, Markham, Ontario, Canada L3R 1B4
Penguin Books (N.Z.) Ltd, 182–190 Wairau Road, Auckland 10, New Zealand

—

First published 1951
Second edition 1952
Reprinted 1955, 1959
Third edition 1962
Reprinted 1964
Fourth edition 1965
Reprinted 1967, 1969, 1971, 1972, 1974,
1976, 1977. 1979, 1981

—

Made and printed in Great Britain by
Hazell Watson & Viney Ltd,
Aylesbury, Bucks
Set in Monotype Baskerville

THE PELICAN HISTORY OF ENGLAND

CONTENTS

PREFACE

THIS book is an attempt to describe the society of early medieval England without quoting evidence drawn from an earlier or later period than that to which the book relates. I have used the writings of many of my fellow labourers in the field of medieval history, but the absence of footnotes in this book prevents the acknowledgement of my debts. No acknowledgements could ever adequately express my obligation to my husband, who persuaded me to undertake this work, encouraged me to persevere in it, and helped me at every turn. But for him it would never have been written.

D. M. S.

Whitley Park Farm
 Reading

August 1950

I AM grateful to Penguin Books Ltd for allowing me to annotate this book. The notes are printed on pp. 281–98. I hope that they will enable readers to find the sources of my statements. Apart from some corrections and one additional paragraph, the text of this edition is unaltered.

D. M. S.

February 1952

To this third printing I have made a few corrections and some additions to the list of books for further reading.

D. M. S.

August 1954

A THIRD edition of this book has enabled me to rewrite some paragraphs and make corrections where recent work has thrown fresh light on old problems. In particular, I have been able to take some advantage of the remarkable work now going forward on the Anglo-Saxon and Anglo-Norman coinage, which is giving a new impression of the practical efficiency of the late Old English state. *Anglo-Saxon Coins*, ed. R. H. M. Dolley, Methuen, 1961, was published after this edition was prepared for the press. In addition to an important series of articles on the Anglo-Saxon coinage, it contains Mr P. Grierson's convincing account of the circumstances under which the term 'sterling' first came into use.

D. M. S.

5 February 1962

IN this fourth edition the pagination of the book has been changed throughout after page 20 owing to the insertion of a few paragraphs in Chapter I. In previous editions I had said little of the actual introduction of the Exchequer and the resulting changes in the administration not only of the King's finances but of his justice throughout the land. Mr Grierson's definition of the word 'sterling' as an indication of the quality of the Conqueror's English coins is now incorporated in the text. The resetting of the whole book has enabled me to make a number of minor corrections throughout, but I have not rewritten the book at any point.

D. M. S.

30 December 1964

CHAPTER I

THE KING'S HOUSEHOLD
AND GOVERNMENT

THE year 1066 is the one date which everyone knows, however unmindful of the past he may be. In that year William,
duke of Normandy, led the last effective invasion of this
island and by his conquest of it completed the racial pattern
necessary for the evolution of the society of medieval
England. He found a rich island off the coast of Europe of
which the wealth had in the previous thousand years
attracted first the Romans, then the Saxons, then the
Norsemen and Danes. The Romans saw it as a source of
minerals, slaves, and corn. Perhaps, too, they saw it as a
place where individuals ill-endowed or in debt at home
could settle on wide estates in a life as like that of the Roman
countryside as the climate allowed. The Saxons and
Angles saw it as a good land to settle in, to plant with
villages and farms, a land where a nation could be built.
The Norsemen deserting their barren land sought the same
ends. With patient labour the Anglo-Saxons had created a
rich and cultivated society. They had developed a literature
and a complicated system of local government and taxation.
The Danes and Norsemen destroyed much, but even in
destruction they contributed to the last phase of Anglo-
Saxon independence. They brought to the racial brew of
England their own determined individualism, their robust
humour, their love of legal subtleties.

The Norman followers of Duke William came to a land
of old-established traditions which were still a barrier to
true political unity. After the Danish wars of settlement the
kings of Wessex had won something more than nominal rule
over the whole land. In conquering the king of Wessex the

Danish Cnut had taken his place. In Edward the Confessor's days, on the eve of the Norman Conquest, a writer in York could pray 'that this land might remain one kingdom for ever', but it may be that he was more enlightened than his contemporaries. Even now Englishmen are in general very conscious of the past and are moved by its influence. In the eleventh century the influence of the past was even stronger. The Englishmen of the far north retaining their dim traditions of long-past glory, the Norsemen of Yorkshire with their memories of an independent kingdom of York, Mercia – the land between Oxford and Chester – with its memories of Offa's greatness in the eighth century, the half Danish shires to the east with their determined independence already deeply rooted in the land might all give recognition to the king who ruled from West Saxon England, but would be slow to give unquestioning support to one who was not strong enough either to rule or to defend them effectively.

The Norse and Danish foundation of Normandy was not a national migration like the settlement of the Danes in England. The northmen who followed Rollo to Normandy were Viking chiefs with their men whose presence in northern France was reluctantly accepted by King Charles the Simple in 911 in order to keep out others. In the next twenty-five years they were using the lands they had won as a base for winning more. The boundaries of Normandy were never stabilized until after 1204, when the duchy itself passed to the rule of the king of France. The Viking spirit remained alive. It drove out younger sons to fight in Spain and found states in southern Italy and Sicily. It drove the Duke himself to attack the rich and ancient kingdom beyond the Channel. It was sublimated in the early Crusades. In 1066 the Normans were still, in fact, a race of fighters who could more easily be brought to follow their Duke in an aggressive war than to cultivate the arts of local government at home.

William of Normandy brought no great following to England. The army which defeated Harold near Hastings was no more than 6,000 or so, and of them many were mercenaries hired for the adventure and dismissed in 1070 when the north had been cowed into quiescence and Chester had submitted. The Norman invasion was not, like the Saxon or Danish invasions, a national migration. It was an aristocratic conquest led by a man who won a kingdom for himself and distributed estates among his followers. This new aristocracy replaced the English nobility who had formed the court of the Old English kings. It soon came to dominate rural society and local government as well. But the Frenchmen, as contemporary English writers called them, were at first merely the top layer of a society in which the slow routines of the agricultural year remained the basic facts of life, and Englishmen pursued them as they had done for centuries before Hastings was fought and lost.

The Norman and Englishman of the eleventh century were in a real sense complementary to each other. The English had much written and unwritten law. They had an elaborate system of courts of justice, and pleasure in long-drawn-out litigation. The last Old English kings had a highly-trained clerical staff which the wealth of England had allowed them to recruit from the best brains of Europe. They had devised the writ, a most convenient instrument of government, for by it the king could send well authenticated information or commands about the land. The Anglo-Saxon writ was simply a letter beginning with a greeting to the person or persons to whom it was sent and telling them what the king wished them to know. The recipient knew it was genuine by the king's seal which was attached to it. The Anglo-Saxon kings had also worked out a system of national taxation which was capable of adjustment and development. They had provided themselves with the best currency in western Europe, pennies neatly designed, competently executed, and made of good silver. The work of English goldsmiths, silver smiths, and needleworkers was famous on the continent. The king had a household force of picked men trained for war and he could supplement it by summoning all free men to fight in defence of the land. But as a nation Englishmen cared more for the arts of peace than for aggressive war. They had no desire to send their ships to far waters in search of problematical adventure. Individuals found excitement enough in distant trading expeditions and in pilgrimages to Rome or Jerusalem. But they could rise with great courage to meet a national emergency and in the bleak months of 1066 they fought two great battles in the north against the last and most formidable of the Viking invaders before they met and after a hard day of fighting were with difficulty defeated by William of Normandy near Hastings.

William of Normandy won the battle of Hastings because he and his men specialized in the art of warfare, whereas the English did not. They still fought on foot, depending on resistance rather than attack and using the battle-axe as their characteristic weapon. The Normans fought on horseback. They had learned the value of archery as well as the sword and the lance. But Englishmen were slow to accept defeat and by repeated rebellions they prevented William I from creating, as he at first desired, an Anglo-Norman state in which Englishmen and Normans could work together under a Norman king recognized as the heir of the last king of the West Saxon line. Inevitably, men of English blood ceased to control affairs and by the time Domesday Book was compiled in 1086 only two of the king's leading tenants were men of English descent. Some Englishmen had gone to Scotland to serve king Malcolm, others had fled to the service of the Eastern Emperor at Constantinople. William I was an autocrat who seized the opportunity of conquest to gain a power new and unprecedented among European kings. The theory that by right all land was the king's and that land was held by others only at his gift and in return for specified service was new to English thought. It gave a new unity to England when great men accepted as axiomatic that they held their land by service performed to the king, whether the land lay in the north, the centre, or in the old West Saxon shires.

But the new lords like the king had to make the victory of

Hastings effective before they could enjoy its fruits. Before 1066, although every ancient borough was defensible, Englishmen had not learned the newer arts of castle building to which the Normans had devoted themselves. The Norman castle brought home most forcibly to the English the fact of conquest. The king himself saw to the building of a castle in every county town and generally many houses had to be destroyed to make room for it and for a clear space about it. A constable was appointed to look after the castle and command its garrison. At a number of other strategic points besides county towns castles were built and maintained at the king's expense. The first castles the Normans built in England were at Pevensey and Hastings to protect the harbours which they themselves had found vulnerable. Before 1086 Corfe castle had been built to guard Poole harbour. The significance of Dover was so apparent that a castle had been built there before the Conquest. Windsor, a hill which commanded the Thames roughly midway between London and the county town of Wallingford, was a natural defensive site. Moreover, William I allowed his men a free hand in the building of private castles to defend their new lands, for in the first years after Hastings his interests and theirs were one.

In construction these Norman castles have a deceptive simplicity which generally hides great skill in the choice and the use of the site. The general plan of almost all of them is the same, a mound of earth called a motte, generally with a ditch around it, and a courtyard or bailey below it, also enclosed with a ditch and bank. Occasionally, as at Peak castle in Derbyshire, the site chosen was so precipitous that the usual motte was not necessary. In the first period after the Conquest these castles were very primitive buildings. A stockade round the bailey formed the outer defence. The ditch round the motte was filled with water and bridged across. The bridge could be drawn up when the castle was besieged and the bailey had been taken by storm. Like the bailey, the motte was defended by a stockade. Wooden huts within the bailey, the spaces between the uprights filled with wattle and daub, housed the first generation of the conquerors. It was impossible to build in stone on mounds newly made, nor was stone for building often ready to hand. The Tower of London and the keep of Colchester belong to this age, but London was of particular importance, and at Colchester the bricks of the Roman city were there to use; perhaps, too, the builders were tempted to experiment by the signs of the rectangular Roman building on the site where the castle stands. The king expected his greater barons to secure their lands by building castles at their chief places of residence. In this way, by means of royal and baronial castles, the land was pinned down and revolt was hopeless before it had well begun.

The fortunate survival of the Bayeux Tapestry, which was made to commemorate the conquest less than ten years after the actual battle of Hastings, has preserved in skilful needlework a lively picture of the main events leading to the end of Anglo-Saxon England. Limitations of needlework and the inability of the artist to cope with problems of perspective do little to diminish the value of the work as a contemporary representation of masculine society in regard to building and dress, armour, furniture, and meals. The castles of Dol, Rennes, Dinan, and Bayeux are shown as almost exaggerated mottes. At Dol, Dinan, and Bayeux the bridge over the moat or ditch between the motte and the bailey is painstakingly portrayed. At Bayeux the Duke is about to ride his horse over the bridge. The feast after the dangerous Channel crossing is depicted from the catching of the animals to the flushed repletion of the Duke and his half-brothers on a seat just big enough for three. Some of the meat was cooked in a cauldron hanging on a bar between forked stakes. The fire beneath it appears to be made in an iron receptacle on legs. Another fire was made on the ground below a large cauldron on three short legs with a ring on each side of the rim. Serving-men are handing spits with meat to the men who set the table for the feast, putting the meat in bowls before each place. A man with a horn seems to be summoning the Duke to the feast. In the next picture the Duke and his chief men are seen sitting before the table set with bowls of food and shallow cups of wine. They are waiting while the bishop of Bayeux, the king's half-brother, says grace. A servant with bended knee is holding a bowl while a cloth is draped over his arm – that is, a finger bowl and cloth for wiping off the stains of food.

The circumstances of the feast pictured on the Tapestry were often reproduced at the ever-moving court of the Norman kings of England. William I was constantly moving about the land, mainly to secure the obedience of remote parts, partly to save the expense of sending the produce of royal manors about the country, and partly also to enjoy hunting in the royal forests. Many of his meals therefore must have been in the nature of highly organized and rather formal picnics. On a smaller scale the same is true of his magnates. All of them had manors scattered in many shires and none of them remained constantly in one. All through the period with which this book deals there was an ever-moving stream of traffic on the roads of England; great men, their families and retinues, moving from manor to manor. William I made a practice of holding three great feasts a year at which he wore his crown and entertained in state his bishops, abbots, earls, and barons with a great crowd of knights attendant on them. At Easter the party met at Winchester, at Whitsuntide at Westminster, and at Christmas at Gloucester. These were the great social occasions of the year, but they were much more than that. A contemporary writer stresses the fact that foreign ambassadors were invited to attend these ceremonies. They were also, and primarily, the times at which the magnates met the king in council. In a feudal state all authority ultimately lay with the king, who was expected to act with the advice of his great council of tenants-in-chief. These three great feasts were thus the relaxation and reward of the men who had come from all parts of the land to prove their loyalty to the king by their presence at his court, to hear about such plans as he might wish to talk over with them, and to act when need arose as the highest court of justice in the land.

These solemn feasts in the hall of Westminster, Winchester, or Gloucester were the high-lights of the social year in the Conqueror's reign; the occasions that the chroniclers wrote about, when public business was openly discussed before the whole body of the king's great men whom it concerned. The making of the Domesday survey was ordered at the Christmas feast and Council of 1085. What happened on other days than these great festivals is in some ways more interesting, both because the life of the court was very like that led in other great households, and because it was the king and the people who were with him from day to day who really governed England. Of necessity William I's court was an armed camp as it moved about the country to impress the fact of conquest upon Englishmen. It was the austerity of his character and his love of hunting that his English subjects noticed most about him. His son and successor William II was as great a hunter as his father and it was while he was hunting in the New Forest that he was 5 'shot with an arrow from among his own men'. Henry I, the Conqueror's youngest son, succeeded his brother and, after he had suppressed a serious baronial revolt, ruled the land in peace for more than thirty years. A generation of peace meant an easing of strains in court and country alike and allowed Englishmen and Normans to feel themselves a single nation.

Walter Map, a member of the court of Henry II, grandson of Henry I, wrote a book about court life as he had known it, and, looking back on the days of Henry I from the end of his grandson's reign, he stresses the contrast between the ease and friendliness of Henry I's court and the uncertainties and changes of his own day. Walter Map praises the wise and controlled generosity of Henry I, whose household was governed by customs written down by his 6 orders. Walter describes how arrangements for its transport and the places at which it would stop were made far ahead and known to all, so that there was always enough to eat, how the great men who came to his court had their accustomed allowances, as did all of his household. 'If we can believe our fathers,' he says, 'his age can be called the age of Saturn, ours, of Jove,' by which he means that Henry I's court was ruled over by a kindly and sympathetic head and Henry II's by an incalculable power. In Henry I's day it was like a fair wherever the king moved, for the route which the court would take and the places it would stop at were planned far ahead; foreigners as well as Englishmen came to it and found many merchants and ample wares. The old, and men of dignity and wisdom who desired audience of the king were summoned before dinner; after the midday meal those who were there for pleasure were admitted. 'The court was a school of virtue and wisdom before dinner, after it a place of companionship and respectful mirth.' Elsewhere in his book Walter Map again 7 makes all these points about Henry I's court, saying that the young men of his household were not allowed access to him before dinner nor the old after, 'unless they were there at his wish that they might learn or teach'.   8

'Who,' says Walter Map, 'can conceal the little jests of so merry and gracious a man, not so much the emperor or king as the father of England?' The king's chamberlain, Pain fitz John, every night took a single measure of wine in case the king was thirsty during the night, and he never asked for it more than once or twice a year, so that Pain and the servants often safely drank it all early in the night. One night the king looked for the wine and it was not there. Pain got up and called the servants but found nothing. The king caught them hunting for the wine and not finding it. 'What's this,' said he, to a trembling and fearful Pain, 'do you not always have wine ready?' Pain timidly replied: 'Yes, my lord, every night a single measure, but you are so rarely thirsty that we drink it either late at night or after we have slept awhile, and having told the truth we throw ourselves on your mercy.' Then the king said 'Do you get no more than one measure a night?' 'No' said Pain. 'That,' said the king, 'was very little for the two of us; in future get two measures from the butlers every night, one for you and one for me.' Pain fitz John was one of those to whom 9 personal service to the king brought a rich reward. A contemporary chronicler records that Henry I specially favoured him. He was given extensive lands in Herefordshire. His daughter and heiress married the son of another of Henry I's young men, Miles of Gloucester, whom the king's daughter, Maud, made earl of Hereford. The great earthwork in Radnorshire still known as Painscastle preserves his name today.

Henry I looked out for talent and gathered about him able men – described somewhat unfairly by a contemporary chronicler named Orderic as 'of low origin, whom for their obsequious services he raised to the rank of nobles'. Orderic names some of these faithful servants of the crown, but at this point omits the greatest of them, Roger, a clerk from Avranches, whom the king brought to England early in his reign and appointed as his Chancellor. Roger held this office for about a year but before the end of September 1102 he had been chosen by the king as bishop of Salisbury and had given up the chancellorship to undertake the more onerous duty of supervising the king's finances. It was bishop Roger who introduced from the mathematical schools of northern France a more elaborate calculating machine or abacus than had been used in the English kings' treasury in Saxon days. Edith the wife of Edward the Confessor could use the 'one stringed abacus', that is a string of beads, for adding and subtraction. More difficult operations could be performed only by the use of counters on a chequered cloth. Clerks needed some mechanical aid even to do simple sums, for arabic numerals were unknown as yet in England and it was impossible easily to add up a column of figures set out in Roman numerals. They are not only cumbersome but have the additional weakness of providing no figure or device to indicate that nothing is to be added to a column of figures. At least by the year 1110 the sheriffs were attending twice yearly at an office already known as the Exchequer to render account to the king's ministers of the money they had previously paid in the royal Treasury. Late in the reign of Henry II bishop Roger's great-nephew, Richard fitz

Nigel, the royal Treasurer, described in detail the Exchequer and its work. There can be no doubt that the oblong exchequer table which he described, with a ledge around it to prevent the counters falling off, covered by a chequered cloth bought new every year, and surrounded by benches to accommodate the chairman at the head faced by the sheriff at the foot of the table, and the clerks along one side of the table opposite the calculators along the other side was the plan laid down by the great originator, Roger, bishop of Salisbury.

The other chief ministers and household officers of the king, the Chancellor, the Treasurer, the two chamberlains, the constable and the marshal each had his appropriate seat at the exchequer board and there was room for other men sent by the king to oversee or take part in the work. In bishop Roger's day he must himself have occupied the chair. His only recorded official title – *Regni Angliae Procurator* – indicates the overriding importance of his financial duties, but he himself was generally described in his own writs as bishop of Salisbury, although the manner in which he wrote to others and was addressed by them indicates his pre-eminent position in the land. Only the king was his superior and after the queen's death in 1118 and in the king's absence he ruled the land as regent. When Richard fitz Nigel described the Exchequer in Henry II's reign its chairman was the Chief Justiciar, but there is no sign that this title was used in the reign of Henry I. Nevertheless the establishment of the exchequer board at which all the king's chief ministers were bound to meet in solemn session twice a year had created a new centre of government. Long before Henry I's death it had become a court of justice as well as an accounting office. Its officers were described by the king as 'My barons of the Exchequer' and its proceedings were recorded in rolls. One roll and one only, that of 1130, has survived from Henry I's reign, the first of a noble series which ends only in 1832. 12

The great rolls of the exchequer is the proper title of this long run of records, but in familiar speech they soon became known as the Pipe rolls, for rolled up and packed away into their cupboards at Westminster they had very much the appearance of a stack of pipes. The fortunate survival of the Pipe roll of 31 Henry I for the year 1130 makes plain how dynamically the Anglo-Norman kingdom has developed under its first three Norman kings. England has become a centralized realm. The king has in his service a body of judges who are sent in groups of two or three to sit in every shire and hear both criminal and civil pleas. The evidence of this first Pipe roll supports, and is itself supported by that of individual chroniclers and a large and increasing number 13 of isolated writs and charters.

All these contemporary sources taken together display an elaborately ordered kingdom in which, under the general oversight of the king and his other self, Roger bishop of Salisbury, a 'Justiciar of all England' was in charge of a highly efficient judicial machine. The first holder of this office was probably Ralf Basset, who was succeeded in 1127 by his son Richard. The surname Basset recurred for many generations among the royal judges. The judges who went out from the king's court to visit the shires were supported by local judges who were responsible for hearing pleas of the crown in the counties to which they were appointed. In this position they enjoyed some measure of control over the sheriffs who presided in the ancient shire and hundred courts of the Saxon days where much of the nation's litigation still had its place.

But the Exchequer even at the end of Henry I's reign was still essentially a department of the royal household and it was still the king and his household which governed the land. The accuracy of Walter Map's description of the court and the life the king and his servants led is strikingly borne out by a document which comes from the earliest 14 years of Henry I's successor, King Stephen. It was probably written as a guide to the new king about court customs and the pay and allowances individual members of the court, both high and low, were accustomed to receive. It shows that the royal household was organized in three main divisions, the chapel, the hall, and the chamber, with two subordinate departments, under the marshal and the constables, responsible for the order and safety of the court and the control and employment of the outdoor servants. The account begins with the chapel, of which the chief officer was the Chancellor. He received the largest daily salary of anyone in the king's service, 5 shillings a day, one loaf of the best quality and 2 ordinary loaves, one measure of the best wine and one of ordinary wine, one wax candle and 40 candle ends. This allowance of bread, wine, and candles was the perquisite intended for the sustenance and comfort of the recipient in his private chamber of an evening, additional to the two meals a day which he ate at the king's expense and table. The chancellor's second-in-command was called the master of the writing office, who 'at first' had '10 pence a day, one ordinary loaf, half a measure of ordinary wine, a large candle, and 12 candle ends. But king Henry so increased Robert de Sigillo that on the day the king died he had 2 shillings a day, one measure of ordinary wine, one little wax candle, and 24 candle ends.'

These two men were evidently very much more than mere household officers. The Lord Chancellor of modern days is the direct successor of the Chancellor of the Norman kings. In the twelfth century the idea of public service distinct from service to the king was far in the future. The great officer of state of later days was still a household servant in daily attendance on the king, keeping his seal in his own custody and personally responsible for its use. The master of the writing office is the twelfth-century parallel to the head of the civil service today. Already in the second generation after the conquest the work of the king's clerks has so much increased that the head of the office has had his salary raised.

'The document goes on to say that the chaplain who keeps the chapel and relics has the allowance of two men, that there were four servants of the chapel each with double food, and two pack horses each with a penny a day and a penny a month for shoeing. For the service of the chapel two wax candles were allowed on Wednesday, and one on Saturday, and one to burn every night before the relics and 30 candle ends. A gallon of the best wine was allowed for mass and on Holy Thursday a measure of ordinary wine was allowed to wash the altar. On Easter Day one measure of the best wine and one of ordinary wine were allowed for the communion. These arrangements were not lavish for the private chapel of the king. It went about with him on his travels, carried on two pack horses. Its porterage was still being managed in the same way in king John's reign. His annual accounts have for several years in succession a payment for a pair of panniers for the king's 15 chapel. In the king's lodgings the king's clerks sat at their work behind a screen which separated them from the people in the hall, but they were ready at a call to write the documents, the writs or charters, which the business of the day demanded. The name of the head of the office, the Chancellor, comes from the Latin word *cancella*, a screen. Every baronial household of the day had its chapel, simpler, but modelled on the same lines as the king's. In every noble household there was certainly a clerk whose duty it was to look after his master's seal and to write his business and personal letters. He must have been as necessary a member of the day to day retinue of the baron as the chancellor was 16 of the king's.

The central point in every household, whether royal, baronial, or that of the simple country gentleman, was the hall, where meals were served and the public life of the household was passed. Two officials of equal standing presided over the two departments which provided the necessities of daily life in the hall, food and drink, the steward and the master butler. Each had as daily payment the same as the Chancellor if he ate outside the house, that is 5 shillings, but if, like the Chancellor every day, these officers ate within the house they received only 3 shillings and 6 pence, two ordinary loaves, one measure of ordinary wine, and a full allowance of candle. They were in fact on a considerably lower rate of pay than the Chancellor. The steward's responsibility, food, was dealt with in two parallel offices, the pantry and the larder. There were two master despensers, one of bread and the other of the larder, each with 2 shillings and 10 pence a day, one ordinary loaf, one measure of ordinary wine, one small candle and 24 candle ends if they ate outside the house, but with 2 shillings only, and half a measure of ordinary wine and a full allowance of candle if they ate within the house. In both the pantry and larder there were a number of despensers who took turns to serve, receiving 19 pence a day plus their allowances if they ate out and 10 pence plus allowances if they ate in the house. Also attached to the pantry was the man who looked after the cloths, whose predecessor appears on the Bayeux Tapestry armed with his bowl and napkin. He had customary food, 3 halfpence a day for his man, a penny for his pack horse and a penny a month for shoeing. The usher, the man who looked after the pantry door, had the same except for the pack horse, and the man who counted the loaves had customary food. The larder door, too, had its usher with the same allowance as his opposite number in the pantry. The larder maintained 4 slaughterers who had customary food only; the pantry four bakers, two of them working in the bakery and two going out to purchase flour for the bread. There was a man who made wafers, and there was a man to look after the tables. He had a pack horse with its livery. 'The bearer of the alms dish shall eat in the house.' The royal kitchens must have been scenes of great activity. The document enumerates a number of cooks and other kitchen workers, each of whom apparently had a man whose daily wage was 3 halfpence. The cook of the king's privy servants stands out among the rest, for he received the same pay and allowances as the despensers. Attached to the great kitchen, where the meals for the vast daily crowd who fed at the king's expense were cooked, was also the servant who received the venison as the hunters brought it to the hall.

The sequence of officials and offices was much the same in the butler's sphere. The master despensers of the cellar had the same allowances as their fellows of the pantry and larder, except that, as the document says, 'they had more candle'. There were, as in the kitchen, an usher and a number of men with 'customary food and three halfpence for their man'. Some of them were responsible for providing the receptacles for the wine and beer, the 'hose' and the butts, some were simply workmen. There were 4 cup bearers serving in turn, each with his man; a fruiterer, and a carter, who had customary food and livery for his horses.

Everyone, king or magnate, freeman or serf, regarded his bedroom as the safest place in his house and kept his treasures there. It was in the king's chamber that the Treasury had its origins and in this first description of the king's household beside the master chamberlain, who is the first officer of the chamber, is the Treasurer, who, the writer says, 'has the same allowance if he is in the court and serves in the Treasury'. By this date the Exchequer had become a firmly established institution. One of the nephews of bishop Roger of Salisbury, Nigel bishop of Ely, was treasurer, and the document seems to be implying that he received his 5 shillings a day while the Exchequer was in session and that he was employed there, wherever the king himself with his immediate household might be. After the Treasurer, the document mentions one of the chamberlains by name, William Mauduit, who had 14 pence a day and 'continuously eats in the house and has one large candle, 13 pieces of candle, and 2 packhorses with their livery. The porter of the king's bed eats in the house and has 3 halfpence for his man and a packhorse with his livery. The chamberlain who serves in turn has 2 shillings a day. . . . "The chamberlain of the candle" has 8 pence a day. The king's tailor eats in the house and has 3 halfpence for his man. The chamberlain without livery eats in the house if he wishes. The ewerer has double food and when the king goes a journey a penny for drying his clothes, and when the king has a bath 3 pence, except on the three great feasts of the year. Touching the laundress there is a doubt.'

There is a curious mixture of simplicity and formal

splendour in these arrangements. The charter by which Henry I in 1133 granted the office of 'master chamberlain of all England' to Aubrey de Ver has survived in a facsimile copy. The king made this grant to Aubrey 'in fee and inheritance with all the dignities and liberties and honours which belonged to it'. In 1141 Aubrey became earl of [17] Oxford. The master chamberlain was a great man, far too great a man to perform menial services even about the bedchamber of a king. His successor today is the Lord Great Chamberlain. The office of Lord Great Chamberlain continued in the family of Ver, descendants of the first earl, until 1625 when the direct succession came to an end. [18] William Mauduit, who ate continuously in the house, was a baron whom the king wished to have with him but did not expect to concern himself with domestic duties. Presumably the man who saw that the bed was made was the usher of the chamber who is entered towards the end of this document among the workmen and serjeants. He had 4 pence a day for the king's bed every day when the king went a journey. The king's bed was probably a fine feather bed, which with appropriate coverings of linen sheets, rugs, and furs travelled slung across the back of a packhorse. The man who looked after the curtains and hangings, presumably those for both the hall and the chamber, ate in the house, and when the hangings had to be carried about had an allowance for a man and a horse. By taking with the king's travelling household a sufficiency of tapestry or plain curtains a primitive building could be transformed into a dignified setting for the king. The king's tailor and his men were only a small staff for looking after the king's clothes. A single officer was responsible for drying them when they got wet and for providing the infrequent royal baths. At this date there seems to have been some doubt whether there was anyone retained to do the washing at all.

The earliest household accounts which have survived come from the reign of king John. They show the precise [19] number of the baths which king John took between 29 January, 1209 and 26 May, 1210. Over seventy years have passed since the description of the household of Henry I was drawn up and in the interval the ewerer, who originally merely had 'double food', has acquired the daily wage of a halfpenny. Between 29 January and 17 June he was paid 5 shillings and 10 pence for 140 days. The price of the king's bath has gone up, too. Except on the three great feasts of the year when he paid nothing, Henry I paid 3 pence for his bath. In 1209 William the ewerer was paid '4 pence for a bath made for the lord king at Marlborough, 5 pence for another bath made at Northampton, 5 pence halfpenny for a third bath made at Nottingham, 5 pence for a fourth bath made at Gloucester, 5 pence halfpenny for a fifth bath made at Bristol, 5 pence for a sixth bath made at Bramber, 5 pence halfpenny for a seventh bath made at Aldington'. But the eighth and last bath of the six months' account cost the king only 2 pence. On 3 November at Nottingham William was again paid at the rate of a halfpenny a day for the 140 days from 18 June to 4 November. He was also paid 'for the bath made for the lord king at Marlborough 5 pence, for another bath at Nottingham 5 pence halfpenny, for a third bath at Northampton 5 pence halfpenny, for a fourth bath at Gloucester 5 pence halfpenny'. William was not paid again until late in May 1210, when for the period 5 November to 26 May he received 8 shillings and 6 pence halfpenny. At the same time he was paid 6 shillings and 1 penny for 'eleven baths for the use of the lord king'. The places where king John enjoyed them are not given in detail. From other evidence John seems to have been particularly interested in clothes and jewels, so that it may be fair to assume that he had a higher standard of personal cleanliness than many of his contemporaries. By this date the 'doubt' about the laundress has been settled, for Florence the laundress periodically received, like the other humble members of the household, 18 pence for shoes.

There remain to be described those two interlocking departments of the constable and the marshal. Three constables are mentioned by name. Their salary and allowances were the same as the steward's and so was that of the master marshal, John. While the constables were responsible for the protection of the household and the control of royal forces in time of war, the marshal had duties more intimately connected with the king's daily life and routine. He had to keep all the receipts of the payment of gifts and allowances from the king's treasure and chamber. His subordinates, also called marshals, were responsible for arranging lodgings for the whole court as it moved about the land. They were often sent as messengers by the king. The document notes that they are paid 8 pence a day if they are on the king's business away from the court but only 3 pence a day when they are with the household. The miscellaneous crowd of necessary workers – ushers, watchmen, 20 serjeants, huntsmen – all are gathered up into this department, for the marshal was responsible for the order and comfort of the court as the constable was for its safety. There was a man called the hearthman, *focarius*, who always ate in the house and from Michaelmas to Easter had 4 pence a day for making the fire in the hall. The usher of the chamber and the man who looked after the curtains have already been mentioned. There were 4 hornblowers who had 3 pence a day each, a rate which recognizes that some skill went to their blowing. Huntsmen were more highly paid, the knights among them 8 pence a day, hunters of the wild cat, 5 pence. The archers who carried the king's bow had 5 pence, as did the other archers.

These varying rates of daily pay in pennies raise the question as to the real value of the rewards which the king gave his servants for their daily tasks about his person and court. The silver penny was the only coin minted at this date, a small thin coin of good silver with the king's head and name on one side of it and the name of the moneyer who made the coin and the place where he made it on the other. Modern discussions of this period often suggest that coined money was scarce, but the Pipe rolls, the annual accounts of the English kings, which survive from about the middle of the twelfth century, show how substantial was the volume of actual coined pennies in circulation at that time. To attempt to equate the pounds, shillings, and pence of the twelfth centry with those of pre-war days is an almost hopeless task, but as a rough guide it is perhaps permissible to regard twelfth-century money as from fifteen to twenty times as valuable as its early twentieth-century counterpart. If the higher rate is taken, a huntsman with his 5 pence a day and his food was reasonably well paid even by modern standards, while the Chancellor with his 5 shillings a day was in receipt of a dignified remuneration.

To estimate the real value of the food and lodging these royal servants enjoyed is equally difficult. The enforced simplicity of life and the scarcity of goods made for high prices. Everything was scarce. The widespread love of hunting had a solid economic basis in the endless search for food. The great royal forests up and down the land where game was strictly preserved for the king's hunting played an important part in feeding the vast household which daily looked to the king for meat. Enough had to be provided for two main meals a day, leaving enough over to be salted down against the winter. Salt was dear because it was a necessity of life. It was provided by salt-pans on the coast and by the salt works of Worcester and Cheshire. Salters' carts taking their wares to the main centres of trade were a feature of the period. Pepper and the spices of the East were dear, for they were scarce. The peppercorn rent, which today means something purely nominal, goes back to the time when men were very glad to take a rent in pepper. The importance of such fresh-water fish as pike, roach, bream, and dace and the high esteem in which eels and lampreys were held were not caused merely by the necessity of providing food for the fast days of the Church. Such things were an essential supplement to the meat, game, and fowl which most men preferred. The earliest account rolls of the royal household show that at that date, 1209, king John was accustomed to pay 9 shillings and four pence halfpenny to 100 poor men when 'he ate twice on a Friday', doubtless eating meat or fowl because he wearied of fish. In 1212 he spent 27 shillings and 1 penny on one 24 occasion feeding 100 poor men with bread, meat, and ale for the soul of his father and another 100 because Geoffrey fitz Peter and William Briwerre ate meat on that same Wednesday. Such vegetables and fruit as the seasons offered were of poor quality. At the beginning of the period honey provided what sweetening there was, although in 1176 Henry II bought for his own use 34 pounds of sugar at the rate of 25 9 pence a pound. It is very rarely mentioned and must have been exceedingly scarce. John spent £3 on sugar and 26 other spices in 1206. During the thirteenth century luxuries of this sort seem to have become somewhat more accessible with the increase of trade, but they remained out of reach of all but the rich.

The men who served in the king's household were in a real sense a race apart, an aristocracy of service, protected from the harsh austerities of medieval life. All the greater offices and many of the less important ones as well secured to their fortunate holders not merely a daily wage, food, and allowances, but an estate in land. In the generations immediately after 1066 the king had more land at his free disposal than at any other period in English history. He needed an infinite variety of service about his court and his person, for his hunting and his wars. It was easy for him to give a manor in return for some specific service and by the time of Domesday Book in nearly every county a number of men called 'servants of the king' were holding land in return for some personal service to him. It was a transitory phase in national development, for it proved an unnecessarily lavish way of reward. William I cannot have known at all accurately the value of the land he gave out so readily in early days. As the twelfth century wore on such grants became fewer and by the end of it have almost ceased. Their place has been taken by the grant of an annual sum of money payable either from the farm of a shire by the sheriff or direct from the Exchequer. But the practice of establishing serjeanties was in full vigour when the royal household 27 was taking shape.

From the first the highest household officers performed their menial tasks only on great feast days, when, as their fee, they received some of the instruments of their labour. At the time when this description was written the chief butler was William de Aubigny, who had been given the office by Henry I together with substantial Norfolk lands. He married the widow of the king himself and was later raised to the earldom of Arundel. Such a man would not serve daily as butler. But when the king was crowned and the great coronation feast was held in splendour these officers wished, and indeed insisted on their right, to perform 28 their duty to the king. There exists a careful description of all the arrangements for the coronation in 1236 of Eleanor queen of Henry III. On that day the chief butler, the earl of Arundel, was under sentence of excommunication. The earl Warenne served in his place as chief butler and after the banquet had as his fee the cup which he had handed filled with wine to the king at the feast. Beside the earl Warenne there served master Michael Belet, who handed the earl the cup filled with wine for the king. As his fee he had the earl's robe. The mayor of London claimed to stand before the king in master Michael's place, but the king rejected the claim, saying that no one ought by right to 29 serve there but master Michael, so that the mayor served the two bishops who sat beside the king. Michael was descended from the John Belet who in Henry I's day was holding the manor of Sheen, or Richmond, in Surrey, in return for butler-service. Michael Belet was a judge and held Oxfordshire lands as well as the Surrey manor. He could not serve daily in the king's hall. It is significant that after the coronation feast in 1236 he gave his own robe to his kinsman Henry de Capella 'who was wont on other days in the year to serve the king with his cup'. The record adds that Michael was not bound to make this gift had he not wished to do so. Other services about the king's cellar and butlery carried with them estates in land. The man responsible for transporting the 'hoses' of wine, receptacles shaped rather like a Wellington boot but capable of being closed up for transport, held the manor of Creswell in the parish of Bray in Berkshire by that service. The office of usher in the butlery was held by the Kivilli family whose land lay in Essex, and the duty of buying the king's beer was rewarded 30 by a small estate at West Hendred in Berkshire. Offices about the king's household were hereditary with the land that went with them, but the king always extracted a present from the heir before he was allowed to enjoy his inheritance or exercise his right to perform his inherited service.

But such concrete rewards as money, food, allowances, and land were by no means the end of advantages which the men about the court enjoyed. Walter Map, writing at the very end of Henry II's reign, told the story of a quarrel between Thurstan the despenser and Adam of Yarmouth, whose duty it was to put the seal on official documents. Thurstan wanted a writ sealed free of charge, but Adam refused to do it for him because Thurstan had refused to let Adam have two of the king's cakes when he had guests. Henry II himself intervened to stage a reconciliation scene in which Thurstan with bended knee handed two cakes becomingly enveloped in a napkin to Adam, who handed him the document duly sealed. The king declared that his ministers should not only serve him to the best of their ability but also serve one another. 31

The king himself was a good and considerate master, providing not merely wages and food but clothes also for his servants. The Pipe rolls of the early thirteenth century show that he was generous in his gifts of robes to members of his household and chaplains in royal castles about the land. These robes were all-enveloping garments of thick cloth suitable to protect their wearers from the draughts in contemporary halls and churches. Academic robes are the stylized successors of the robes that all who could afford them owned in the twelfth, thirteenth, and fourteenth centuries. In the early years of the thirteenth century such garments for household servants cost from 25 to 28 shillings apiece, although 13 shillings and 4 pence appears to have

32 sufficed for a chaplain on occasion. Robes are not mentioned in the description of Henry I's household arrangements, but before the end of the period covered by this book the amount which each member of the household should have for robes was nicely graded in accordance with his rank in the king's service. Masters and knights expected to have robes with squirrel's fur on them. Lesser men had to be content with rabbit fur. Edward I issued an ordinance for his household in 1279 which shows the departmental heads such as the steward and the marshal receiving for robes 8 marks, that is £5 6s. 8d., and lesser officials 3 marks, or 33 sometimes 3 marks and a half, £2 or £2 6s. 8d. a year. In 1318 in the days of Edward's son, Edward II, a far fuller ordinance for the king's household was drawn up. It defines with precision the rights and perquisites of each officer and the number of subordinates he is allowed to maintain at the king's expense and the perquisites of each of them. By this date the organization is far more elaborate, food is more plentiful, and clothes are dearer. Rank is carefully defined. A banneret received 16 marks a year in two equal portions for his robes, a simple knight received 8 marks. The two clerks who sat at the accounting table received 2 robes a year in cloth or 46 shillings and 8 pence. Grooms in the various departments received one cloth robe a year or one 34 mark, that is 13 shillings and 4 pence. The ordinances of Edward I and his son are careful to say that clerks shall receive an actual wage in money only until the king has 'advanced' them, that is, provided them with a benefice at the expense of the Church.

The description of the king's household of about 1135, the account rolls of 1209, and the ordinances of 1279 and 1318 mark the stages in the development of the king's household during this period. The description of Henry I's household was written down just in time to preserve an impression of the original simplicity of organization while revealing the way in which the great departments of state arose there. In 1135, although the Exchequer has been set up to control the collection of the king's income and keep his accounts, those who sat about the Exchequer board were still regarded as members of his household. The Treasurer, although he had no strictly household duties, was a household officer. Of the Chancellor and the Chancery the same is true. By 1209 things were very different. The Exchequer was a department of state in almost permanent session at Westminster Hall, with a subordinate department, the Treasury, each of them entirely separate from the household. The only connexion that remained was the right which household officers retained, but rarely exercised, to a seat at the Exchequer board. The king was still the effective head of the state and his household the centre of policy. The Chancellor was in constant attendance on him and Chancery clerks were ever at hand to write and seal the necessary documents. But the Chancery, too, had outgrown its place in the king's hall. Its head was a great magnate with affairs of his own to order. From 1199 to 1205 the archbishop of Canterbury himself, Hubert Walter, was Chancellor. In his time the practice of keeping office copies of documents issued by the Chancery began and the great series of Chancery records soon came to rival the records of the Exchequer itself.

The peace and order of Henry I's reign died with the king. He left no legitimate son, and his nephew Stephen, who seized the throne, was ill-fitted to the position. 'Of outstanding skill in arms, but in other things almost an idiot, except that he was more inclined towards evil,' is how Walter Map describes him. The attempt of Maud, daughter of Henry I, to acquire the throne failed, for she was too haughty to win and keep the loyalty and affection which alone could have secured recognition of a woman's claim to rule. Walter Map says of her: 'Daughter of the best of princes and of the holy queen Maud and mother of a good king, she herself was the very worst between good men.' Her attempt brought civil war. Apart from the 35 devastation to which her claim gave rise, the whole land missed the guidance and control of a strong king. Stephen gave away lands, titles, and royal rights to gain support.

Maud did the same. The sheriffs failed to collect the royal revenue and the Exchequer ceased to function. Itinerant Justices no longer visited the shires to hear pleas and keep the whole land in touch with the crown. In 1153, disheartened by the death of his eldest son, Eustace, and wearied by his efforts to force his will on a reluctant baronage, Stephen was ready to make terms with Maud's son, Henry. A rich endowment was secured for William count of Boulogne, Warenne, and Mortain, Stephen's 36 younger son. The succession to the throne was transferred to Henry, who in the next year became king as Henry II.

His accession brought England to a leading place among European powers, for he was already in right of his mother Duke of Normandy, by inheritance from his father Count of Anjou and Maine, and by right of his wife Duke of Aquitaine. His lands stretched from the Solway Firth to the Pyrenees. His court was a place to which the able and ambitious were inevitably drawn. Everyone was conscious of relief and joy when he became king. He was a young man of twenty whom Walter Map describes as of middle height, handsome and good to look at, unsurpassed in agility and reasonably literate. He understood every tongue spoken between the Channel and the river Jordan, speaking Latin as easily as French. Wise in drafting laws and correcting the government of the state, a subtle deviser of the unaccustomed or concealed judgement, he was affable, modest, and humble. He was always travelling about on intolerable daily journeys which seemed twice the normal length and he was merciless in this to his household which followed him. He was most skilled in regards to hounds and birds and most eager for that sport. He worked far into the night. Those about him ascribed his perpetual labours to fear of getting 37 too fat.

This zest and energy was in violent contrast to the lethargic government of his predecessor. A jury of Henry III's reign giving a verdict about the tenure of a small property in Warwickshire told a story which shows how humble people were affected by the personality of the king. The jurors said that in king Stephen's war an itinerant soldier called Warin of Walcote passed through the dwelling of Robert of Shuckburgh who had a daughter named Isabel. Warin loved her and took her. Robert refused to give him Isabel as his wife and he could not have her both because of Robert himself and because of Robert's son, William, who was a soldier. But William went out to fight and was killed in the war. When he heard this Warin came with a multitude of men and took Isabel away by force and held her for a long time. 'At length, after the death of king Stephen, when the peace of king Henry was proclaimed, Warin fell into poverty because he could not rob as he used to do, but he could not refrain from robbery and he went everywhere and robbed as he used. And King Henry, having heard complaints about him, ordered that he should be taken. At length, when he was sought out and ambushed, he came and hid himself at Grandborough in a certain reedy place and there he was taken and led before the king at Northampton, and king Henry that he might set an example to others to keep his peace, by the counsel of his barons ordered him to be put in the pillory and there he was put and there he died.' 38 Isabel went back home, married again and had a son. Her first love story has been rescued from oblivion because her descendants by her two husbands quarrelled about the ownership of the 4 virgates of land which had formed Robert of Shuckburgh's modest estate.

Walter Map could find little to blame in Henry II, for no one, he said, could be more gracious and affable than the king or bear more patiently the jostling crowds. He did nothing for pride's sake, but was sober, modest, and pious, faithful, wise and generous. Nevertheless, owing, as Map says, to his mother's teaching, he protracted business to such an extent that before their case was dealt with many died or were forced by hunger to withdraw from the court, 'sad and empty'. Another of his faults was that when he stayed in a place, which he rarely did, he did not show himself abroad as his good people wished, but in inner chambers he was generous to those who seemed unworthy of it. Stephen's 39 reign had shown how necessary to the welfare of everyone was a strong king. The years after his death passed in a turmoil of business. Henry II wasted no time, but there was so much to do, so many law suits arising from the days of anarchy which only the king could settle, so much land and so many royal rights granted away by Stephen which the king must recover, that inevitably justice seemed slow. If the king stayed long in one place in those early days it was because business kept him there. Moreover, he had always to keep in mind his lands across the Channel. The French king was watching them closely, ready to take advantage of any weakening in the hold of the English king. For just over a year from his coronation on 19 December Henry was moving about in England, in the midlands, the north, and the west country, forcing men who had built private castles in the previous reign to destroy them and dealing with such public enemies as Warin of Walcote. But in January 1156 he went to Normandy. He was bound to do homage to his overlord, the king of France, and he found himself obliged there to make war upon his own discontented brother. It was not until the spring of 1157 that he was free to return to England, and in the summer he opened war upon the Welsh. When that was over the king again showed himself in many parts of the land, the far north, both Carlisle and Newcastle, the midlands, the south and the west, before his affairs took him to Normandy in August 1158. During this visit to France Henry was obliged in 1159 to make war upon the count of Toulouse.

It is against this background of political distraction that his people saw the king. A very curious document has survived from the early years of the reign in which a pertinacious litigant called Richard of Anstey has set down how much he spent and how many horses he and his messengers killed in following up his suit for the inheritance 40 of his uncle William. It shows the king's court from the angle of a subject who must do business there. Richard had one important fact in his favour: he was a leading tenant of Richard de Luci, jointly Justiciar of England with the earl of Leicester, so that he knew well many of the people about the court. They gave him advance news of the doings of his adversaries. The suit was complicated, for it rested on the question whether the woman who was in possession of the land, the daughter of Richard's uncle William, was a bastard or not. Bastardy was a matter for the Church court. When the archbishop's court had proved itself unable, or unwilling, to deliver a verdict, Richard, with the king's permission, appealed to Rome. He had already spent a great deal of money, sending in the first place to the king in Normandy for a writ, sending about England for counsel, obtaining the record of a divorce case over fifteen years old, collecting his witnesses, his clerks, his friends, and his helpers on the various occasions when his suit had been summoned for a hearing in the archbishop's court, going to the king in Gascony to get a writ ordering that the plea should go forward despite the summons to the army collecting for the war in Toulouse. The appeal to Rome involved sending and keeping clerks there at considerable cost.

At last Richard secured a decision from the Pope, who issued three writs in his favour, one addressed to the archbishop, one to Richard de Luci, and the third to Richard himself. With them he went to Romsey, where Richard de Luci was awaiting the king's coming from Normandy. 'Thence,' says Richard, 'I followed the court three weeks before I could make fine with the king and in that journey I spent 5 marks of silver. And because the king was vexed that the lord Pope had sent no writ to him, I forthwith sent off my messenger to the lord Pope to fetch a writ directed to the lord king, which my messenger afterwards brought me at the close of Easter at Windsor, and in that journey he spent 50 shillings. After I had made fine with the king, my lord Richard de Luci by the king's command gave me a day for pleading at London at mid Lent. And there was a council then, and I came with my friends and my helpers, and because he could not attend to this plea on account of the king's business I stayed there four days and spent 50 shillings. Thence he gave me a day at the close of Easter when the king and my lord Richard were at Windsor . . . and because my lord Richard could not attend to this plea on account of the plea of Henry of Essex' (then under suspicion of cowardice shown in the war in Wales) 'the judgement was postponed from day to day until the king should come to Reading.'

'At Reading,' continues Richard, 'in like manner it was postponed from day to day until the king should come to Wallingford, and in that journey I spent 6 pounds and 5 shillings. And thence, because my lord Richard was going with the king to Wales, he removed my plea to the court of the earl of Leicester in London, and there I came and in that journey I spent 35 shillings. And because I could not get on at all with my plea I sent to my lord Richard in Wales so that he might order that my plea should not be delayed, and he ordered that Oger the steward and Ralf Brito should do justice to me without delay and they gave me a day in London, and that messenger spent 5 shillings. Therefore I kept my day in London with my friends and my helpers and there I spent 27 shillings and 4 pence. From there my adversaries were summoned by the king's writ and by the writ of my lord Richard de Luci to come before the lord king. And we came before the king at Woodstock and there we remained eight days. At last by the grace of God and the king and by the judgement of his court my uncle's land was adjudged to me and there I spent 7 pounds and 10 shillings.' Richard adds that in the king's court he spent 16 and a half marks in gold, silver, and horses and in addition to this he gave 36 and a half marks to Ralf the king's doctor, 100 marks to the king, and to the queen one mark of gold.

This naïve account of the expenses of conducting a suit at the exalted levels of the royal and papal courts illustrates as does no other contemporary document the multiplicity and variety of the business dealt with by the king and those immediately about him. The two Justiciars, the earl of Leicester and Richard de Luci, were two of the greatest magnates in the land. Nevertheless they were content to hold office under the king and spend laborious days in the detail of public business. The Justiciar was the man who took the king's place in his absence, who acted, in fact, as an extension of the person of the king. He was the second man in the kingdom. That Henry II appointed two co-equal justiciars at the beginning of his reign may perhaps suggest that he feared that a single great officer of state might become too powerful. Richard de Luci outlived the earl and held the position alone for the last ten years of his life. He was succeeded by an East Anglian baron named Rannulf de Glanville, who had made the royal service his career. Henry II was fortunate in his servants. The names of the men who came and went about his court can be known from the lists of witnesses to the charters issued from his chancery. Beside the Justiciar, the Chancellor, and the men who held positions within the household itself, such as the stewards, the chamberlains, and the butlers, were bishops and barons from different parts of the country. The men whose names recur most often in these lists must have formed, in fact though not in name, an inner council among the great men by whose advice the king ruled his land.

But it was the personality of the king that knit these men together to form a court and government and create an administrative system unique in the medieval world. No other country in western Europe could boast of a department of state comparable to the Exchequer of the English kings, where under the chairmanship of the king or his Justiciar the great men of the land gathered about the chequered cloth to deal with the king's accounts and withdrew to an inner chamber to discuss matters of high moment or settle knotty points of law. Walter Map praises the Exchequer and contrasts it with the church courts. 'The Exchequer,' he says, 'is a unique place in which there is nothing miraculous, for the eye of a just judge is ever upon it. When I once heard there a full and just judgement in favour of a poor man against a rich man, I said to the lord Rannulf, the chief Justiciar, "Although justice for the

poor man may be put off by many digressions, it has
achieved a swift and happy judgement." Then Rannulf said
"Indeed, we decide cases much more quickly than your
bishops do in the Church courts." To which I said "That is
true, but if our kings were as far from you as the Pope is
from the bishops I think you would be equally slow." He
41 laughed and did not deny it.' But the Exchequer sat in
almost continuous session at Westminster while the king
moved about the land, staying for a time at some favourite
place like Clarendon in Wiltshire or at some important
centre like Northampton or Winchester. The Exchequer
was the first of all government departments, but the spirit
and heart of the government was with the king as he moved
about the land with his court and household.

Those about the court and household of king Henry II
were clearly conscious of the greatness of their king and of
the new prestige which his power and capacity had given
the land. Walter Map says that 'the convincing proof of our
king's strength and justice is that whoever has a just cause
wants to have it tried before him, whoever has a weak one
does not come to him unless he is dragged. I speak,' he says,
'of king Henry II whom Spain chose as the judge of the
ancient and cruel controversy between the kings of Toledo
and Navarre, although the custom of old of all the kingdoms
was to prefer the court of the king of France before all
others. Now by the merit of our king our court is preferred
before all others and this ancient dispute is brought to a
42 fair decision.' That the king himself was conscious of the
quicker tempo that life and government had assumed in
his days there can be no doubt. It is a proof of his proud
assurance that from the latter part of his reign come two
books which could have been written only with his consent
and goodwill, if not at his direct command. An account of
the law and practice of the king's courts of justice, a manual
for the guidance of both the judges and litigants in the royal
courts, is associated with the name of Rannulf de Glanville,
43 the king's chief Justiciar. A detailed account of the working
of the Exchequer system, describing the sources of the

king's income, the method of making up the royal accounts, and the duties of the officers of the Treasury and Exchequer, was written by the king's Treasurer, Richard, son of Nigel bishop of Ely.

44

The monarchy was in this age the guarantee of stability and peace and it was inevitable that a strong king should want to rule according to his own mind. But the king was bound to keep on good terms with his great men on whom his military strength depended. Much as the kings of this period would have liked to rule as despots they could not long keep up despotic power. Henry II did not really try. He associated his great barons with him in his government by discussing every change in council before he issued the assizes which made his decisions known to the men of the land. Many of his Justiciars were barons by inheritance. It may well have been the stringent enquiries which he instituted in 1170 into the relations not only between sheriffs and the men of the shires but between barons and their own men that brought some of the English earls and barons to support the king's discontented sons in the revolt of 1173–4. But even the active aid of the kings of France and Scotland could not bring victory to the rebels, since in England the weight of the baronage held with the king. The suppression of the revolt meant that the king could continue his reforming policy with the cooperation of his subjects. It is probable that few of the barons who used the king's new writs of novel disseisin and *mort d'ancestor* realized what their inevitable, though remote, result would be.

Thirty-five years of strong rule by a king who kept a close watch on every aspect of government, who heard pleas himself and was prepared to spend sleepless nights evolving the exact formula of a judicial writ meant that by the end of his reign Henry II had collected around him a group of able men trained in the administration of a centralized government. Their skill and judgement were severely tested in the reign of Henry's son and successor, Richard I, who regarded his crown as so secure that he could treat England merely as a source of supplies for overseas adventures. Only

45 twice in his ten years' reign did he visit the country. He crossed from Normandy on 13 August, 1189, for his coronation at Westminster on 3 September, but he left England again on 12 December. 'Almost everyone,' says one chronicler, 'was angered that a noble king about to set out to distant regions should leave his own kingdom with so little ceremony and should have, as he left it, so much less care for it than he ought.' The four months he had spent in the country were largely occupied in raising money to meet the heavy charges of his journey through France and Italy and his crusade in Palestine. 'I would sell London if I could find 46 a bidder,' he is reported to have said. His arrangements for the government of England were a matter of financial bargaining and it was not surprising that disturbances broke out before the king had left Sicily for his journey over the great sea.

Richard I left his Chancellor in supreme authority in England, making him also Justiciar and procuring for him from the Pope the office of papal legate. William de Longchamps had risen by service in Richard's household while he was Duke of Aquitaine and, like his master, knew little of English conditions. His real difficulty was the anomalous position of the king's brother, John. Richard had given him the earldom of Gloucester by right of his wife and had also granted him six shires so freely that the officers in charge of local government looked to John and answered at his exchequer, not at the king's. Nevertheless John was not allowed to regard himself as the heir to the throne should Richard, as yet unmarried, die on his dangerous journey. Before he left Sicily for Palestine in 1191 Richard sent home to England to control the contesting parties an old servant of his father's, Walter of Coutances, archbishop of Rouen, a man trained in the exchequer tradition. With the support of the judges inherited from Henry II's days, archbishop Walter held the land for Richard when the news reached England that the king had been captured in December, 1192, on his way home from his crusade. That was the real test which proved the strength of Henry II's

work. John's attempt to seize the kingdom of his absent
brother was quelled and a vast ransom raised and despatched to Germany. Richard undertook to pay 100,000
marks to the Emperor of Germany and 50,000 marks to the
Duke of Austria who had first seized him. This large sum of
money, £100,000, would amount today to considerably
more than £2,000,000. Not all of it was paid and some of it
may have been raised in Richard's French lands, but the
greater part of it was certainly paid, and from England,
before Richard secured his freedom in February, 1194.

As soon as he was free Richard returned to England to
show his subjects that he still lived and reigned, to punish
the rebels, and to undergo a second coronation. He landed
at Sandwich on 13 March, 1194. Rebels were dealt with in
a great Council held at Nottingham and the stain of
imprisonment was washed away in a coronation ceremony at
Winchester, equally solemn though less elaborate than his
original anointing at Westminster. On 12 May he crossed
the Channel for the last time. Again the dominant note of
the king's visit was financial. Even the rebellion could be
turned to profit, for the lands of the rebels were taken into
the king's hands. Philip II of France was pressing his attack
on the duchy of Normandy and mercenary soldiers were
necessary for its defence. The military service which
Norman and English barons owed for their lands could not
maintain a standing army for the defence of Normandy.
Welsh foot and horsemen and Brabantine mercenaries were
paid largely by treasure sent to the king from England.
The government of England was entrusted to Hubert
Walter, who in 1193 became both archbishop of Canterbury
and Justiciar. He was the nephew of Rannulf de Glanville,
Henry II's last Justiciar, and he had been brought up in
Rannulf's household. When Hubert gave up the office of
Justiciar in 1198 his successor was Geoffrey fitz Peter,
whom Hubert Walter himself had trained. From 1191 to 47
the end of the incurious Richard's reign the tradition of
Henry II controlled the land.

The virtues of his servants protected Richard I from the

troubles which generally came upon a neglectful king, and his crusading exploits, his skill in war, and dignity in captivity won him the respect of contemporary chroniclers. Modern historians, following this tradition, have often awarded him praise he never earned, while they have poured upon his brother and successor, John, an equally undeserved reprobation. But when John died Normandy had been lost to the French king, England itself was a papal fief, and the English barons were in revolt and had invited a foreign prince to take the title of king in England. This succession of disasters inevitably influenced historians writing in the days of John's son. John was discredited and nothing was too bad to say about him. The political failure of his reign is there for all to see. There is, however, another side of the story. John was the true son of the king who devised writs to bring business to the royal court of justice, who watched over the Exchequer, and supervised the justice his judges administered in the shires. It was John who appointed Hubert Walter as Chancellor to bring order to an office used by Richard I as an instrument of financial
48 oppression. Like his father, John kept watch on the Exchequer officials, sometimes sitting at the Exchequer board, sometimes ordering special inquests into moneys owed to the Crown. No king has ever known England better than John, for no king has ever been so continuously moving
49 up and down its roads.

John succeeded to the throne when Henry II's new forms of action had had time to prove their worth. Richard's Justiciars had followed the wise policy of sending judges round the country frequently, so that if Richard's subjects never saw the king, at least they knew that his justice was being done. The regular appearance of royal judges made it worthwhile to use the writs which initiated suits before them. The work of these judges, whether they were sitting in what was by this date called the Bench at Westminster, or were itinerant in the shires, was creating a new source of income for the Crown and adding very considerably to the
50 work of the Exchequer. More important than the financial

aspect of their work was their influence on the common law of England which they were daily making in their courts. That John realized to the full the implication of this work there can be no doubt. He encouraged the purchase of writs which brought new business to the courts held by his justices. Martin of Pattishall, one of the two justices on whose judgements Bracton afterwards based his classical exposition of the common law, was learning his business in these years as a clerk of Simon of Pattishall, a judge constantly in the king's company. As John went about the land he himself sat as a judge and encouraged the purchase for small sums of writs which brought cases immediately before him. His lively mind and keen intelligence played upon these cases. There can be no doubt that the personal influence of the king had much to do with the rapid expansion of royal justice in this age. 51

No king of England was ever so unlucky as John. From the moment when France came to the strong hands of Philip II his conquest of Normandy was only a matter of time. Richard staved off its loss by a fierce concentration on its protection and by reckless expenditure on defence and allies; expedients that brought their own unfortunate consequences for John. Barons who resented both fighting and paying to keep their king's continental lands resented the loss of them only when they found to their surprise that it meant the loss of their own lands in France as well as the king's. After that, there was never confidence and trust between the king and his barons. Each felt resentment against the other. Rumours that the king himself was responsible for the murder of his nephew Arthur created an atmosphere of fear, a feeling that the land was ruled by a tyrant, and through a bureaucracy which held all men in its clutches. This sense was heightened when pope Innocent III laid an interdict on England because John would not accept Stephen Langton as his archbishop of Canterbury; for John took hostages from his subjects to forestall any move against him. With two such enemies as Innocent III and Philip II watching his every move, the one with powers of binding and loosing from the most sacred oaths and the other ready to risk even the invasion of England itself, John dared trust no one who was not bound by self-interest to his service.

Hence the apparent paradox of John. There is the John who interests himself in the administration of justice, is ready to listen to the cry of those whom contemporary 52 practice would bar from immediate access to his presence, and makes available the new judicial practices to his Irish 53 subjects. There is the John who can organize defence and attack on the grand scale, so that it seems as though English 54 naval history must begin with him. There is the John who introduces new fat pennies to take the place of an outworn 55 currency, who sees the possibility of a Merseyside port and 56 founds Liverpool. There is the John who writes to those who live in the diocese of Lincoln thanking them 'for their gifts and alms put to the construction of the new work at Lincoln,' that is St Hugh's choir, 'earnestly asking' them 'to 57 finish that which' they have 'so laudably begun'. There is the John who proclaims that 'if we granted our protection to a dog it ought to be inviolably observed. Henceforth,' he says, 'we commit the Jews dwelling in your city to your charge; if anyone attempts to harm them do you always protect and assist them; for in future we shall require their blood at your hands if through your default any evil happens to them, which Heaven forbid; for we know that these things happen through the foolish people of the town, not the discreet, by whom the folly of the foolish should be 58 restrained.' There is the John who orders that anyone 59 harming a clerk shall be hanged from the nearest oak. There is the generous, able, and lavish king.

In considering the other side of the picture it must be remembered that for lack of evidence judgement must be 60 reserved about the blackest charges against John. Nor should present-day standards of morality be used for judgement of only the unsuccessful kings. Nor should any chronicler be believed who is not strictly contemporary, and is not supported by record evidence when he makes extravagant statements about the king's evil deeds. But when all has been said which may lighten the picture of this most enigmatic king, there remains the mistrustful sovereign who binds his subjects to him by taking their sons as hostages for good behaviour, who charges individuals, even his best servants, with an insupportable weight of debt, who forces every debtor to find sufficient sureties to cover the whole obligation so that the sureties themselves become enmeshed, who seems as irresponsible in his occasional pardons as in his impositions; the king whose arbitrary conduct drives his subjects to rebellion. 61

This is not the place to discuss the concessions wrung from the king and embodied in the Charter authenticated with his great seal at Runnymede in June, 1215. It should be noted that there was no one authoritative text of this momentous document, nor was it enrolled in the chancery files. John was making promises to every freeman in his 62 land and his chancery had to make and seal enough copies of the charter for one to be sent to every shire to be publicly expounded by the sheriff in the full shire court. A great deal has been written about the Charter and the last word has not yet been said. No single state document has had more influence on the course of history and its influence is even now not spent. It is the forerunner of the great constructive statutes of the thirteenth century, the first detailed review of necessary reforms. It points the way to the new age, to a kingship controlled not by fear of revolt but by acceptance of the restraint of law. To John it seemed that in making such promises he made himself a slave, and indeed the Charter marks the first long step towards the constitutional kingship of a far later day. No medieval king was ever allowed to forget that his predecessor had granted this Charter to his subjects. Every king in turn confirmed it until the days when the middle ages ended in confusion and an autocrat was needed to re-order the land.

John's heir and successor, Henry III, was only a child when his father died in 1216. Barons who had invited a French prince to be their king in place of John had soon

begun to doubt the wisdom of their action and were glad to
be able to return to their allegiance, justifying their ready
change with the platitude that the son should not suffer for
63 his father's sins. The men who formed the young king's
council for the rule of the land took over a governmental
machine made stronger and more supple by the restless intelligence of John and the ability of the men who had served
him. The fragments which survive of John's household
accounts show how great a part in the government of the
land had been taken by the men who were daily with the
king. The household staff was largely responsible for the
64 organization of his Scottish expedition of 1209. It paid the
mercenaries and advanced money to them and to the king's
65 own subjects on his Irish expedition of 1210. Custodians of
the lands of the bishops who had joined Stephen Langton
in exile sometimes accounted for the profits of those lands
to the officials of his chamber, rather than to the Exchequer.
It is very soon evident in Henry III's reign that the king has
now three departments of state, the Exchequer, the Chancery, and the Wardrobe.

The word wardrobe begins to appear in the chancery
records of John's reign and at first seems to mean no more
than that part of the household which has the custody of the
king's most precious possessions as he travels about the land,
his jewels, his documents, his robes, and his money. A small
or privy seal was kept there and used for the king's private
business or for any purpose that seemed more suitably
served by the use of a lighter seal than the great seal. Royal
houses in which the king stayed had a wardrobe where these
things were put. It was a dressing room, a store room, a
66 lavatory, adjoining the king's bedchamber. In Henry III's
reign the word gradually acquires a more definite meaning
and the clerks of the wardrobe come to be the administrative staff of the king's household. This change had been
effected before Henry came of age. The earliest surviving
wardrobe account covers the years January 1224 to April
1227 and shows that there was a twofold aspect of the king's
personal finances: the necessary expenses of the king's

lodging and the necessary expenses of the wardrobe. Under the former heading the ordinary expenses of running the royal household are entered and under the latter the extraordinary expenses which were undertaken by the household. The ordinary expenses of the king's establishment came in those years roughly to about £2,000 a year. The expenses of the wardrobe were uneven and depended upon the political demands on the king's immediate servants. The wardrobe paid for the siege of Bedford castle and the suppression of Faulkes de Bréauté in 1224. It paid also for knighting the king's brother in 1225 and for equipping the expedition which was sent with him to Poitou.   67

It was to the wardrobe clerks that Henry III looked when he first tried to throw off the control of the great officers of state who had been ruling the land during his minority. Hubert de Burgh, the Justiciar, and Ralf Neville, the Chancellor, were such great men that Henry III may well have felt himself hampered and repressed. It was not until 68 fourteen years after he began his reign that in December 1230 he was so far emancipated from the Justiciar's control that he could have a privy seal of his own. The needs of state had forced the Justiciar to allow Henry to be declared of age as early as 1223 in order that there could be a great seal for public business. With the aid of his chief wardrobe clerk, Peter de Rivaux, Henry succeeded in overthrowing Hubert de Burgh in 1232 and in taking over himself the direction of affairs. Peter de Rivaux was the nephew of one of the ablest ministers of king John, Peter des Roches, a Poitevin knight who became a clerk and was rewarded with the see of Winchester for his services to the king. He was the only English bishop who remained loyal to John and stayed in England at his post throughout the Interdict. This loyalty made him obnoxious to the clerical party in England and in consequence he was, as a foreigner, deprived of the office of Justiciar after the issue of the Charter in 1215. It was to this man, an adroit diplomatist and a skilful administrator, that John had entrusted the education of the young Henry. Although he held no office when Henry made his first attempt at self-government, there is no doubt that he was the king's guide.

The king's character may have been in part shaped by this astute cosmopolitan who had spent his best years in the service of John. Since John's death the Charter had been three times re-issued. The omission of the clauses which most closely limited the royal power in no wise lessened its virtue. The rule of the Justiciar and council during the minority had underlined the idea of cooperation in government between the king and his barons. That Henry III should try to turn back the clock was to be expected. The wardrobe officials and the wardrobe seal were his instruments. His first attempt was thwarted and Henry showed his essential poverty of spirit by his ready acquiescence in the dismissal of his Poitevin ministers in 1234. Foreign clerks coming to England after 1236 with the Savoyard and Provençal relatives of the queen entered the king's service and aided him in his renewed attempts to ignore his baronial councillors and to subordinate the officers of the Exchequer and Chancery to those of the Wardrobe. One reason, though not the only one, for the baronial revolt of 1258 was the resentment of the barons at their own exclusion from the king's councils, the king's dependence on his foreign wardrobe clerks, and his lavish generosity to his foreign kinsfolk.

Much good work was done by the king's personal ministers between the fall of Hubert de Burgh in 1232 and the outbreak of the baronial revolt in 1258, but it was the unostentatious work of men engaged in perfecting a machine of government and the unpopular work of men reviewing the collection and auditing of the king's revenue. Exchequer, Chancery, and household had been drifting apart while there was no head of the state of full age to act as a focus of all activity. Already when Richard fitz Nigel was writing the *Dialogus* in the 1170s the Exchequer was hidebound and rigid. His successors as Treasurers may have been less bound by convention than he and readier to experiment, but the Exchequer was a conservative office. At whatever dates are chosen for their examination, 1209, 1350, 1650, or later, the Great Rolls of the Pipe, the annual rolls of Exchequer accounts, are the most perfect examples of rigid conservatism that the most conservative government department could ever produce, with their formalized writing and their sterotyped entries. It is easy to see the descent of the last great rolls of the eighteenth and nineteenth centuries from the roll so lovingly described by Richard fitz Nigel. 69 Already in John's reign it needed the impulse of the king himself initiating enquiries to trace some of the moneys owing to the crown. The Exchequer, for example, had allowed successive sheriffs of Warwick and Leicester to pocket the special aid imposed on the knights of the earl of Leicester as a punishment for the earl's part in the rebellion of 1173-4. This fact was only revealed by inquest in 1209. Exchequer officials sometimes needed to be 70 reminded that they had some responsibility for the collection of the king's revenue as well as the duty of producing neatly audited accounts. As treasurer of both Exchequer and Wardrobe, Peter de Rivaux could survey the whole financial field. At his impulse the financial position in the shires was reviewed. Reforms begun at the Exchequer by this household officer in the years 1232-4 were carried to their logical conclusions in the years 1240-58. When the barons' war 71 broke out Peter de Rivaux was Treasurer of the wardrobe again.

Parallel with this attempt to draw Exchequer and Wardrobe more closely together went a review of the other great department of state, the Chancery, which was, in theory at least, still a part of the royal household, following the court as it moved. But the Chancery was a rapidly growing office. Its records were getting more bulky every year and some permanent home was becoming necessary. It was an anachronism that the clerks who were employed in writing writs of common form which needed no authorization by the king or minister should be obliged to move about the country with the court. In 1232 Ralf Neville bishop of Chichester, then Chancellor, received a grant of oaks from an Oxfordshire royal forest for the house at Hensington near Oxford which he was building as official quarters for these clerks. He was given further help towards his stables there in 72 1234. The clerks who wrote the administrative writs dealing with matters which came up in the ordinary course of daily business were called clerks *de precepto* because they wrote writs in accordance with the precepts given them for each individual occasion. In time it became unnecessary for those clerks also to remain with the court, for the practice was developed of issuing a writ under the wardrobe seal to authorize the chancery clerks in their turn to issue a writ under the great seal. This procedure was not fully elaborated until much later in the century, but in 1265 the first steps were taken to provide the Chancery with what became its permanent home on the site where the Public Record Office 73 stands today in Chancery Lane.

The most striking reform in the Chancery during this period was a drastic reduction in the Chancellor's share of the money paid for the use of the king's seal. Every time the king's seal was used for the authentication of a document issued on behalf of one of the king's subjects, whether it was a grant of land or of privilege, the recipient had to pay for the sealing. When Richard I wanted to raise money he had a new seal made and declared that all charters issued under his first seal must be brought for confirmation and 74 reissue under his new seal. In his day, too, the Chancery officials, from the Chancellor downwards, took excessive fees. John's first official act was to correct this extortion, but he did not attempt to take from the Chancellor the issues of the seal, as these payments were called. Henry III's Chancellor, Ralf Neville, bishop of Chichester, was a man of baronial rank, who like his predecessors had been appointed to his office for life. Henry III could not remove him, though he had for a time taken the seal from him and entrusted it to a wardrobe official. In 1244, the year of Neville's death, the Hanaper – 'hamper' – department was set up. The keeper of the Hanaper received the money paid for the use of the seal and out of this money met the expenses of the Chancery. He accounted for his office to the Wardrobe which henceforward received the issues of the seal. The Chancellors who succeeded Neville were kept in due subordination by the king. They were salaried officials, not independent statesmen of baronial rank.

The period of the barons' revolt and the years which followed (1258–65) are often described as a time of reform. The barons who had felt that the king ignored their advice attempted to recover their power and correct those matters which offended them. They drove out the most recently arrived foreigners and secured the appointment of a Justiciar of their own order, but he, like the Chancellor, was a salaried official answerable to the council. 'Be it remembered,' said the baronial Provisions, 'to amend the hostelries of the king and queen.' But beyond replacing prominent foreigners by Englishmen little was done in the household, nor were its activities materially changed. The best work the baronial reformers did was in the field of local government, and there not all the barons spoke with one voice. Simon de Montfort, earl of Leicester, himself a foreigner when he came to England to claim his earldom in 1233, was the leader of the more extreme reformers. Those who felt that he went so far that he put baronial interests in jeopardy fell away from him and rejoined the king. Henry III challenged his baronial masters, but was defeated in battle and for a short time was under restraint. The death of Simon de Montfort in battle at Evesham against Edward, the king's son, and Edward's capture of Kenilworth castle put an end to the effective opposition to the Crown. By the last years of Henry III the wardrobe was accepted as a third department of state. It kept the king in touch with the exchequer and chancery and through them with the judges and officers of local government.

The outstanding experiments in government in the thirteenth century were born of this atmosphere of strain between king and baronage, the legacy of John's last unhappy years. In the meetings of the great council the barons could voice their doubts and criticisms when the king expounded his policy to them, as by tradition he was bound to do. Inevitably when they disliked his policies they criticized his choice of councillors, of the men whom he kept about him to advise him and to discuss with him the day-to-day affairs of state. That such a body as a select council, in addition to the great feudal council of the king's tenants in chief, was necessary no one doubted. The complexity of the affairs with which the Crown must deal, justice and order, war and peace, everything that might touch the welfare of Church or state, demanded the service of the best brains of the time. It was this need which brought and kept this select council in being. The less frequent meetings of the old great council tend as the century wears on to be called by a new name, Parliament, which stresses one side of this council's work, for the name parliament comes from the French word meaning discussion. The increasing wealth of the nation, the importance of the knights of the shire and the citizens and burgesses of the cities and towns, meant that both the king and his whole baronage realized that knights and towns must also be considered when great issues were at stake. Hence the tentative beginnings of summoning to great parleys generally held in the spring or autumn, now representatives of the shires, now of the towns and cities.

No contemporary chronicler ever realized the significance of constitutional changes which were going on before his eyes, and even so acute an observer as Matthew Paris, the most brilliant historian of his age, failed to see that a new institution was being born. He uses the word parliament, but means no more by it than council. There is no hint that he is conscious of any change, save perhaps his occasional use of adjectives such as 'most general' or 'very full' to describe a meeting of the great council or parliament. Simon de Montfort has earned a place in every history of Parliament because he was the first to summon representatives of the shires and the boroughs to the same assembly when he was in revolt against the king in 1265. His reason was purely practical. He wanted the widest support he could get for a policy of reform which was losing its power to hold his baronial adherents. But there could be no turning back. Nor under such a king as Henry III's son and successor, Edward I, was there any desire to turn back. For his ambitious projects he must mobilize every resource of his kingdom and he must carry his subjects with him so that their imaginations followed his. He proceeded by a series of experiments varied in accordance with the needs of the moment and the opinions of those whom he wished to take into counsel. He summoned knights and burgesses, sometimes to the same assembly and sometimes separately. Occasionally, as in 1283, he summoned two assemblies, one for the north and one for the south of the country. He summoned representatives of the clergy to attend such meetings, but they preferred to sit apart from laymen and make a separate financial bargain with the king.

By the end of the period with which this book deals it is clear that a new institution has come into being, created by imperceptible growth from the great council of earlier days. The king in council in Parliament has become the supreme governing body of the land, having all the powers that had lain in the king in council of earlier days, but with the added prestige of an occasion of great solemnity. It was the supreme court of justice in the land. It was the place where the king tested national opinion on his policy and asked for financial support to carry it out. Legislation, formerly sanctioned as the pronouncement of the will of the king with the consent of his great council, assumed a new formality when it was introduced by the king in council in parliament and emerged as a 'statute', a written document, embodying the will of this august assembly. Edward I used his parliaments to carry through a great series of reforming statutes reviewing every aspect of government and administration from the conduct of Exchequer officials to the clearing of bushes from the sides of the king's highway. The king still has his select council with its undefined power of justice, a power which the new institution has in no wise limited. But he has as well 'his court in his council in his parliaments in the presence of prelates, earls, barons, nobles, and other learned men, where judicial doubts are determined, and new remedies are established for new wrongs, and justice is done to everyone according to his deserts'. This contemporary definition of the Edwardian parliament stresses that side of its work which made inevitably for its permanence – to provide 'new remedies for new wrongs'; to give effect to the subject's right, or it might even be his duty, to present petitions. 'We bid you,' wrote Edward to his Chancellor on 5 February, 1305, 'along with the Treasurer, to whom we have issued a similar command, to proclaim that all those who have petitions to bring to us and our council at our forthcoming parliament, shall bring them day by day to those who are assigned to receive them between now and the first Sunday in Lent. And do you and the others of our council in London deliver,' that is, deal with, 'as many of these petitions as you can before we come, so that no petitions shall come before us in person, save only those which cannot be delivered without us, and these last you are to have well 76 tried and set in good order.'

The history of the growth of Parliament is the history of the constitution, but it belongs in some part to the history of society as well. Men from all parts of the land came to the king's parliaments. Friendships made there led to marriages, so that the pattern of society was vitally affected. But this belongs to the future. Despite his 'Model Parliament' of 1295, when Edward I died the constitution of Parliament was very far from settled. The Commons, that is the knights and burgesses, were not yet a necessary part of a true parliament, nor is there any evidence of their talks together from which the House of Commons ultimately grew. But the germ of all future growth was there.

Nevertheless when Edward I died on his way to Scotland in 1307 the centre of power was still with the king and his immediate household and court, a very different household from that of the Norman kings. The old departments can still be dimly seen, the chapel, the hall, and the chamber.

But the business centre of the household is no longer dependent on the chapel and housed in a corner of the hall. The Wardrobe is a department of state. Its officers could look forward to a distinguished career of public service to be rewarded by ecclesiastical preferment. The household ordinances of 1318 reveal an unwieldy company. New sub-departments of the household have multiplied the size of the king's entourage. So vast has it become that the right or duty of dining in the king's hall was strictly defined, for the kitchen accommodation was breaking down under the strain. The problem of lodging the king's servants, their men and their horses, is acute. 'The hideous plaints and cries' made daily about the crimes and quarrels of the court-followers of both sexes necessitated a careful definition of those who could claim lodging near the court. It is a far cry from that good if simple dinner depicted on the Bayeux Tapestry with which it all began.

CHAPTER II

BARONS AND KNIGHTS

THE great men who followed their duke to England and helped him to win the kingdom expected land as their reward; enough land to enable them in turn to satisfy the expectations of their own men who had accompanied them on the adventure. The process of rewarding these services began at once and proceeded through the early months and years of William's reign while Englishmen were becoming painfully convinced of the finality of their defeat. William had visited England only once before 1066, and he cannot have known in any detail how its lands lay, how the estates of individual Englishmen were distributed, or of what extent they were. The obvious way of rewarding his expectant followers was to give them the lands of one or more of the Englishmen whose resistance to the invasion had ended in death or flight, so that their lands were at the disposition of the new king. In this way he could at once begin to satisfy his land-hungry followers. Such an opportunity as that enjoyed by William I has come to few kings. He had conquered a kingdom and could make something approaching a new start. Unlike other rulers of the day, William had no immediate need for anxiety about the loyalty of his chief men. Their future depended on his continued tenure of the English kingdom. William was therefore able to impose such conditions on them and to demand such services as were necessary for the security of his rule.

An army to maintain his control over the conquered Englishmen and to defend his new kingdom against attack from abroad was William's first necessity. In return for the land which he was giving them he therefore demanded from his men knights to serve him in war. He knew more about what he wanted than about what he had to give and the bargains he drove with his men were far harder than those which any of his predecessors had been able to make with their men in Normandy. He could not under the conditions of 1066 make any precise equation between the value of the land and the number of knights demanded in return for it, but he could and did ask for a definite number of knights, generally reckoned, for convenience, in multiples of five. Having insisted on the general principle that all land was held of the king in return for some specified service and indicated to individual barons what their service should be, William could leave to them the business of securing their properties and providing the service which they had promised him. How his barons found the knights they brought to the king's army, or who these knights were, does not seem at this date to have concerned the king. If they liked, the barons could provide the requisite military service by hiring knights, if they could get them. They could, if they liked, maintain a force of knights in their households ready to perform the service on demand, or they might give men land in return for their promise to perform some part of the service that their lord owed the king.

The men described in contemporary documents as knights were a very miscellaneous class. Romantic literature from Geoffrey of Monmouth to Sir Walter Scott and Lord Tennyson has cast an unreal glamour over the figure of the medieval knight. His shining armour, his lance, his spirited horse, his readiness to rescue alike the beauteous damsel in distress or the aged and no longer lovely woman, his watches and vigils in church, his valour in the tournament are all part of the fiction and far removed from the reality of 1066. The knights of the time of the Conquest were essentially soldiers, trained in the household of some great man in the art of fighting on horseback. It was not until the practice of hiring foot-soldiers had gone far that knights abandoned their horses in battle. The Latin word for knight was *miles*, soldier, and it was their capacity to fight on horseback that in this age qualified them for knighthood. Twenty-one has become the accepted age of maturity because young men of that age were regarded as of full strength to bear and use the arms of a knight. But the knights of this age were bound also to attend on their lords, and conquered Englishmen observing the social relationships of their conquerors regarded the knights as essentially retainers, men at the service of their lord for war or peace. They saw nothing noble or impressive about them as a class. Hence they called 78 them *cnihtas*, serving youths, retainers. The word knight slowly changes its implications as the status of the knight himself changes.

While the future of the Norman conquerors in England was still uncertain every Norman lord must have retained bands of such men in his household. In the far north, where the fact of conquest was slowly and unwillingly accepted, household knights were a necessity long after a south-country magnate could live without a retinue of armed men 79 in being and at a moment's summons. But the expectation of peace in this period was never high. All through William I's reign there was constant fear of foreign invasion, both from the Danish kingdom, where the memory was ever present that king Cnut of Denmark had also been the ruler of England, and after 1071 from the county of Flanders, where William I had supported an unsuccessful claimant to the county. In 1085 Danish preparations for the invasion of England were so menacing that William imported a larger mercenary force than the land had ever seen and billeted them upon his great men. The French king's hostility, owing to the overwhelming resources which the conquest of England had given the Norman duke, might easily have led to an invasion of England had the French king ever felt strong enough to attempt it. The long peace of Henry I's reign in England was felt to be phenomenal. It was followed by the nineteen unhappy years of Stephen's reign when there was no central authority to protect a stretch of countryside from devastation by the military retinue of an ill-intentioned magnate. In Normandy the dukes had never in the years before the conquest of England succeeded in stopping private war, although they had tried to insist that disputes should first be brought to the Duke's court so that an attempt could be made to settle them peacefully. The new power that conquering a kingdom gave to William I enabled him to prohibit private war altogether and to insist that quarrels between his great men must be settled in his court. But even when private war was forbidden the households of great men were the schools in which knights served an apprenticeship to their trade.

The young men and boys who entered noble households for education and training came from all the higher ranks of feudal society. Some were the eldest sons of very great men. They would one day inherit wide estates and must be bred in all the knightly arts. The sons of the very greatest magnates would probably enter the household of the king himself for training. The feudal practice of maintaining the integrity of an inheritance by passing it intact to the eldest son meant that provision for younger sons was always a problem and often caused bitter quarrels. Clever ones could look for a career in the Church, but the majority preferred to seek a training in the art of war. Younger sons were an unfailing source from which feudal retinues of knights could be recruited. Placed in a baronial household, these youths learned their trade and hoped that their father or their patron would provide them with an heiress or a widow to give them a stake in the country. Such men existed in great numbers all over feudal Europe. They flocked to any theatre of war in hope of gain. The mercenary soldiers hired by William I were of this type and origin. Such men from the estates of William's great men followed their lords or their lord's sons to England in 1066 hoping to join the landed classes in the conquered country.

They were crude, rough men, toughened by war, with a keen eye to their personal advantage. They had no elaborate equipment as knights. Their armour was a one-piece garment of interlinked riveted rings of metal, falling from neck to knee, the lower part shaped into two leg pieces. It was probably worn over a padded undergarment and for

transport was threaded through the arms on a pole,
80 borne shoulder high by two men. A sword, lance, helmet,
and shield, high leather boots with spurs, a saddle, reins,
bridle, and stirrups completed their equipment. The helmet
was of iron with a long piece coming down to protect the
nose. The shield was kite-shaped. It might bear markings,
but as yet they were mere devices of decoration. The heraldic
coat-of-arms was slowly evolved during the twelfth century
from elementary beginnings first discernible in Stephen's
reign. The new feudal society of Anglo-Norman England
was in the last resort built up by such men as these. These
men dealt more directly with the English people than their
lords could do. Some married Englishwomen. All had to
adapt their lives to the conditions of an economy rooted in
the past which they could not sever. The process of fitting-
in, of accommodating habits of thought and speech to a
new land, was not easy and must often have been painful
to the old inhabitants. The king left it to his barons and
their men to manage as best they could.

But William I had no intention of allowing his tenants-in-
chief to approach the state of independence which he himself had enjoyed before 1066 in regard to the king of France.
By 1086, twenty years after the battle of Hastings, they
had had time to make at least preliminary arrangements
about the military service they owed the king. At Old
Sarum in that year William took homage and an oath of
fealty in person from 'all the land-holding men who were of
any account' – a phrase covering all those men who had
been enfeoffed with more than a modest estate in return for
knight service, whoever their immediate lords might be. The
satisfaction of the demand that such men as these should do
homage directly to the king himself established a most
important precedent. Not only was William I the ultimate
lord of all land in England, but all who held land owed an
immediate duty directly to the king himself. It was not until
the reign of Henry II and exactly a hundred years after the
battle of Hastings that the English king advanced to the
logical conclusion of these arrangements. In that year

Henry II asked all those men who held of him in chief to inform him in sealed letters how many knights had been enfeoffed on their lands before the death of king Henry I, how many since, and how many knights were left to be provided from the private resources of the tenant-in-chief himself when the king called out the feudal army. He also asked for the names of the knights, so that all those among them who had not yet done homage to him and of whose names he had no record could do it before a certain date. The replies of the barons to these instructions were copied into two memoranda books at the Exchequer and form the first comprehensive review of the new feudal society which the Norman kings had established in England.

The Salisbury Oath of 1086 was the first public indication of the Conqueror's attitude towards the internal organization of the estates of his great men. Before he died he had taken a further step which even the members of his immediate circle must have regarded with doubt and apprehension. A contemporary records how in the Christmas council of 1085 the king had 'very deep speech with his wise men about this land, how it was peopled and by what sort of men. Then he sent his men into every shire all over England and caused it to be found out how many hundred hides were in the shire and what land the king had, and what stock on the land, and what dues he ought to have each year from the shire. Also he caused it to be written how much land his archbishops, bishops, abbots, and earls had, and, though I may be somewhat tedious in my account, what and how much each landholder in England had in land or in stock, and how much money it might be worth. So minutely did he cause it to be searched out that there was not one hide or yard of land, nor even (it is shameful to write of it, but he thought it not shameful to do it) an ox, or a cow, or a swine that was not set down in his writ. And all the writings were brought to him afterwards.' Searching 81 enquiries like this were bound to arouse deep feelings of resentment. In some parts there were riots and so many false statements were made that the counties had to be visited a second time in the same year and many people were punished for perjury. The inevitable comparison of this unprecedented enquiry with the last great Day of Judgement meant that in the twelfth century the book in which the results of the inquest were recorded was known as Domesday Book.

The writings brought to the king for digestion were the verdicts of the Frenchmen and Englishmen who spoke before the commissioners, answering the king's questions on behalf of their own villages. Their verdicts, made up village by village, and giving an account of the whole village as a unit, were either destroyed or allowed to disappear when they had been summarized and re-cast in the form desired by the king for record and reference. Two books contain the results of these labours. The returns for Essex, Norfolk, and Suffolk make up the Little Domesday Book. In the greater Domesday Book are the returns for all the rest of England covered by the enquiry. The clerks seem to have begun their task on East Anglia and Essex. Their work is less accurate but includes far more detail than appears in the shires entered into the main volume. It is significant that the king should have thought it worthwhile to set his clerks to so laborious and complicated a task as the compilation of these books from the original returns of the juries. By their work the clerks changed the whole character of the record. They made it a directory of aristocratic land-holders. In nearly every county the same form was adopted. A description of the county town and any other borough important enough to have a separate account precedes an index of the chief landholders in the country beginning with the king, passing through archbishops, bishops, abbots, earls, and barons, to the king's servants and landowners of English birth. Under the names of the king and of each tenant-in-chief there then follows a description of the estates which each held within the shire. The work is as competent and accurate as that of any modern government department working with all the apparatus of card indexes and typewriters. By this time, twenty years after the Conquest, many Normans had been trained to serve as royal clerks. They dealt adequately and competently with what must have seemed to them exasperating puzzles of English place and personal names and gave a new though purely superficial tidiness to the vagaries of English tenurial practice.

Although this great record was made up into two books it is always referred to in the twelfth century and afterwards as though it were a single volume. It was laid up in the Treasury at Winchester where it could be consulted on questions of land tenure and taxation. In the early twelfth century it was referred to as 'the book of the Treasury', for the name Domesday Book was a popular name, given, according to the Treasurer, Richard fitz Nigel, by the native English. He himself described it in about 1179 as the book of judgement, *liber judiciarius*, 'not because it contains judicial sentences on doubtful matters, but because it is not possible for any reason to depart from its judgement'. The [82] reason for the compilation of this work given by Richard fitz Nigel is worth consideration, for though he was living a hundred years after the book was written, he was its official custodian and knew how it was used in the courts of justice: 'so that every man may be content with his own right and not usurp with impunity the rights of others'. [83] The uses to which such a survey could be put were many and various, but above them all there rides the king's own personal desire to know the condition of the kingdom he had conquered twenty years before.

The magnates of Domesday England were not a [84] numerous class. So far as can be seen William I relied for an army of at least 4,000 knights upon a group of barons whose number can hardly have reached 200. The Conquest had given him the power to exact knight service from the ancient English churches, a source from which he obtained 780 knights in addition. The lands held by a great baron or an important church were collectively and indifferently known as a barony, a 'fee', or an 'honor'. Fee means simply those lands with which the tenant, lay or ecclesiastical, is 'enfeoffed' by the king to hold freely by definite service. 'Honor' seems a vague term, indicating as it does by origin merely that which gives honour to its holder, but it was a very useful collective description of estates, which, often lying scattered widely over the map of England, were yet bound together by a close-held feudal tie. 'Honor' is essentially a feudal term. The greatest honor of all was the king's, his realm of England.

Two principles seem to have guided William I in his distribution of rewards. He was first of all concerned to guard danger points, the coast of Sussex, whose vulnerability he had himself proved, the coast of Kent, East Anglia, the northern border, the passes through the Pennines to the Vale of York, the Cheshire plain between the Pennines and the Welsh mountains, the Welsh border, the south-west peninsular. In all these parts he was content to see trustworthy individuals, sometimes kinsmen of his own, holding what were in the first generation military commands. He made England an embattled island taut against imminent peril. But the possibility of danger from within was always near the thoughts of a king in the feudal age. To prevent a great man in rebellion from relying on a countryside entirely in his economic power William seems to have aimed at spreading and extending the territorial interests of great men. How this policy worked from the point of view of the lands of a single individual, a man close in the Conqueror's confidence, can be pleasantly illustrated from the description given by the seventeenth-century scholar, William Dugdale, in his great book, *The Baronage of England*, of the position and power of Henry de Ferrers, the founder of the family of the Ferrers, earls of Derby. After pointing out that Henry was one of the commissioners who went round the country on the Domesday Inquest, Dugdale continues 'That he was a person of much eminency both for his knowledge and integrity there is no doubt; otherwise it is not like he should have been trusted in so high and weighty an employment: neither of less Power and Wealth, as may seem by the Lands he then possessed, which were twenty lordships in Berkshire, in Wiltshire three, in Essex five, in Oxfordshire seven, in Warwickshire six, in Lincolnshire two, in Buckinghamshire two, in Gloucestershire one, in Herefordshire two, in Hampshire three, in Nottinghamshire three, in Leicestershire thirty-five, in Derbyshire an hundred and fourteen; and in Staffordshire seven besides the castle and borough of Tutburie; one of which was Chebsey whereunto that part of Stafford appertained wherein the king appointed a castle to be built, instead of that which was then demolished. Near unto the castle of Tutbury, he founded a goodly monastery for Cluniac monks, and amply endowed it with Lands and Revenues.' The new society of the Norman age 85 ignored the ancient divisions of shire and hundred. Few honors lay within the borders of a single shire.

As this description shows, the lands of Henry de Ferrers lay scattered in fourteen counties. Although the weight of his power lay in Derbyshire, Staffordshire, and Leicestershire he could never ignore the outliers of his honor in Essex, Berkshire, or Hampshire. This subtle interlocking of the landed interests of the feudal nobility made for the strength and stability of the new society. It forced the Conqueror's great men to work with him in running the whole land since they could never treat their own estates as a geographical or economic unit. It spread their immediate interests into every county where they held land. It made it easy for them to endow their anxious followers in return for the knight service which they themselves owed the king. In the first age of English feudalism the magnates who held these widespread honors were unwilling to allow even the smallest and most remote of their dependent holdings to slip from their feudal authority.

The problem of keeping an honor together so that the lord could be sure of getting the services due to him and through him to the king from all the tenants on his estates was not an easy one. The affairs of a great honor like that held by the Ferrers earls of Derby were only less complicated than the affairs of a kingdom. Like the king the head of an honor had certain outstanding tenants with whose

counsel and advice he conducted the affairs of the whole honor. The letters sent to Henry II in 1166 show that in every important honor a group of tenants stand out above their fellows. They owe their lord the service of 3, 4, or 5 knights, sometimes they owe him even more. Sometimes they hold land of other tenants-in-chief or even of the king himself. When the actual holdings of such men within an honor are tracked down it often appears that they are dispersed among their lord's lands as his are dispersed within the kingdom. A good example of this can be given from the Ferrers honor. Hubert de Curzun held 3 knight's fees of the earl and his land lay in 4 counties, at Fauld in Staffordshire, at Lockinge in Berkshire, at Diseworth in
86 Leicestershire, and at Sibford Ferris in Oxfordshire. The earl Ferrers's letter of 1166 shows that he had an unusually large number of tenants like Hubert de Curzun, holding as much or more land. Such men as these had their own problems of administration. They, too, held their court to which their tenants must come and bring their pleas. They were often the equals of their lords in social status, and within and without the honor they were regarded as barons.

It was only by insistence that the duty of attending the honor court lay on all those who held of the honor that the scattered estates of which it was composed could be kept together. This duty of attendance at the honor court is stressed by a legal writer of Henry I's day. He says 'It is lawful for every lord to summon his man to right in his court, and if the man is resident in the remotest manor of the honor whence he holds, he shall come to the plea if his
87 lord summons him.'

The court of the honor was, in the early part of this period at least, held at the head of the honor, the place where the lord had his principal residence. Tutbury in Staffordshire was the head of the Ferrers honor and to the court there men must have gone even from Berkshire and Hampshire in the twelfth century. No roll of the proceedings in any honor court has survived from this age, so that it is impossible to find out for how long a lord was able to maintain the practice of a single court for the whole honor. There is no doubt that later in the middle ages a number of courts were held in central manors of groups of estates, so that long journeys were avoided. The absence of record evidence also means that it is impossible to know much about the sort of business that was done in an honor court. Nevertheless, the charters which have survived from this age throw a little light on this obscurity. When one of the king's tenants-in-chief made a grant of land in this period he frequently addressed the charter which was evidence of his gift to 'all his barons and men, French and English'. The details of this formula of address varied with the circumstances and the taste of the individual drafter; sometimes the charter was addressed to the men of a specific county or manor; but whatever phrase a magnate or his clerk favoured, the intention and reason of it was the same. The honor was a unity of which the identity was maintained by the common knowledge and the common interest of all its members.

Occasionally, too, a charter preserves a record of a particular transaction carried out in an honor court and names the members of the court who were present. A very interesting document coming from the early twelfth century records a grant made by one of the king's despensers, William de Anesye, in the court of his lord, Henry de Port, at Basing in Hampshire, the head of the honor of Port of Basing. William announced to all his own men, French and English, that with the consent of his heir he had granted land of his own acquisition to his younger son for the service of one knight. The way he made the grant is then set out. He says that with the counsel of his friends and peers – that is, men of the same feudal standing as himself in the honor of Basing – he has surrendered the land to his lord who has forthwith given it to William's son and taken his homage for it. It is noted that William's service to his lord was in arrears and that, in return for the grant, his son has paid his father's debt. No less than 36 witnesses to the deed are named and the presence of 'many others' is recorded. Five of the witnesses were members of the lord's family and bear the surname Port, and among the others are many fathers and sons recorded together. It must 88 have been a very full meeting of the honorial court.

During the hundred years between the battle of Hastings and the baronial letters of 1166 the king's tenants-in-chief were gradually elaborating the organization of their estates and completing their arrangements for providing the king with the knights he demanded. The letter sent in by the contemporary earl Ferrers illustrates how gradual was the building up of this complicated tenurial arrangement. He distinguishes between the knights his father had enfeoffed, those his grandfather had enfeoffed, and those established 89 on their knights' fees before 1135. The great men who granted land in return for knight service in the first generations after the conquest certainly did not envisage the momentous consequences of their acts. They were concerned with the immediate problem of finding knights for the king and tended to consider their grants of land as sometimes of a temporary and always of a conditional character. They did not promise to warrant the holder of the land against all men and women as later grantors did. The possession of land, even of a small estate sufficient to maintain one knight, gave its holder a settled and established feeling. Such men more often than not passed their land on to a son, and insensibly the feudal rules of inheritance came to apply to knights and their fees as they did to earls and barons and their baronies. A very interesting document coming from between 1162 and 1166 shows the court of William de Ferrers witnessing an agreement between two of its number who were the sons of one and the nephews and heirs of another of the chief tenants on the Ferrers honor. By this agreement the elder of the two made his younger brother the heir of the two baronies which their father and uncle had held of the earl. The elder brother received certain lands, set out by name, and caused his own son to become his brother's man so that the exchange should be perpetuated. These men were under-tenants, but 90 thought of themselves as barons and men of position. They could reverse the feudal rules of inheritance with the good-will of their lord, but the arrangement necessitated a long and complicated agreement made in the honor court.

The tenants of these great honors must never be thought of as mutually exclusive groups, for a man might well hold land of more than one lord. He must do homage to every lord of whom he held – 'touching life and limb and earthly honour, in what is honest and profitable, keeping his counsel to the best of his power, saving his faith to God and the ruler of the land'. But there was a special bond between 91 a man and the lord to whom he owed what came to be called liege homage, for a man could be the liege man of one lord only, namely the lord of whom he held his chief residence. He must never sit in judgement on this lord, he must follow him in war against everyone but the king, and his lord must act as his surety when necessary. The germ of the public relationship which later ages were to know as allegiance lies here. The kingdom which William the Conqueror founded came into the fullness of its stature when, after Normandy had been lost, the king's tenants-in-chief were forced to realize that they could do liege homage to only one king and that neither the king of England nor the king of France would be content with less than full allegiance.

The practice of holding land of more than one lord made it impossible to secure the personal service in the field of all who held land by knight service. Very early in the Norman age it must have been necessary on occasion to allow a man who owed knight service to perform that service by deputy or pay a sum of money to exempt him from personal service in the king's army. Illness and old age were obvious dis-abilities to which a tenant by knight service would sooner or later succumb. The succession of a daughter to a knight's fee was inevitable when once the heritable character of the knight's fee was accepted by law. The answer to this problem was scutage, shield money, payment of money

instead of performance of service. In about 1125 the son of a
man who was holding land when Domesday Book was
compiled gave an estate in Warwickshire 'for the third part
of the service of a knight, so that he ought to redeem his
whole service each year for 20 shillings, paid half at Easter
92 and half at Michaelmas'. The word scutage was already in
93 use by the year 1100. By the middle of the twelfth century
it was a long-established institution. It was generally paid
at the rate of 20 shillings on the knight's fee for each knight
whose service was not performed in person. The lord was
charged with the whole sum due from all his men and was
authorized by the king to collect the individual sums from
his tenants. Scutage made it possible for their holders to
split up knights' fees if piety, economic pressure, or the need
to provide for a daughter or a younger son made it necessary. It allowed small pieces of land to be granted in return
for a small fraction of the service of a knight. A grant of land
for the twentieth of a knight's service comes from Henry I's
94 reign. From Henry II's reign comes a grant for the hun-
95 dredth part of the service of a knight.

There is no early and general definition of the actual
amount of service in the field which could be expected from
a knight, nor are the other implications of his tenure fixed
and clear. But it so happens that towards the year 1150
John son of Gilbert, who served Henry I, Stephen, and
Henry II in turn as Marshal, granted an estate for the
service of one knight with the express stipulation that the
recipient 'if there is war shall find for me one knight for two
months, and if there is peace, for forty days, doing such
96 service as the knights of barons ought reasonably to do'.
No one in England was better qualified than the king's
Master Marshal to define the service of a knight, and the
words which have been quoted are good evidence that in
this age the service of a knight must be performed each year,
that it was longer in war than in peace-time, and that in
times of peace a knight's services might be used in any way
that was not derogatory to his station. A lord needed a
garrison for his castle and help in its maintenance. He

needed an escort for himself and his family as they rode about the land from one to another of their houses. When twelfth-century charters are closely compared it becomes apparent that the services of a knight fell under three heads – service in the field or scutage in its place, castle guard or money for a substitute, and escort duty. A great magnate 97 needed a sufficient number of enfeoffed knights to secure the performance of all these peace-time duties by groups of knights serving in turn.

When the lord had particularly heavy expenses to meet custom allowed him to take an 'aid' from his free tenants. The king himself could similarly take an aid from his tenants-in-chief. There was a continual struggle between tenant and lord about the occasions when such a payment might reasonably be taken by the lord and the amount that he might reasonably exact. The first occasion when a compromise was set out was in the Great Charter of 1215, when the king promised that he would give no one permission to take an aid from his free men save for the ransoming of his body, making his eldest son a knight, and marrying his eldest daughter for the first time. But this concession made no mention of the amount of the help that could be asked for. It was not until the Statute of Westminster in 1275 that the king set a limit to the amount a lord could ask. Then the rate was laid down at 20 shillings the knight's fee or 20 shillings for £20 worth of land held at a rent. At the same time the king forbade the taking of an aid for the knighting of the eldest son until he should be 15 years of age, and for the marriage of the eldest daughter until she should be 7 years old. 98

In addition to service in the field, castle guard, escort duty, and the aids which the lord could take from his men, he had other rights which came into operation when his tenant died. Before a son could enter upon his inheritance he must do homage for it to his lord and pay him a relief, a fine for permission to enter upon his father's lands. This death-duty, for it amounted to that, fell very heavily on all feudal tenants, whether they held directly of the king or of another lord. Here again it was not until the king granted the Charter of Liberties to all free men in 1215 that he made any concessions about the amount of the relief which feudal tenants paid. Then it was laid down that the relief of a barony should be £100 and the relief of a knight's fee 100 shillings. Before that, although there was general agreement that the sums laid down in the charter were reasonable, the king took all he could get, and there is no doubt that his barons did the same. If the heir were under age when his father died the child was in the wardship of his lord together with his lands. The lord could farm the land himself and take the profits, or sell the right to another man. The heir's upbringing and education must be looked after, but there was no power which could force the guardian to farm the land honestly. He could sell off the stock and let the buildings fall into disrepair. Few, if any, guardians were honest enough to farm the land soberly in the heir's interest and husband his resources. This uneconomic behaviour was expected and custom decreed that if an heir had been in wardship he should enter upon his lands without paying a relief. No heir who had been long in wardship would have been able to raise any considerable sum of ready money.

The marriage of the heir, too, was in the lord's gift, and he would sell it unless he had a daughter or some other female relative for whom he must needs find a husband. The widow of a military tenant, also, was of financial value to her lord. Her dower of the third part of her late husband's land together with whatever her father had given her as a marriage portion often made her a desirable match. She might well find that she had to pay the lord a sum proportionate to her financial resources to secure the right to live unmarried or marry a man of her own choice. In the Charter king John promised that widows should not be forced to marry if they wished to live without a husband. The record which most clearly shows the tight bonds which bound the feudal world in this respect comes from the year 1185 and is called the 'roll of ladies, boys and girls for twelve counties'. A typical entry runs 'Sybil of Harlton, who was daughter of Roger de Gigney, is in the king's gift and she is 70 and over. She has Harlton of the honor of Giffard and £10 worth of land. Roger of Huntingfield is her son and heir and apart from him that lady has 9 children.' 99 Great ladies were helpless before the king's demands for money or re-marriage, particularly in the reigns of Richard I and John, when the king was trying to raise money for foreign war. One of the greatest ladies in the land, Hawisa, in her own right countess of Aumale, and widow of the earl of Essex, was married by Richard I to a Poitevin, William de Forz. She tried to refuse him, but was obliged to give in because the king ordered her goods to be seized into his hand. A marriage of this sort, when an heir or heiress 100 was forced to marry someone of a lower social standing, was resented by the barons. In 1215 the king promised that an heir should not be disparaged, should be married, that is, to one of his or her own degree.

Daughters who were not heiresses, but for whom some marriage portion must be found, were often difficult to provide for. Some women desired the religious life, but even for that they needed some endowment. Great magnates with a large number of dependent knights often looked for husbands for their daughters from among their own tenants. But even then they were obliged to make some provision which would attract the man to make the marriage. In the latter part of Stephen's reign the earl of Warwick gave his daughter Alice in marriage to Geoffrey of Glympton, the king's chamberlain, who held 17 knights' fees of the earl. Alice's marriage portion from her father was a reduction in the number of knights her husband owed his father-in-law to 7. It may be assumed that the earl did not 101 regard this marriage as disparagement, although Geoffrey's father had been one of the young men raised from humble station by Henry I as a reward for his service to the king. A similar marriage portion for a daughter was provided by the Lincolnshire magnate, Gilbert de Gant, in the early thirteenth century. He agreed to reduce the knight service of Henry de Armenteres from 10 to 8 knights, to pay him 60 marks, and to pay the expenses of knighting his son, Geoffrey, who was to marry Gilbert's daughter, Juliana. This was a complicated arrangement, because Gilbert de Gant was concerned to find somewhere for the young couple to live. He therefore arranged that Henry de Armenteres should settle a manor on her with the proviso that Henry himself should receive the profits of that manor for his life. Gilbert de Gant fully realized the possibilities of friction that such an arrangement might create in the Armenteres family, but he did his best for all parties by promising to help Henry de Armenteres to suppress Geoffrey if he tried to prevent his father enjoying the income of the manor during his lifetime.

From the lords of the greatest honors down to the holders of a fraction of a knight's fee everyone was on the watch to maintain or improve a position dependent entirely on what could be wrung from the land by the men sitting on it. No refreshing stream of wealth derived from trade could be looked for in this age. Marriage was the simplest way of acquiring unearned wealth and in the marriage market hard bargains were struck throughout the middle ages. Like Galiena de Damartin, heiress of land in Essex and Suffolk, who was barely 7 years old when she was married to the first of her three husbands, most heiresses were married while they were still little children. The feudal rule that a man's inheritance should pass undivided to his eldest son preserved the unity of estates sufficiently large to enable the holder to do something for his other children without endangering the heir's position. The smaller honors did not permit of such arrangements. By feudal law the inheritance was divided between the daughters if a man left no son. Save in the case of the largest holdings, division often pointed the way, if not to debt and poverty, at least to a lowering of the standard of life to which each partner in the division had been bred. It must not be assumed that the feudal ranks of society were static, that a great lord's younger sons or his daughters could maintain their father's rank.

Amid these fluctuations of family history the status of the knight changed almost beyond recognition from the days when Englishmen equated knights with serving youths. A stake in the country was the first step which led the knight to the dominant position in local government which he had achieved by the middle of the period covered by this book. The amount of land men were offered and accepted in return for the service of one knight varied both with the relative value of the land and the individual lord's conception of what a knight needed to maintain him in that degree, nor was it of necessity all in one village or even in one county. There was policy behind the king's distribution of the lands of his greatest men about the land; it may well have been policy which led those men to scatter the holdings of their own barons. It is curious to find a magnate giving his steward for the service of half a knight lands which lie more than a hundred miles apart. 104 Each bargain made between a lord and a man who received land in return for performing knight service to the king on his lord's behalf was a separate bargain struck between two individuals. Many lords in the early part of the twelfth century considered that land worth £10 a year was adequate return for the service of one knight, but few of the men enfeoffed in the years before Domesday Book was compiled can have received as much land as this. It was on value rather than acreage that early grants for knight service were based. 105

From the early part of the twelfth century it is necessary to keep in mind the distinction between tenure by knight service and knighthood itself. As soon as the principle of scutage was accepted it became possible for men with no qualification for fighting to accept land for military service with the intention of discharging their service in cash. Such tenants were not knights and most of them had no hope or intention of ever entering the knightly order. Another distinction, too, should be remembered; the distinction between the landless knight and the enfeoffed knight, the lord of an estate sufficient to maintain him and enable him to meet any calls his lord might make. This last distinction was a real and urgent one from the knight's standpoint. Throughout this period more men were trained to fighting than could ever hope to be provided with a landed estate. A youth won his training in the household of some lord. When he had finished this apprenticeship and become skilled in arms, some gentleman of position, his own lord or another, must formally initiate him into the knightly order before he could style himself a knight. But it by no means followed automatically that he obtained a settlement in land. The landless knight in this period, as in the seventeenth century, was generally able to find occupation in the service of those who made war. Such men were 'knights bachelor', the 'bachelery of England' as they themselves declared. Some of them would in due time inherit land and others would marry into it, but until they did so they were an uneasy restless group.

Some ceremony must always have marked the end of a young man's apprenticeship to arms. As the nations of western Europe emerged from the chaos of the Dark Ages and, in the first half of the twelfth century, became conscious of new strength, social habits became more elaborate. Knighthood, chivalry, and nobility of birth became associated with one another and the ceremony of knighthood became applicable only to those of gentle birth. Men who had no claim to gentility must remain mere fighting men. A description, written about 1170, of the knighting by king Henry I of the young Geoffrey of Anjou at the time of his marriage to the king's daughter in 1127 illustrates the dignity and importance of the act. Geoffrey was ceremonially clad in robes and armour everywhere decorated with the emblem of the lion. He was marrying a king's daughter and the widow of an emperor. His knighting was a great and solemn occasion. For lesser men as well, the ceremonies which accompanied the acquisition of knighthood became more elaborate with the passing years. A night's vigil in church and a ritual bath, the provision of a mattress and costly robes, became indispensable to the making of a knight. By the end of the twelfth century these decorative social customs had taken firm root, encouraged by the rapid increase in wealth during the period. The king's accounts show that in 1204 he spent £33 on 'three robes of scarlet and three of green, two baldekins, one mattress and other necessaries for making one knight'. 107 The knight's name is not recorded, but in all probability the episode took place while king John was spending Christmas with the archbishop at Canterbury. In the same year at Bristol on 17 July king John knighted one of his valets, Thomas Esturmi, but spent no more than £6 10s. 0d. on his robes.   108

In England the reign of Stephen (1135–54) seems to mark a definite period in the social evolution of the baronial and knightly classes. The long peace of king Henry I's reign had given them wealth and leisure to develop the arts of civilized life. It was in Stephen's reign that Geoffrey of Monmouth was writing his romantic history of the Britons, describing the splendour of king Arthur's court. Part of this account Geoffrey dedicated to Robert earl of Gloucester, 'accomplished scholar and philosopher, brave knight and skilled commander,' and part to Alexander bishop of Lincoln, 'a 109 prelate of the greatest piety and wisdom. There is no one among the clergy or the laity attended with such a train of knights and nobles whom his established piety and great munificence have engaged in his service.' These phrases 110 suggest a new social ease. Inhabitants of Britain in the days of Arthur would, from Geoffrey's account of them, have felt quite at home in the England of the early twelfth century. Geoffrey set down a romanticized vision of the life of his contemporaries seen through a golden haze. He describes Arthur's fine armour, each piece of which was known by its personal name, and the feasts and sports by which Arthur's coronation was celebrated. The knights sported in imitation of a fight on horseback while the ladies watching from the walls encouraged the competitors. Geoffrey is referring to the tournaments which in this age became a frequent and regular feature of social life.

Successive popes forbade 'the detestable fairs which the vulgar call tournaments' and in 1179 Pope Alexander III declared that although their repentance must be accepted, yet those who were killed in a tourney must be forbidden 111 Christian burial. Nevertheless, the tournament throughout the twelfth century was the accepted training ground for war. The aged pope Celestine III admitted this when in 1193 he forbade the tournament on the ground that young men could learn the art of war as effectively and far more usefully by going on crusade and helping to recover 112 the Holy Places from the infidel. Papal prohibitions had little effect, for tournaments were the particular enjoyment of young noblemen. They gave rise in this period to an elaborate and increasingly formal system of devices on the helmets and shields of knights to make them easily recognizable when, clad in full armour, they rode into the tournament field. Heralds who knew the coats of arms were expected to call out the names of the competitors as they 113 rode on. Such formal devices took the place of the indeterminate markings which had decorated the shields of earlier generations. Geoffrey of Monmouth talks of the figure of the Blessed Virgin Mary painted on Arthur's shield to remind him constantly of her; an indication that Geoffrey had not 114 met the science of heraldry. But by the middle of the twelfth century the leading families of England, like those of France, had chosen their emblems or devices. A family might well have some inherited connexion with the device which it adopted. The fleur-de-lis by long tradition was associated with the family of the kings of France and the dragon with the kings of England. The coats of arms which derived from the twelfth century are generally very simple and clear, for families were not as yet hampered in choosing their devices by the necessity of avoiding infringement on the arms of others. A carefully thought out vocabulary grew up to describe the arms borne by different families. Families linked by kinship or dependent tenure with a dominant line often bore the same arms, but with a difference, that is, with some modification of the original design.

The science of heraldry was well established in England by the middle of the thirteenth century, but France was its origin and home, and the French romances of this age are the best source of information about the atmosphere of the tournament.

In England it was always something of an exotic plant. When Geoffrey de Mandeville, son of Geoffrey fitz Peter earl of Essex and Justiciar, was killed in a tournament in 1216 the chronicler Ralf of Coggeshall says that he died 'of a wound received while, in the French manner, riding horses very quickly they mutually attacked each other with lances and spears'. The spirit of William the Conqueror, 115 who would allow no private war, lived on in his descendants and successors. Stephen's love of tournaments was part of his grievous unfitness for the duties of a king. The chronicler William of Newburgh says that 'this mimic warfare, undertaken without enmity and as a trial of strength and valour only, never existed in England save in the days of king Stephen, when owing to his softness there was no vigour in public discipline'. But even Stephen tried to prevent his 116 subjects from holding tournaments and at least on one occasion early in his reign he prevented two of his greatest magnates from holding a tournament at York. When he 117 was in urgent need of money for his war with France, Richard I, another irresponsible ruler, used this eagerness for tournaments to fill his privy purse. He issued a charter from France addressed to the archbishop of Canterbury, who was ruling England on his behalf, to the effect that tournaments could be held in five places in England, between Salisbury and Wilton in Wiltshire, between Warwick and Kenilworth in Warwickshire, between Stamford 118 and Wansford Bridge in Northamptonshire, between Brackley and Mixbury in Northamptonshire and Oxfordshire, and between Blythe and Tickhill in north Nottinghamshire and south Yorkshire. Three earls were sureties that those who wished to enjoy this privilege would pay 10 marks for the king's charter.

Even Richard I felt it necessary to state in this document

that his peace must not be broken, nor the power of justice be diminished, nor wrong done in his forests. An earl must pay 20 marks for permission to engage in a tournament, a baron 10 marks, a knight who had land 4 marks, and a landless knight 2 marks, but no foreigner must engage in the sport. On the day of the tournament the Justiciar must have two clerks and two of his knights present on the field to take oaths from all the earls and barons and knights that they will pay before they engage in the sport, and to keep a record of their names and their payment. There survives a copy of the carefully worded 'form of peace' to which all 119 who engage in the tournament must subscribe. It was probably the work of the archbishop who tried to anticipate and guard against the worst evils that might arise. From the time anyone left his house to go to the place of tourney until he came home again he must take nothing unjustly and without permission, but must buy at the usual markets. In going and coming he and his men must give offence to none. If they themselves meet with trouble and cannot right it, they shall report it and it will be amended. All who go to a tournament shall swear that they will be in the justice of the lord king and keep his peace, going and coming and while at the tournament, in particular as to the king's forests and markets. How much money came to Richard I from this concession will never be known, for it was not paid into the Treasury nor accounted for at the Exchequer. 120 It is therefore not recorded on the Pipe rolls.

Those who engaged most eagerly in this social pastime were young men of the baronial class who had nothing to do and landless knights who made war their profession. There was no better training for war, for a tournament was a mimic battle, a general engagement taking place over a wide area, and though knights rode on and off the field at pleasure the prize went to the one who fought hardest. The five places which Richard I licensed were all stretches of open rolling country either on or near a great main road. Tournaments were very dangerous, for no rules could control excitement. One of Henry II's sons, Geoffrey,

husband of the heiress of Brittany, was killed in a tournament in France in 1186. He was thrown and trampled on
by his horse. In 1286 the heir of the earl Warenne was 121
killed in a tournament at Croydon. These were by no means 122
isolated instances. The French king's authority in the
twelfth century was too restricted for him to have prevented
tournaments even had he wished to, and English knights
were free to attend them as long as the two kings were at
peace with one another. When they were at war occupation
was ready at hand without the fictitious excitement of the
tournament. In the days before Normandy was conquered
by Philip II the upper ranks of English society had such
close ties with northern France that they were slow to
develop a purely English outlook. They were inclined to
take their fashions in sport as in dress from their French
neighbours whose language they spoke. When John
imported mercenaries from the south-west of France they
probably wanted some entertainment in England as well as
the labours of a Scottish expedition, for on one occasion the
king gave two of them an allowance to buy themselves linen
armour, that is, the costume worn on the tournament field. 123

When the barons were holding London and waiting there
in revolt against king John for help to come to them from
France they planned to hold a tournament at Stamford.
Belatedly they realized that Stamford, that is, the tournament ground between Wansford Bridge and Stamford, was
so far from London that they might lose the city if it were
left unguarded. They therefore wrote to William de
Aubigny of Belvoir who would have gone to Stamford
direct from Belvoir to tell him that under these circumstances they were putting off the Stamford meeting, but
proposed to hold a tournament near London on the heath
of Staines. They urged William to come to the tournament
so provided with horses and arms that he might have
honour therein. 'He who shall do best there will have the
bear which a certain lady will send to the tournament.' 124
The commanders of the baronial forces doubtless regarded
this meeting as a means of keeping fit for the coming war

with John. It is not surprising that the council which controlled the land for the young king Henry III found that the rebellion and war had left much unrest behind it. While many young men went off on crusade others showed a zest for tournaments which the council tried in vain to curb. The papal ban on the sport pronounced in the interest of the crusade was used in the hope of keeping the peace. When a tournament was arranged the chief ecclesiastical members of the king's council pronounced a sentence of excommunication against all who should take part in it. This did not mean that the meeting was put off. In 1219 even the presence of Stephen Langton, archbishop of Canterbury, on the tournament field was not enough to 125 stop play. Had the attendance been restricted to landless knights the danger would have been less acute. It was the eager participation of the irresponsible young noblemen with their personal followers wearing their livery which made the occasion a menace to society.

Henry III tried to maintain the royal prohibition of tournaments. He himself cared nothing for the sport, for his interests lay in art and fine buildings. His health was poor and his temper uncertain. He found it particularly difficult to insist on obedience to his orders to abstain from tournaments because in his reign so many foreigners came to England to seek their fortunes, and they expected to enjoy the sports of France. The queen's relatives began to come over immediately after the marriage in 1236 and his own relatives by his mother's second marriage as soon as they were old enough to come. But even before 1236 English knights had discovered the delights of local competitive sport, and tournaments between north and south roused the excitement of a cup final. At Oxford, too, students had violent affrays between northerners and southerners. In 1236 a tournament between the northern and southern knights was held in Lent. Long before the victory of the southerners was at last admitted the game had turned into a real battle. The papal legate, Otto, was called in to 126 appease the venom of the contesting parties. When the

Frenchmen began to swarm into England tournaments between English and French were the obvious means of passing the time. In 1247 two of the king's half-brothers arrived in England, Guy of Lusignan, who was already a knight, and William de Valence, who had not yet been knighted. Guy de Lusignan and the earl of Gloucester 127 arranged a tournament in which they should be the leaders of the contesting sides. The test was to be held between Dunstable and Luton. Henry III forbade it, fearing that Guy would be killed because of English jealousy of the king's favour to his foreign kinsfolk.

128

In Michaelmas of that year the king summoned all his barons to London for the feast of the Translation of St Edward a fortnight after Michaelmas so that they might be present when a gift of the blood of Christ brought from Jerusalem was taken in solemn procession to the church at Westminster, and when also the king proposed to confer the honour of knighthood on his young half-brother, William of Valence. After the solemn service at Westminster, the king, wearing a small golden crown and sitting on his throne, caused William to be summoned. He came attended by a great company and the king knighted him and some of those with him. On this occasion he agreed that a 129 tournament should be held so that William and his companions might gain skill in knightly arts. The earl of Gloucester gladly challenged William to come to a general tournament at Northampton, for the English nobles were seeking an occasion to reduce the pride of the newcomers. When the appointed day drew near the king in council forbade the meeting, fearing trouble. At last, however, on 130 Ash Wednesday 1248 the king was brought to allow it, and it began and ended in good order. William of Valence showed great spirit, but could do little against the hard and warlike knights of England. He was unhorsed and given a good beating to initiate him in knightly practices. William's 131 enthusiasm was in no wise diminished and when, in the next year, the king forbade the Ash Wednesday engagement at Northampton William sent word to the contestants that

if weather permitted they should not fail to attend, promising that he would shield them from his brother's wrath.
132 A foot of snow prevented the engagement taking place. Later in the year knights from all over England gathered at Brackley. The earl of Gloucester, who had hitherto led those who challenged the foreigners, on this occasion
133 changed sides. William of Valence and his supporters thoroughly defeated the English knights. They had their revenge in 1251 in a bitter tournament at Rochester where they returned with interest the blows they had received at
134 Brackley.

It was impossible to maintain the royal prohibition of tournaments against such men as the earl of Gloucester and when, too, it was generally accepted that the man who shunned the tournament forfeited the esteem of his fellows. A man beaten in the tournament must try to win back his renown. In 1252 the earl of Gloucester was obliged to go abroad to restore the credit of his brother William, who, having been shamefully overthrown, had lost all his horses and arms in a tournament. The earl won back all his brother had lost, 'returning with the greatest honour to his
135 own land, having almost annihilated his adversaries'. In the middle years of the century the fashion in tournaments was changing in response to the influence of the romantic legends of the British past. Already in 1252 Matthew Paris describes how 'not in that sport vulgarly called the tournament but rather in that game of chivalry called the Round Table' knights gathered at Walden from the north and south as well as many from abroad. This meeting had an unhappy ending, for on the fourth day, while two knights renowned for their prowess were within the lists, one of them was killed, his adversary's lance having pierced his throat between the joints of his armour. No suspicion of foul play arose until the earl of Gloucester dug out the point of the lance and found that it was not blunted as it should have been, but sharp as a dagger. Then it was remembered that the dead man had in a previous tournament broken the leg of the man who had just killed him. Matthew Paris remarks

that of this God alone, the searcher of hearts, knows the truth.   136

Despite this unhappy event the Round Table was a less barbarous affair than a mimic battle which might so easily turn into a real one. The knights who attended a Round Table engaged in individual joustings with blunt weapons and light armour rather than in the confused general engagements of the formal tournament. They feasted at tables set around the walls of the hall, leaving the centre an open space for minstrels and the servers of the feast. The rise of this fashion in England showed that the tournament in some form or other had been accepted by authority. Henry III's son, Edward, the future conqueror of Wales and, for a time, of Scotland, was growing up in this atmosphere of warlike endeavour. He had none of his father's dislike of the tournament, for he grew up tall and handsome, fit to engage in the sport. In 1260 Edward took a great company of knights abroad to tourney and was soundly beaten, losing all he had. In the summer of 1262 he was abroad again, having, with difficulty and with his mother's help, raised money from Italian merchants to retrieve his previous losses. But instead he was beaten and severely wounded and lost all he had taken with him. In the life of 137 Edward I foreign tournaments were indeed the training ground of a great king.

Although there is no doubt of the reality of English interest in tournaments, there is equally no doubt that the men who were most drawn to the sport in the thirteenth century were the magnates who had competent servants to look after their lands and hold their courts, so that they were left with little to do. Such men set the fashion. Inevitably landless knights were drawn into their ambit in the hope of getting a settlement in land. Young men who would one day inherit land but for whom there was not yet a place in England had always found, or hoped to find, profitable adventure in going abroad to tourney. In Henry II's reign William the Marshal, later earl of Pembroke and at last regent of England for Henry III, was learning the art of

138 war by going to tournaments in France. But there is no doubt that in Henry II's reign those men who had received land in return for knight service or had inherited land given to their fathers or grandfathers were finding that the settled estate in land, with its interests and responsibilities, tended to distract their attention from what had originally been their reason for existence. The average holder of a knight's fee in Henry II's reign was more interested in his land and in his hopes of increasing the family estate by arranging provident marriages for all his children than in the service for which the land had originally been granted.

In 1181 Henry II found it necessary to issue an Assize of Arms in which he set out the weapons and equipment appropriate to the knight, the freeman, and the burgess. He sent Justices to each shire to enforce this Assize. Every holder of a knight's fee must have a coat of mail and a helmet, a shield and a lance. Those of the king's tenants-in-chief who had omitted to provide for all their knight service by the creation of knight's fees must possess enough armour to arm the knights for whom they were personally respon-

139 sible. Throughout this period armour was becoming heavier, more elaborate, and consequently more expensive. The representation of a knight fully armed on horseback which appears on the seals of all men of rank in the latter part of the twelfth century is good evidence for the trend of

140 fashion in armour. Towards the end of the century men began to protect their horses with something that would at least turn a glancing blow. Leg pieces which look like iron stockings, gloves of mail, and a padded waistcoat to wear under the coat of mail added to the knight's safety but were a costly addition to his equipment. Every extra piece of armour meant a stronger and more costly horse. When at the end of this period plate armour was coming into fashion for man and horse the price of a war-horse rose steeply. Over his armour the knight wore a surcoat of fine stuff or silk which might be richly decorated. But already by the early years of Henry III's reign many holders of one or two knights' fees must have felt that there was little to be gained

from learning the art of war. It was cheaper and safer to pay scutage and stay at home. Men who thought along these lines inevitably went on to wonder whether there was much to be gained by undergoing the ceremony of becoming a knight. The necessity of procuring armour and a horse suitable to the occasion, the cost of the entertainments expected by kinsfolk, men, and friends made knighthood appear a luxury readily foregone.

From 1194, when Richard I returned home from captivity in Germany, to 1204, when John lost Normandy to Philip II, war between France and England was almost continuous, although broken by occasional truces and treaties. After 1204 it was not until the battle of Bouvines in 1214 made it evident that the loss of Normandy must be accepted in England that the English king ceased to press for a renewal of war with France. These years of overseas war mark a change in the character of the knight's service, for they force upon the attention of king and baron alike the question of how much service the king could exact from each individual knight. Legal documents avoid precision on this vitally important issue which was one of the causes of the break between king and barons in 1215. Even the Great Charter makes no more than the discreet promise that no man shall be forced to do more service for a knight's fee than he ought to do.

It is possible that the theory that a knight's service should be limited to forty days arose from a custom which demanded that amount of service yearly from each knight in time of peace. For campaigns at home to suppress a rebellious baron or avert a threatened incursion of the Welsh there was no need for long-term service. A succession of campaigns across the Channel made urgent a question which earlier sovereigns had not been concerned to raise. Richard I and John needed a standing army. Richard I met the problem in part by hiring Welsh foot soldiers and Brabantine mercenaries, but he could not afford to make war with them alone. A foot soldier was paid 2 pence or 3 pence a day and a horseman 4 pence or 6 pence, but these were the rank and file, hired in hundreds. Archers, mounted or on foot, formed a small minority of these forces. Knights to officer them were essential, and companies of mounted knights were still a vital part of an army in the field. Prices were rising fast. In the middle of Henry II's reign 142 a knight could be hired for 8 pence a day. Knights who were expected to command foot soldiers seem to have been 143 paid 12 pence a day. At the end of the century a knight 144 could demand a daily wage of 2 or 3 shillings.

In 1196 while a truce with France was still in force, Richard I wrote home to the archbishop of Canterbury, saying that he expected war rather than peace with the king of France and asking that his tenants-in-chief should come prepared to stay with him in Normandy for some time. To lighten their burden he suggested that each should 145 be accompanied by at most seven knights. This letter is the first sign of what became the solution of the problem, a reduction in the number of knights which each tenant-in-chief was expected to bring to the royal army. In 1198 Richard I asked through the archbishop that his English tenants should either send him a force of 300 knights to serve with him in Normandy for a year, or help him with the money necessary to hire such a force at the rate of 146 3 shillings a day for each knight. Knights with responsibilities to their English lands would certainly be unwilling to stay abroad so long and it was money rather than men that Richard expected and did in fact receive. The king's need for knight service meant that individuals who wished to purchase from him land or privilege occasionally offered knight service as a bribe. In 1204 a member of the Neville family paid 60 marks and a palfrey to have Jordan de Aneville's widow with her land and promised, in addition, that 'he will serve the king as a single knight with horses 147 and arms for a year at his own cost'. In 1205 John was planning a major assault on France and was particularly vulnerable to bribes of this sort. Richard of Herriard, a judge, in that year agreed to pay the king 100 marks and 'send one knight into the king's service' in return for being allowed 'to put himself on the grand assize for the land he was claiming against Gilbert de Hauville'. As a judge, 148 Richard knew all too well that the plaintiff had no right to ask for the grand assize. In that year John demanded that all knights in every shire should be constrained by the sheriff to send to the royal army one from every ten knights in the shire, to be armed and paid by the other nine at the rate of 2 shillings a day. The length of service required 149 is not specified, but the implication is that the knights must remain with the king while he needs them. No one realized more clearly than king John that the arrangements made by William the Conqueror to provide himself with an army were out of date in his great-great-grandson's days. The army of 1205 gathered as the king commanded, but it never crossed the Channel. Almost the last public act of archbishop Hubert Walter was his successful protest, with William Marshal earl of Pembroke, at the renewal of the war with France. 15c

If knights whose ancestors had accepted land in return for service in the field found that active service was ceasing to be their primary obligation to the king, they found simultaneously that their civil duties were rapidly increasing. When William I was king, he was forced to use his greatest men, his more important tenants-in-chief, for every variety of public service. They were his advisers and judges, the commanders in his armies and the agents of his government in the shires. His sons bred up a race of officials, civil servants trained to the work of government and making a career in public administration. The fact that many of them were rewarded by marriages or lands which carried them into the baronial class does not affect the fact that a new reservoir of administrative talent had been found. Into this group, able young men were constantly being recruited. At the same time the descendants of the rough fighting men and the younger sons who had made up the Conqueror's army – the miscellaneous crowd of men who had won knights' fees – were getting rich. In the courts of their lords' honors they had experience of law and practical business.

Within a wider field they were steadily being drawn more closely into the work of local government. Inherited from the Anglo-Saxon age, the courts of shire and hundred presented a field of opportunity to those who were interested in the affairs of the countryside. William I and his sons preserved the shire and hundred courts, in which since days beyond the memory of man free men had met under the chairmanship of the king's representative to settle their 151 disputes in the traditional way.

As a result of these influences there came into being in every shire a group of men who were beginning to be thought and spoken of as the knights of the shire. It was to twelve knights of the shire that Henry II entrusted the supervision of his venison in his forests. To four knights of the shire was assigned the oversight of forest pasture-rights. From a still earlier date, men of this type had repeatedly been called into service on the juries summoned to answer questions about local boundaries or local customs. To the knights of the shire in the first place and only after them to the great body of free and lawful men, the reforming administrators of the age looked for the more frequent juries upon whose work the new developments depended. It would have been an intolerable burden on what must always have been a small class to demand that all the men should be knights who served on the juries in the new forms of action, on the juries which informed the king of crimes and accusations of crime, on the juries which answered innumerable questions on small matters of fact put to them by the king and his ministers. But the king insisted that the juries of Grand Assize, by whose verdict the ownership of land was settled, should be composed of knights. Four knights of the shire where the land at issue lay chose twelve knights of the same shire to give a categorical reply to the question 'Who has the greater right to this land?' Knights were sent by the king's court to view the infirmity of such litigants as pleaded that they could not be present in court by reason of sickness that confined them to bed. When a litigant wished to appoint an attorney to plead his case for him and was unable to come to the court to name him, knights were sent to learn the litigant's choice. When the court needed an impartial view of land or common rights of which the ownership was in dispute, knights were sent to make the view. When the king's court at Westminster needed information about the progress of a suit in the shire court two knights were sent to 'bear the record of the shire'. An individual suspected or accused of felony might be put formally by the court in the custody of a group of knights who would be responsible for holding him and producing him when required. Every one of these pieces of business involved more than one appearance in a court of justice and many of them called for tiresome and sometimes distant journeys.

Such work, all of it unpaid and time-consuming, increased greatly with the increasing popularity of the royal courts of justice. It is not until 1202 that the records of judicial proceedings in a single county survive completely enough to give an impression of how these burdens were being met by the men of the countryside. In that year king John sent a company of judges to ride the circuit Lincoln, Leicester, Coventry, Northampton, Bedford, Dunstable and so back to Westminster. The complete rolls of proceedings at Lincoln survive, also a rather battered roll from Northampton, and the short roll compiled at Bedford. In 152 this year a number of knightly tenants were on active service in Normandy with the king or were waiting to cross the sea. Twelve such men are mentioned by name in the Lincoln roll. But there is nowhere in these rolls any hint that there were not enough knights in the shires, and, indeed, present in court, to meet the demands of justice. In Lincolnshire 140 men served in this year on juries on which only knights could serve, predominantly juries of grand assize. Most of them served on only one assize, but a number on two or three; several served on four, two on five, and one, William son of Amfrid, on six. He must have been one of those men, like some hardworking county councillors today, who spend their lives in county business.

Seventy-nine undoubted knights can be counted among the names which appear on the Northampton roll and 38 on the Bedford roll. These figures do not suggest that at the beginning of the century there existed any unwillingness among the lesser gentry in the shires to take up the burden of knighthood.

Nor does the roll of civil proceedings at Lincoln in the winter of 1218–19 suggest that the business was at all held up 153 for lack of knights. It is true that only 42 knights can be identified from their jury work at Lincoln in that year, although the business far exceeds that of 1202. But by 1218 the grand assize was far less popular than it had been at the turn of the century. It was slow and cumbersome. It turned on a categorical answer that a jury more often than not found itself quite unable to give. Other simpler and quicker processes had been devised which a jury of free and lawful men could settle. In 1208 Robert son of Ralf of Massingham paid 5 marks to be quit of service on juries and inquests except those which concerned the king's rights 154 when a dispute had arisen between the king and others. Such quittances increased in popularity until the barons complained in 1258 that the king had given them so freely in many counties that no grand assize could be taken for 155 lack of knights, and plaintiffs therefore could not get justice. The reformers of this time found a work of fundamental importance for the knights in every shire and no exemptions from jury service were valid with regard to this new work. In every county four knights were to be chosen. They were to attend every meeting of the shire court and make a list of all complaints of injuries brought by individuals against 156 sheriffs and other government officials.

The change in outlook which resulted in this unwillingness to accept the burdens of knighthood must have developed rapidly in the early years of Henry III's reign. Jury service must have been light in the closing years of John's reign when no itinerant justices were at work and the bench at Westminster was almost idle, but as soon as Henry III became king and rebels began to return to their allegiance the services of juries who knew what lands rebels had held before the war were much in demand all over England. The council devised a 'common writ' which men who returned to the allegiance of Henry III could buy. It instructed the sheriff to put the purchaser into possession of such land as he had held before the war and had lost by reason of the war. Each writ of this sort meant work for a [157] jury. Dislike of these unpaid obligations and the increasing professionalism of war worked together to bring about a minor social revolution. The social standing of the knight no longer seemed to compensate for the work he had to do. From the king's point of view this was unfortunate. He was less concerned about jury work, for most of that could be sustained by the increasing band of freemen. But young men who held knights' fees and remained simple freemen would in all probability abstain from purchasing the armour suitable to their station. They could not be counted on as effective fighting men in case of need, even for the defence of England.

The king's counter to his subjects' reluctance to be knighted was a general order in 1234 to all sheriffs that they should proclaim throughout their bailiwicks that all men who held one or more knights' fees in chief of the king should procure arms and cause themselves to be knighted. [158] But the full effect of this and later proclamations of the same type was to a certain extent hampered by exceptions which the king showed himself ready to grant to individuals. Only a month or two after the 1234 proclamation, for example, Henry III exempted Andrew Blund 'valet of the archbishop of Dublin' from the order. Such exemptions at [159] any rate served the useful purpose of bringing money in to the Crown. But that the Crown had in mind the military situation in particular is suggested by the order of 1282 that all men with £30 worth of land should provide themselves with a horse and armour. They need not, that is, be knighted, but they must have the weapons of war. In 1285 all freeholders worth more than £100 a year were to become knights; in 1292 the income level for compulsory knight-

160 hood was lowered to £40. It is difficult to find evidence about the success of these orders and there is no doubt that they were used as a means of raising money by the sale of exemptions. Nevertheless it is clear that through the greater part of the thirteenth century the government was trying by the artificial means of general orders to keep in being a military form of society which was out of date.

It was probably with this end in view that kings stressed the pageantry of the ceremony by which men were admitted into the order of knighthood. The fashion of knighting a group of distinguished people at the same time and making a social occasion of it made for the same end. In 1225 Henry III gave his brother Richard the knightly belt 'and
161 with him ten nobles destined for his service'. Richard was at this time sixteen years old. He was sent off a little later in the year with two older and experienced men and an escort of 40 knights to take over the rule of the English possessions in south-west France. In order to stress the solemnity of the occasion 15 other youths were knighted in 1241 with Peter of Savoy, one of the queen's uncles, to whom Henry III had
162 given the earldom of Richmond. In 1252 Alexander III of Scotland married Henry III's daughter at York and on the day before the wedding in order that he 'might show reverence and honour to his lord, his neighbour, and his future father-in-law' Alexander was knighted by Henry III. Twenty other young men were knighted with him, all clad in exceptionally fine garments as befitted so important a
163 ceremony. A month before he died in 1272 Henry III knighted his nephew, Edmund, and invested him with his earldom of Cornwall. At the same time Henry de Lacy earl of
164 Lincoln and fifty English and foreign nobles were knighted.

With a programme of wars ahead Edward I from the beginning of his reign tried to encourage young men to become knights by every means in his power. If his direct orders that men should be knighted were largely ignored, his temptations were more successful. The conquest of Wales was celebrated by an elaborate 'Round Table' held in the
165 heart of the Snowdon country. Tournaments became part of

the accepted social scene in Edward's reign. He encouraged the deliberate archaism which regarded the conquest of Wales as an adventure like those undertaken by Arthur's knights of the Round Table. The search for the Holy Grail, Parsifal, and the swans belong to the continental strain in the romance of medieval knighthood, but Edward drew on that, too, in his efforts to stimulate the sluggish imaginations of young men. His most elaborate temptation to youth was offered in his old age. In 1306 Robert Bruce made his bid for the crown of Scotland, newly conquered after stupendous and long drawn out campaigns by the English king. Bruce began his adventure by murdering, in church, the man who stood in his way and would never have agreed to join him. In that year Edward prince of Wales was twenty-two years old and he had not yet been knighted. The king proclaimed that all who wished to be knighted with the prince should come to London and that the cost of the ceremony would be borne by the king. The 267 young men who presented themselves provided their own horses and armour, but the king gave them their knightly robes. The prince was knighted by the king in private and then came out into Westminster abbey church and knighted his companions. A particularly splendid feast was held when two swans decked with golden chains were brought into the hall and the king swore on the swans that he would avenge the murder with which Bruce's rebellion had begun.

Edward I realized that knighthood must be tied to the court and the glamour of the court if young men were to be drawn into the knightly order. But this richness and display, this feasting and jousting had but a remote bearing on the life of the man of substance in the countryside. It might make him feel that the expense of knighthood was worth while so that he could be akin to the world of fashion and for a moment figure in the court. But many men must have felt that they could remain useful members of society, attending their shire courts and serving on juries, farming their estates, and marrying off their children, without taking up the status of a knight.

CHAPTER III

THE COUNTRYSIDE AND
ITS INHABITANTS

The Forests

FROM the crowded streets of a modern city it is difficult if
not impossible to look back in the mind of the countryside
of the twelfth and thirteenth centuries. But the effort of the
imagination is well worth while and in some parts of England
these centuries do not seem so very far away. Their influence
is apparent in the aspect of most country scenes to those who
have any knowledge of past history. One dominant element
in country life in these centuries has long passed away. The
king's forests are no longer protected by a special forest law.
In these centuries the vital distinction in the countryside
was between land subject to the forest law and land which
lay outside the boundaries of the king's forests. The law of
the forest, as the medieval people knew it, was not the slow
growth through centuries of settled government, but a
Norman innovation due to the love of hunting which in
William I and his successors amounted almost to a passion.
'The forest has its own laws,' said Richard fitz Nigel in the
Dialogus, 'based not on the common law of the realm, but
166 on arbitrary legislation by the king.' When the Normans
came to England the land had been subjected for centuries
to the gradual encroachment by the plough on waste and
forest. It was still a well-wooded land and even in those
parts where the richness of the soil had encouraged early
clearance and more intense cultivation – such a district as
the Vale of the White Horse in Berkshire – there were still
more trees than the modern eye would expect to see.
Nevertheless, had the forest law not been introduced to
curb, and in some measure direct, the subjection of virgin

soil to the plough, the beasts of the forest would have vanished from the English scene perhaps a century or more before they did.

'In the forests,' said Richard fitz Nigel, 'are the secret places of the kings and their great delight. To them they go for hunting, having put off their cares, so that they may enjoy a little quiet. There, away from the continuous business and incessant turmoil of the court, they can for a little time breathe in the grace of natural liberty, wherefore it is that those who commit offences there lie under the royal displeasure alone.' Asked to define the word forest, Richard said 'The king's forest is the safe dwelling place of wild beasts, not of every sort, but of the sort that dwell in the woodlands, not in any sort of place, but in certain places suitable for the purpose.' In reply to the query whether there were royal forests in every county, the Treasurer said 'No, but in wooded counties where the lairs of the wild beasts are, and very rich feedings.' In the days of Queen 167 Elizabeth when the forest law had long been in a state of decay, John Manwood wrote a treatise about it. He began by defining the word forest. He described it as 'a certaine territorie of wooddy grounds and fruitful pastures, privi- ledged for wild beasts and foules of the forest, chase, and warren, to rest and abide in the safe protection of the king for his princely delight and pleasure'. Manwood elaborates 168 the phrase 'wooddy grounds and fruitful pastures', saying that 'a Forest must be stored with great woods or coverts for the secret abode of wild beastes and also with fruitful pastures for their continual feed: for the want of either of these two, doth cause the exile of wild beastes from the forest to some other place, for that the nature of the wild beaste of the Forest is, to flie into the thicke coverts for places of Secresie to rest in, whereof if there be none within the Forest, then they leave the Forest, and wander up and downe untill they find coverts elsewhere, which being with- out the bounds of the Forest, where those wild Beastes are so found wandering, then they are hunted and killed to the utter destruction of the Forest: and in like manner it is, if the wild beastes have not those fruitful pastures within the Forest for their feed, then they pine away and starve, or else they are forced to forsake the forest and to seek for food without the Forest, where they can find the same, and then they are likewise hunted and killed, whence it is manifest that a Forest cannot have continuance without wooddy grounds and fruitful pastures. And so consequently it followeth, that to destroy the coverts of the Forest, is to destroy the Forest itselfe; Also to convert the pasture grounds, meadowes, and feedings into arable land, is likewise to destroy the forest.'

How much of England lay within the borders of the royal forests in this period is a very difficult question to answer. Nor would an accurate answer tell how much of the country was dense woodland. Whole villages with their appropriate complement of arable and pasture lay within the boundaries of royal forests and were subject to the law devised to protect the king's beasts of the chase. That William the Conqueror created the New Forest is one of the commonplaces of historical knowledge. It is not always remembered that he could not by an act of royal power make of a stretch of fertile countryside a dense forest suitable for his hunting. What he did was to declare that a stretch of rough forest and common land, within which villages and hamlets lay in forest clearings, was subject to the Forest Law, and to put in it beasts of the chase to breed and multiply for hunting. The whole land was indeed set about and studded with forests preserved for the enjoyment of the king. Some counties were so closely populated and tilled that the Norman and Angevin kings made no attempt to create forests in them. Kent is a notable example of a county which even in this stage must already have shown something of its garden-like character. Bishop Odo of Bayeux whom the Conqueror made his earl in Kent created a Park for beasts at Wickhambreux, but he had to give to the archbishop four stretches of swine pasture in exchange for the 25 acres he enclosed. Norfolk and Suffolk, too, escaped the forest law, but Lincolnshire men who lived in 'the marsh' were

subject to it, for 'Pleas of the forest touching the marsh'
appear in the Pipe rolls. They seem to refer to the lowlands
of Kesteven, once long ago a forest, but showing little signs
of it in the twelfth century.   171

Epping Forest is the meagre remnant of the days when
almost all Essex lay within the king's forest and was
described as the king's forest of Essex. But in that county
were many ancient villages, as its place names prove. From
the Thames, which for many miles was the northern
boundary of Windsor forest, a man could in these days pass
southwards, bearing in a somewhat westerly direction
through the woods of Eversley or Bagshot into Pamber and
so into Bere Forest and finally into the king's New Forest
which was bounded by Southampton Water and the
Channel coast. Throughout his journey he would be within
country which lay under forest law, and far on his either
hand forest jurisdiction spread. In the thirteenth century
officials could talk of the great expanse of country which lay
in the Midlands, north and north-east of Oxford, as 'the
forest between the bridges of Oxford and Stamford'.
Within its borders lay the forests of Shotover and Bernwood,
Whittlewood, Salcey, and Rockingham. The Hay of Hereford which was under forest law was a district about six
miles in length which included part of the town of Hereford
itself. Sherwood forest in Nottinghamshire is part of our
common literary inheritance, but that the High Peak in
Derbyshire and Macclesfield below it were forest is less
generally realized, for the High Peak was a mountain
wilderness, very different from the oaken glades of Sherwood. In Yorkshire Galtres, immediately to the north of
York, and Pickering were royal forests and covered many
square miles. A great area in Northumberland was forest
and in Cumberland lay the wide forests of Allerdale and
Inglewood. In Lancashire Lonsdale and Amunderness at
one time were subject to forest law. But there were still 172
vast areas of wild land in the north which lay outside the
forest law. The king's favourite hunting places lay in the
south, south-west, the west, and the midlands.

The English forests in this age were the relics of the primeval woods with which the land was in remote days very largely covered. By this time the majority of the noxious wild beasts of ancient forests had been eliminated. In the early twelfth century earl Alan of Richmond blamed his steward and constable for allowing wolves to congregate in the Yorkshire dales round Byland abbey to trouble the country folk, but in the thirteenth century few wolves can have survived to be a nuisance. For many generations they had been regarded as the enemy of the countryside. 'Let him bear the wolf's head' was the traditional sentence on a man who was being outlawed from the society of his fellows. Like the wolf, the outlaw could and should be killed at sight. A few wolves occasionally bred in the English forests and in the mountains of Wales, Westmorland, and the Peak in the early years of the thirteenth century. Those who killed wolves in forest country could be sure of a reward from the king. In 1210 king John gave 15 shillings to two huntsmen who killed two wolves at Gillingham in Dorset and another at Clarendon in Wiltshire. That he gave so much suggests that he was not often called upon to pay it. All through these years the Worcestershire wolf-catcher received 3 shillings a year from the sheriff, but there is no evidence that he was ever expected to account for the wolves he killed. The beasts protected by the forest law were the red deer, the fallow deer, the roe, and the wild boar. The last of these was becoming scarce and by the middle of the thirteenth century there can have been few left. In Edward III's reign, after the period covered by this book, the roe deer ceased to be protected by the forest law, because, it was said, it drove away the other deer. The impression the records give of the forests of this age is that the English kings were trying desperately to cling to a rapidly vanishing past, when the forests were alive with game for the pleasure of the king.

It was mainly for the purpose of protecting these cherished animals that the king assumed the right of allowing certain of his subjects the privilege of hunting other wild animals regarded as harmful to the beasts of the chase. The animals which were the subject of such grants were the fox, the hare, the cat, and sometimes the badger and even the squirrel. The wolf was often included after the fox for good measure, and the coney, though not specifically mentioned, seems to have been included in practice with the hare. The earliest grants of hunting rights of this nature do not specify the animals to be hunted, but merely state that the king is granting rights of warren. The bishops of Lincoln, whose see covered much of the centre and east of England, received from successive kings a long series of charters granting them rights of warren. Henry I gave to bishop Alexander warren over all his land in Lincolnshire and Nottinghamshire. Henry II confirmed his grandfather's 177 grants to bishop Robert II. In giving him warren over the 178 lands between Newark and Stow, the king stressed the amplitude of the gift – 'whosoever the lands may be'. 179 This was unusually generous. The normal practice was for the king to confine such rights to the recipient's own estates. Many men whose lands lay within counties under forest law received charters allowing them rights of warren in their lands within the forest. By these generous grants of warren the common rights of hunting, which in remoter and less populous days, when kings were less autocratic, had been unrestricted, were gradually whittled away, and the scene was prepared for the game-laws of modern times.

The king for his own reasons was generous in his creation of warrens. He was much less willing to allow a subject to have a private forest, although, in the aggregate, grants by successive kings placed considerable stretches of country under the control of individual magnates as private forests, generally called chases. To the people who lived within a chase there can have seemed little difference in the severity of the rules which governed their contact with the country around them and the beasts that lived in it. The foresters who looked after a chase were responsible to a subject, not to the king, and the king's forest justices did not as a rule enter a chase to hear forest pleas. But when king John 180 granted part of the forest of Huntingdonshire to Geoffrey fitz Peter earl of Essex, he promised that the local forest court should still take care of the offences against the forest for that part which he had given to Geoffrey and that 181 Geoffrey should have the profits arising from it. In the north particularly, there were many woods put 'in defence' by their owners – the first step towards the assumption of full hunting rights and the exclusion of others from them.

Magnates who controlled forest country could make grants of woodland in very similar terms to those employed by the king. Between 1253 and 1260 Roger de Quincy earl of Winchester and constable of Scotland granted a stretch of woodland in Shepshed, Leicestershire, to Garendon abbey so that they might 'assart', that is, plough up, 'sell, and make their profit in whatever way they freely wish'. He gave them in addition 'all the beasts of the chase and all woodland beasts of any sort which they have or in the future shall have, or which shall in any way be found in the en- closed wood, to chase and to hunt and to take in whatever 182 way they wish . . . provided that they do not make a deer- leap'. A deer-leap was a sunk fence, or 'ha-ha', up which the deer could leap into an enclosure, but which he could not negotiate in the opposite direction. The king, too, disliked a sunk fence in a park wall near any of his forests. In 1207 Eustace the parson of Lowdham, then in Sherwood forest, had to pay 15 marks in annual instalments of 15 shillings to appease the king because 'he had caused a ditch to be 183 made in the manner of a leap'.

The custom of making parks or enclosures from which the deer could not stray was common all over the country. Windsor Great Park was originally such an enclosure within the greater area of Windsor forest. Billingbear park in east Berkshire was a park of the bishop of Winchester adjacent to the king's forest. Individuals who made a park near the king's forest were well advised to get his permission. If they did not, they might find themselves charged with a consider- able sum to win his favour again. Henry de Pomeroy made a park at Berry Pomeroy in Devon and was forced to pay

10 marks to the king in 1207. In 1230 Alan Basset obtained 184
a licence from Henry III to enclose 3½ acres of his wood in
Wootton Basset, which was within the king's park of
Braydon, and to make a park of it together with his wood
of Vastern which lay outside the park of Braydon. A great 185
many parks were made in the thirteenth century without
the king's permission, for wealth was increasing and a
person of position needed a park with deer to provide meat,
and a fishpond to supplement his Friday and other fast-day
food. There are many old farm and estate names of which
the word 'park' forms a part, particularly in wooded or
wild country like Derbyshire. They all come from this
ancient practice of enclosing land in order to preserve deer
for hunting. In the twelfth century the abbot of Reading
with royal permission made his park on the hills to the
south of the town. Whitley Park Farm, within the borough
of Reading, still preserves its memory today. But a lord
often found that men poached his deer in his park and his
fish in his ponds. In 1236 the king refused to allow magnates
the right of putting these poachers in private prisons of their 186
own. In 1275 king and lords agreed on the way the offender
should be treated. The poacher went into the king's prison,
but the lord received part of the fine imposed on him.   187

The law of the forest was directed to the single end of
protecting the wild beasts so that they might be found in
abundance for the king's hunting. Any action 'whereby the
beasts of the forest are harmed' brought upon the perpe-
trator the displeasure of the king. In a small country like
England deer would have become extinct within a few
generations if hunting had been unrestricted. The breaking
up of woodland, the making of 'assarts', would have
accelerated the process of destruction, as indeed it did,
despite efforts to regulate it. Richard fitz Nigel defined the
word 'assarts' as the result of 'cutting down forest, woods,
and thickets suitable for feeding animals, ploughing the soil
and cultivating it'. If, he says, 'woods are so severely cut
that a man standing on the half-buried stump of an oak or
other tree can see five other trees cut down about him, that

is regarded as waste'. Such an offence, he goes on to say, even in a man's own woods, is regarded as so serious that even those men who are quit of taxation because they sit at the king's exchequer must pay a money penalty all the heavier for their position. The private woods referred to in this passage are those which lie within a royal forest, not those in a chase or in country outside forest law. In 1198 a searching forest-eyre was held, for Richard I was short of money for his French war, and many Berkshire villages were forced to pay for 'waste', Bucklebury, Kentwood, Beech Hill, Grazeley, Whitley (beside the abbot's park), Thatcham, Crookham, Sonning, Earley, and Broad Hinton. In each case the amount charged was half a mark and it was paid up in full.

The ultimate responsibility for administering the forest and preserving the law of the forest lay with the chief forester. In the twelfth and early thirteenth centuries several members of the Neville family in turn held this office. The chief forester was never a popular man, and his officials were distrusted and disliked. Richard fitz Nigel talks of the 'exactions of Alan's gang', one of whom seems to have roused a particular venom among the clerks at Westminster, for someone wrote on one of the rolls 'Richard de Neville is black and a bad man'. At this time Alan de Neville was chief forester. Below the chief forester came the wardens, sometimes hereditary and sometimes appointed at the king's pleasure, responsible for the care of groups of woods. They often carried out their duties by deputy, but it was the wardens who were responsible for the actual administration of the forest. Below them were the verderers, generally four in each forest, chosen in the shire court. They had no pay, but were freed from other unpaid local work, such as serving on juries. Their chief work was to attend the forest courts held every six weeks. These courts were called attachment courts, in which the offences against the forest were first of all dealt with. The ordinary work of the forest, the gamekeeping and all that went with it, was done by foresters, some riding and some walking foresters who sometimes had lads to help them.

A deep smouldering resentment was felt against the strict enforcement of the forest law, for it imposed a double burden on the men of those counties which lay under it. They had the ordinary courts of law to attend and maintain and the ordinary officials of the shire and hundred courts to deal with. In addition they were forced to attend the courts and assemblies held for forest business and keep on good terms with the officers of the king's forests. Forest law in no way superseded the ordinary law of the land; it merely supplemented it. The forests spread before those who lived in or near them many tempting delights; extra meat, if it could be caught without the forester's knowledge; honey, if it could be found and concealed; dead wood for firing; acorns for pigs; live wood for building, if it were worth the risk of the law. The forests added, in fact, a wide variety of offences and penalties for their commission from which those who lived out of reach of the forests were free. It was 191 not until the rebellion of the barons at the end of John's reign that any real concessions about the forests could be wrung from the king. Such disafforesting as had already taken place had been paid for heavily in cash. The Charter of 1215 included certain general promises and in 1217 the young king, Henry III, was forced by his council to issue a long charter of the forests which dealt in some detail with the organization of the forests and provided remedies for the long-standing grievances which men resented most. The Forest Charter took its place beside the Great Charter as part of the foundations on which the English social scene was laid.

It clearly set out the courts and assemblies through which the business of the forest was done. It promised that the 'reguard' shall be held as it was 'in the days of king Henry my grandfather and not otherwise', that is, as the context 192 shows, once in every three years. As its name suggests, this meeting passed in review the metes and bounds of the forest and all matters touching the king's rights in the forest. It was conducted by twelve knights chosen for the purpose and the results of their enquiries were reported to the Justices of the Forest to be recorded in their rolls. Of all the forest regulations perhaps that one was hated most which laid down that dogs kept within the forest must be 'lawed'. The charter defines this as the cutting of three talons from the front foot without the pad. It declares that enquiry into dogs kept in the forest shall be made only at these meetings held every three years and by the view and witness of lawful men, that the owner of an unlawed dog shall pay three shillings, and that the lawing shall be done only in the places where it was done in Henry II's reign.

The business of regulating the use of the woods in the forest was conducted in meetings known by the Old English name of swanimotes. The Charter declares that three only should be held in the year; one a fortnight before Michaelmas to arrange about the pasturing of pigs on the king's acorns; the second about St Martin's day to collect the customary fees for the privilege; and the third about a fortnight before Midsummer, when the forest was closed for hunting because the beasts were supposed to be fawning. In addition to these meetings every six weeks throughout the year the foresters and verderers met in the attachment court to review 'the attachments as well of the vert as the venison'. The 'vert' is the greenwood of the forest and the offences which could be committed against it were manifold. The cutting down of saplings, of branches, or of whole trees were all matters of report. Minor offences against the greenwood were dealt with by fine in this court; the perpetrators of serious offences were attached to appear before the Justices of the Forest. They were, that is, obliged to find pledges that they would appear when the court met. Offences against the venison were the most serious of all forest offences, too serious for action on them to be taken in this attachment court. A forest beast found dead was dealt with in much the same way as a man found dead. A special inquest was held by the four neighbouring villages. The forest charter promised that 'in future no one shall lose life or limb for our venison. But if anyone shall be taken and convicted of stealing venison he shall redeem himself by a heavy payment, if he has that wherewith to do it. If he has nothing wherewith he can redeem himself, he shall lie in our prison for a year and a day. If after one year and one day he can find sureties for good behaviour he shall go out of our prison, but if he cannot, let him abjure the realm of England.' 195

Of a Saxon forest law nothing is directly known save that Cnut had set apart certain districts for his own pleasure within which no other man might hunt. It was in the early Norman period that forest law seems to have been most harsh. Possibly it seemed the harsher then in that the burden was new. The words of the Charter imply that in the past life and limb had been lost for forest offences. Indeed the text of the so-called 'Laws of Cnut touching the forest' show that this was so. Although this most interesting document is attributed to Cnut, there is no doubt that it really comes from that age of law writers, the reign of Henry I. More attention might well be paid to it for the light it throws on the forest law and administration in the early Norman period. In John Manwood's translation these laws declare that 'If any one doe offer force to a Verderer, if he be a freeman, hee shall lose his freedome, and all that he hath. And if he be a villein, he shal lose his right hand.' It continues: 'If such an offender doe offend soe againe, he shall lose his life.' In regard to hunting deer these laws state 'he that doth hunt a wild beast and doth make him paunt, shall pay 10 shillings: If he be not a free man, then he shall pay double. If he be a bound man, he shall lose his skin.' The free man in this connexion is the 'gentle' man, the unfree the 'simple', and the bound man the serf. If a stag were thus hunted, the penalties were proportionately more severe and if it were killed the serf, who received the harshest punishment, as his crime was so much the less appropriate to his station, lost his life. 196

The new power of the Norman kings, exercised with equal force in every part of England, bore hardly on the countryside, and no aspect of their rule illustrates this more clearly than their assumption of tight control over the beasts of the forest and their hunting. There is no doubt that even after the Conquest men could hunt freely in wild country where the forest law did not run, and where royal grants of hunting rights to individuals did not limit ancient customs. But that area was continually decreasing. Royal proclamation could put any stretch of countryside under forest law, and until the end of Henry II's reign the royal forests were constantly expanding. When the growth of royal forests was checked, the hunting rights of barons still grew. Although Richard I inherited his family love of hunting, he preferred the more expensive entertainment of foreign adventure. He was therefore ready to begin the practice of selling immunity from forest law to such of his subjects as were ready to pay enough for it. In the first year of his reign, 1190, the knights of Surrey offered him 200 marks that 'they might be quit of all things that belong to the forest from the water of Wey to Kent and from the street of Guildford southwards as far

197 as Surrey stretches.' A large area of the county was thus freed from forest law. In 1204 the men of Essex offered king John 500 marks and 5 palfreys for the disafforestation of 'the forest of Essex which is beyond the causeway between

198 Colchester and Bishop's Stortford'. In the same year the men of Cornwall were prepared to pay as much as 2,200

199 marks for the disafforestation of the whole of Cornwall, while the men of Devon offered 5,000 marks for the dis-

200 afforestation of the whole of Devon.

It is interesting to see that the men who are offering to pay these large fines for disafforestation are not the magnates of the county. In Surrey it is the knights of the shire, the country gentlemen. In Essex, Devon, and Cornwall it is the 'men' of the shire, by which must be understood all those who met in the shire court, knights and freemen. They must have discussed in those meetings the amount of the bribe they must give to the king. In the agreement with the men of Devon it is specifically recorded that if the bishop of Exeter or the earl of Devon or any other magnate desires to enjoy the benefits of this agreement in respect of his lands he must pay his share of the debt due to the king. The Pipe roll for the year 1207 shows that the bishop owed the king 500 marks 'because he and his men hunted in the forests of Devon and Cornwall and did not share with the knights and other men of Devon and Cornwall in the fine which they made for their liberty'. 201

Despite this extensive disafforestation in the reigns of Richard I and John the Forest Charter promised further concessions. All woods afforested by either of these two kings were to be disafforested at once. This is curious, for 202 there is no other evidence than this demand in the Forest Charter to suggest that either king had increased the area under forest law in his reign. The Charter also promised that afforestations made by Henry II should be viewed by honest and lawful men and that only those should be retained which were the king's own demesne woods. In the years following the Charter the honest and lawful men of the forest shires were doing their work and in consequence great stretches of country were freed from forest law. But the juries were asked to speak of happenings long ago and it is not surprising that their memory was not always very accurate. When Henry III came of age in 1227 he looked into all these matters again and in consequence some areas disafforested earlier in his reign were again put under forest law. Throughout the period covered by this book the forests, the law of the forests and the behaviour of forest officials were standing grievances. The boundaries fixed by Henry III were a constant source of complaint and in 1277, and again in 1297, Edward I ordered fresh perambulations to be made. The honest and lawful men who made them were naturally interested in disafforestation rather than in the preservation of the king's rights. The king's political difficulties, the French and the Scottish wars, forced him to agree in the Parliament held at Lincoln in 1300 to disafforestations, which later he tried in vain to reverse. The area under forest law in the fourteenth and fifteenth centuries was therefore considerably smaller than it had been under earlier kings. Nevertheless it remained an appreciable part of the land.

Now that the forest law has long been forgotten it is possible to think of it dispassionately. It roused bitter feelings of resentment in the most vocal classes of the community, men who owned woods which they could not freely hunt. It seems probable that the common people were less resentful of it. Everyone hated restrictions on hunting for food, for they seemed to rest on no moral basis. No one felt any guilt at poaching the king's deer any more than the Victorian villager at poaching the squire's pheasants. The surviving records of forest proceedings are full of poaching stories and they often hint at the element of excitement and bravado felt by the poacher. The large company of people – thirteen are named – 'and others of their company whose names are to be found out,' who hunted with bows and arrows all day in Rockingham forest in 1255 and killed three deer, were certainly lighthearted in their sport. 'They cut off the head of a buck and put it on a stake in the middle of a certain clearing . . . placing in the mouth of the aforesaid head a certain spindle, and they made the mouth gape towards the sun in great contempt of the lord king and his foresters.' When an inquest was held on this foray it was proved 'by all the verderers of all the forest in Northamptonshire' that a large number of people were involved. Their names show that they came from all over that forest country, but the organizers seem to have been a certain William Tuluse and Simon his son, who lived at Hanslope, just over the border in Buckinghamshire. They killed eight deer altogether and piled the venison on a cart which they drove to Stanwick. They put up for the night at the house of a certain Geoffrey Russell, 'he not being in the house and knowing nothing thereof'. Thence they took it to Hanslope to the house of William Tuluse, where it was divided up and eaten. Eight of the culprits were imprisoned but nothing is recorded about the rest.

Certainly the men who lived near the forest found entertainment and profit in encouraging the king's deer to leave the protected area, for forest beasts found outside the forest could be freely hunted. It was the duty of the foresters to see that they did not stray and, if they did, to drive them back unharmed. In 1269 the Justices in the forest of Rutland were told that when the lord king gave James of Panton permission to take 'two does in the forest the same James took six does . . . and by reason of the noise which he made by beating drums when he beset the does many beasts came out of the forest into the liberty and were taken, to the loss of the lord king and the detriment of the forest'. James was detained in prison. In 1249 'It happened about the Friday 204 next after the feast of St Mary in Egypt that a certain doe escaped from the king's park at Northampton and went into the field of Brampton. When the men of the lady Hugelyn of Brampton perceived it, one of them, whose name is not known, came riding on a bay horse with two greyhounds, one of which was tawny and the other white. And he followed the doe as far as the field of Pitsford and there he took the said doe.' An inquest was held before the verderers and foresters, and the four neighbouring villages came. All that transpired was that the lady Hugelyn's man took the doe and carried the venison to his lady's house, but 'they cannot be attached because they dwell outside the forest'. 205

The records of forest inquests often in a few words present a vivid picture of a forest scene in the thirteenth century, and, incidentally, reveal something of the attitude of the countryside to the forests. 'It happened on Whitsunday (in 1251) that two men with bows and arrows came before the ninth hour from the wood of Twywell, Northamptonshire, making their way to le Rokes with two greyhounds, of which one was black brindled and the other fallow coloured, and a black mastiff; and so they made their way to Hassokes and there they took a doe. And afterwards they returned to Acwellsike and there they were joined by seven men on foot and one on horseback and a lad and eight greyhounds, and they led the said venison covered with leaves and boughs on another black horse . . .' On the eve of Trinity Sunday the foresters and verderers met before the steward of the forest and the six neighbouring villages came, but, being sworn, could tell nothing about the deed. Henry son of John of

Sudborough, the shepherd, gave evidence. 'He says that as he was sitting eating his dinner under a hedge in the field of Sudborough on Whitsunday together with William the son of the winnower and William Russel, the keepers of the plough beasts of Sudborough, and Roger Lubbe, his lord's cowherd, William of Drayton came past them in a green tunic with a bow and arrows and two other men whom he did not know with bows and arrows. He also says that a man mounted on a black horse came after them carrying a fawn in front of him on his lap and he carried venison behind him covered with leaves. He says also that two lads came after them leading eight greyhounds of which some were white, some tawny, and some red. He says also that Roger Lubbe got up and spoke with the said evildoers and led them to Denrode and he fully believes that Roger Lubbe knew them.' William the winnower's son agreed with all that Henry had said, but Roger Lubbe and William Russel would admit nothing. They were therefore committed on

206 bail to the village of Sudborough for production on demand. Their sympathies were clearly with the poachers. At Michaelmas William of Drayton was again in trouble, but he was still elusive. John Spigurnel the riding forester of Brigstock reported that as he was coming from the swanimote with another forester he saw two evildoers to the forest with bows and arrows and they shot three arrows at them. 'They say upon their oath that one of those evildoers was Dawe son of Mabel of Sudborough and the other had a mask over his head, wherefore they suspected that he was William of Drayton, and the more especially as he was accused before of evil in the forest. The said William is with no one continuously, but is sometimes here and sometimes

207 there.'

The forest proceedings show that all classes hunted in the forests despite the law. The Charter allowed the magnates of the land, 'archbishops and barons', as they passed through the forests to take one or two beasts by the view of the foresters if they were about. If they were not about, the hunters were to blow their horns so that they might not seem

to be taking the beasts by stealth. This concession was 208
necessary, for such folk were always on the move about the
land and entertainment was not always easy to secure. All
animals thus taken were reported so that the king's generosity might not be abused. The king's own visits to the forest
when 'he took beasts at his pleasure' were reported also. In 209
1251 three household officials of Richard de Clare the earl
of Gloucester, his master cook, his marshal, and his chamber
clerk, as they went to Stamford to prepare lodgings for their
lord on his way to York took a doe with three greyhounds.
The riding forester informed the earl 'who fully vouched for
the aforesaid men and warranted the deed'. Nevertheless, 210
when the Forest Justices came round in 1255 the matter was
reported to them and, since one of the king's barons was
involved, it was postponed for his consideration. Ecclesiastical persons from archbishops down to unbeneficed
chaplains hunted with zest. At the time of Queen Eleanor's
coronation in 1236 the earl of Arundel could not serve as
butler because he was excommunicated. This sentence had
been declared against him by the archbishop of Canterbury,
the saintly Edmund Rich, because when the archbishop
hunted in the earl's forests in Sussex the earl seized the
archbishop's hounds.   211

This delight in hunting united all classes below the
aristocracy in a common dislike of the forest official. 'I'd
rather go to my plough than serve in such an office as yours,'
a household officer of a Northamptonshire country gentleman is reported to have told a verderer in 1251. That people 212
were unwilling to give poachers away to the foresters is
certain and, indeed, natural. Sometimes this friendliness
went even further than a refusal to answer questions. An
inquest held in 1248 about a poaching episode in Weybridge
forest in Huntingdonshire records how on 2 August 'the
walking foresters were going about midnight to watch over
their bailiwick and met a red greyhound worrying a doe.
They called the greyhound and took it. Afterwards twelve
men came . . . one of them with an axe in his hand, another
with a long stick, and the other ten with bows and arrows.

And they led three greyhounds in a leash, of which one was white, another speckled with black and white, and of what colour the third was they know not. The foresters called the men, who shot six arrows at them . . . and the foresters shot at the men, who entered the wood, and on account of the thickness of the wood and the darkness of the night the foresters know not what became of them.' The foresters recognized one of the men as Gervase of Dene in Bedfordshire, 'who used to be Jeremiah of Caxton's cook and now is with the lord John of Crakehall'. They say that Gervase 'is wont to do evil in the forest and his name is enrolled on

213 the verderers' roll'. A fortnight later, on 16 August, the walking foresters managed to entrap Gervase, as he was riding, using his lord's harness. They entrusted the harness to the three neighbouring villages and put Gervase in Huntingdon gaol. 'After the ninth hour there came to the foresters, Walter the chaplain of Huntingdon and other chaplains of the same place and William of Leicester, the bishop of Lincoln's bailiff, with book and with candle intending to excommunicate all who had laid hands on Gervase, and they sought him as a clerk and a servant of the bishop and commanded the forester to free him from prison.' When the foresters said that it was beyond their power to let him go 'they went to the prison and took the said Gervase as a clerk. And they took off his cap and he had his head newly shaved, and the foresters suspected that

214 it had been shaved that day in prison'. The foresters evidently doubted whether Gervase were a clerk at all. When the Justices of the Forest came round in 1255 Walter the chaplain who had rescued Gervase was summoned to appear and, although he refused to answer in the lay court, he was convicted of the rescue and handed over to the archdeacon of Huntingdon. Gervase, too, was convicted at the same time and handed over to the archdeacon. His lord, John of Crakehall, was in mercy, for he 'received the said

215 Gervase after the deed and still stands by him'. John of Crakehall was archdeacon of Bedford and later became the king's Treasurer.

The hatred felt by the countryside against the foresters was not occasioned merely by the check they kept on hunting of food. Many of the clauses of the Forest Charter were aimed at restricting the oppressions of the foresters. They were forbidden to hold 'scot ales', that is to brew ale and force men who lived in the forest to come and buy and drink it. Such parties were generally an occasion when the men who lived in the forest made payments to the foresters either in kind or money. These exactions were forbidden by the Charter. Nevertheless, throughout this period, unless foresters were definitely appointed as 'foresters in fee', which gave them certain rights and profits and enabled them to 'live at the expense of the lord king', they still preyed on the forest dwellers. As one forest inquest recorded in 1279 'they collect corn or sheaves and other things and make taverns contrary to the Charter of Liberties of the forest'. Foresters in fee, who paid the king a rent for their charge, had certain rights in the taking of what was called 'cheminage', that is, toll, or payment for freedom to cut wood along roads within the forest. The Forest Charter sets out the rules which should guide foresters in making the charge. It is to be taken only at places where it has been taken from old time, and only from merchants who enter the forest by licence to buy wood or charcoal for sale elsewhere. Each cart shall be paid for at the rate of two pence a half year and each pack horse at the rate of a half penny a half year. Those who carry the wood on their back, although they get their living by selling it, shall pay nothing. In 1279 the men of Mendip forest complained that the foresters 'attach every man rich or poor dwelling within the forest with dead wood and with dry wood; from the poor they take from every man who carries wood upon his back six pence, and from the rich as much as they have fortune to make fine'.

The English kings by their forest law were trying to preserve something that was bound to pass away. Civilized man lives by the plough, and not by hunting. The forests were bound to yield to the encroachments of the farmer. Every English forest, even those wild areas such as the

216

217

218

219

High Peak, or the fells of Cumberland, had long before the beginning of this period been penetrated by men desiring land to plough and live by. But the shape of forest settlements was different from that of the villages in open country where for centuries the interest of the village had been centred on its arable fields. The windswept open fields and the close-set villages of the long cleared and settled parts of England contrasted sharply with the scattered hamlets and farms of forest country. As time passed and the plough conquered the forest many forest hamlets themselves grew into villages, but they rarely achieved a village street with the farm houses and yards lying cheek by jowl with one another. Even today the forests of Anglo-Norman England, shorn of their dense woods, subjugated to the plough or converted into pasture land, still speak to the historian of the past. Their isolated farms, the patches of woodland here and there, and the forest trees surviving in midfield or hedgerow proclaim the ancient forest.

The countryside was never static. Increasing population meant that an increasing area of land of necessity came under the plough. The king accepted the fact that encroachments must be made on his forests, but expected to receive a rent from the lands so ploughed up. In the seventeenth century the king's Justice of the forests was still licensing village communities in Sherwood to make temporary enclosures for cultivation within the forest. One of the duties of the chief forester was to license assarts, that is to make a financial bargain on the king's behalf with those who wished to plough up forest land. Richard I allowed the bishop of Worcester to plough up 614 acres of forest land, but the bishop did not plough it all up at once. In 1230 the bishop of that day had some trouble to convince the chief forester that he was ploughing up land in accordance with the licence granted to his predecessor and not making still further encroachments on the forest. The abbot of Pipewell in Northamptonshire was given licence by the chief forester, Hugh de Neville, to plough up land in Rushton, but two suits were brought against him in the first years of the

thirteenth century by men who resented the loss of common 222
rights. One of them was the parson of Rushton. In reply to
his complaint the abbot said that the parson had no
grounds for complaint since he let him have common after
his corn was carried. Judgement in each case was postponed.
In 1221 Thomas of Swanshurst, one of the hamlets in
Yardley parish within the forest of Arden, brought a suit
against nineteen of his neighbours. He had enclosed
common pasture in the forest and they had destroyed his
hedge. In the course of the pleadings Thomas's lord declared
that 'such is the law in Arden that where there is a great
pasture he whose land it is may well make buildings and
raise hedges and ditches within the pasture provided it be
not in the exit or entry' of those who have common 'or to
their hurt'. The nineteen commoners claimed that the hedge
was in their exit. Again judgement was postponed.   223

It was not only the king's forests that were being eaten
into by the plough. Every village had, in addition to its
arable fields, waste or common land where the village
beasts could be pastured. Some of this common land was
woodland, some rough pasture as yet unploughed. A certain
Robert Silac enclosed some of the common pasture of
Broughton in Worcestershire and Hugh of Broughton threw
down his hedges and fed his beasts on the corn Robert had
planted. Having done that he brought an action against
Robert before the king's judges at Worcester in 1221 and
won 4 shillings in damages. Alan son of Humphrey brought 224
an action against William son of Gerard in the same year for
ploughing up 8 acres of common land in Edstone, Warwickshire, and won his case. The courts were constantly 225
being invoked to deal with such cases. Rights of common
were as fertile a cause of quarrels in the villages of thirteenth-
century England as they were of complaints when the open
arable fields were enclosed in the sixteenth, seventeenth, or
eighteenth century. The common land of the village sub-
served the arable and all who had any arable land enjoyed
rights of common on the village waste. These common
rights made it very difficult for the acreage of plough-land

in a village to be increased, since any individual commoner could bring an action and win it against the man who ploughed up the village waste. The necessity of increasing the acreage under corn to feed a growing population meant that in 1236 the king's council declared that the lord of a village could enclose waste land provided he left enough common land to provide pasture for those whose right it was. This declaration, part of the Statute of Merton, made general for the whole country what Thomas of Swanshurst's lord declared was already 'the law in Arden'.

Before the statute of Merton the man who desired to plough up common land was well advised to get the consent of all the commoners if he wished to avoid litigation in which he would probably be the losing side. During the war between king John and his barons the inhabitants of Carnaby in the East Riding of Yorkshire needed to grow more corn than their arable fields would bear. The villagers, men of Roger Mauleverer master of the hospital of St Leonard of York and men of Robert de Percy, ploughed up the common pasture which belonged to both the fees. 'And whoever did not plough it in common with them was subject to a penalty of 12 pence for every unploughed acre, and thus the villagers ploughed up that pasture and carried away the crop in time of war; in time of peace the aforesaid 226 Robert came and carried away the last crop.' The quarrel over the last crop brought the matter into the courts and preserved the memory of this war-time expedient. It would be rash to assume that it was unique. The statute of Merton allowed the lord the right of ploughing up the common provided he left enough pasture for his own tenants; it did not consider the situation which arose when others besides the lord's own men had pasture rights. But in the statute of Westminster in 1285 Edward I gave the lord the right of 227 enclosing the common against others as well.

The Open Fields

During the whole period covered by this book, in the large part of England which was a country of ancient village settlement, the arable land of an ordinary village was cultivated in two, or much more rarely three great open fields, each of them stretching over scores or even hundreds of acres. The origin of this system of agriculture lies far back in a past so remote that no direct evidence about it can be produced. The most recent writers on this subject – people who have both a practical and a theoretical knowledge of farming – have demonstrated that it arose naturally as the easiest way in which a community of men joined together to wring a living from the reluctant earth could reduce virgin soil to the plough. The unit of land was the ploughed 228 strip, sometimes called a 'selion' – from the French word *sillon* meaning 'furrow' – sometimes a 'land'. Its length and breadth were dictated partly by the lie of the land, and partly by the idiosyncrasies of the great plough-team of eight oxen. The farmers ploughed so that the land was turned inwards to make a central ridge down the middle of the selion, the team going up one side and down the other, turning on headlands left unploughed at the selion ends. When the strip or selion had become so wide that the plough-team would have to go too far in turning, the breadth of a furrow was left unploughed, and a fresh selion was begun. The breadth of a selion approximated to the modern perch of 16½ feet – a measure which most probably goes back to the primitive ox-goad, but statutory measures of length were still in a distant future, and early documents sometimes talk of the common perch of the village. This method of ploughing meant that the soil, turned inwards towards the central line, made the selions stand up in curving ridges, dipping on either hand to a furrow; hence the phrase 'ridge and furrow ploughing'. The furrow acted 229 as a drain, and in heavy clay the ridge tended to be markedly high. The selions of old open fields, long ago laid down to grass, can still be traced today in many parts of England. Instead of the straight lines of modern ploughing, the old ploughlands lie curving gracefully across the fields like an inverted elongated letter S, reproduced again and again. The difficulty of controlling an eight-ox plough-team is a convincing explanation of this curious shape, so pleasing to the eye. Even today, the pattern of an immemorial stretch of open field is often revealed to the eye in winter, when snow has melted from the selion ridges but still lies in the furrows on either side. The pattern of ancient arable thus made clear on land which for centuries has been turned to grass corresponds in all particulars with that of the open fields still used for arable in the Nottinghamshire villages of 230 Eakring and Laxton.

The open fields were divided for convenience of ploughing into blocks of these strips, called 'furlongs' or, in parts of England where the Danes settled, 'wongs'. A map of an old open field looks something like a patchwork quilt, for irregularities of contour, problems of drainage and the like made it impossible to plot out the fields in neat parallel square blocks. Some groups of selions lie one way; some another; with here and there unploughable patches left uncultivated. Here and there, too, were odd-shaped bits of land called 'gores' in which the selions grow shorter and shorter to fit into an angle of the field. The holdings of individual farmers lay scattered in strips about the open fields, and within the different furlongs individual farmers held their strips roughly in the same order.

The lord of an open-field village had his share in the common fields. His demesne or home farm lay scattered among the lands of his men. But whereas they counted their lands in strips, his lay in compact blocks, furlongs or the wongs. In the middle of the twelfth century the lord of a manor in Great Sturton, Lincolnshire, gave to Kirkstead abbey in the same county half his demesne in the village. In making the grant he said that 'since the furlongs of my demesne lie mixed among the lands of my men and the monks wish to dwell apart from others I have therefore brought together the land of my demesne and the land of my men in the further part of the fields and I have given that land to the monks to have together, and I have given to my men for their part of the land which they had, an exchange from the land of my demesne at their pleasure'. It is most fortunate that this unique charter has survived to illustrate both the distribution of the lord's blocks of strips about the open fields and the possibility of a rearrangement by agreement between a lord and his men. 231

A great deal of evidence about the way in which the open fields were dealt with can be drawn from the charters which record gifts and sales of land in the twelfth and later centuries. Land was constantly changing hands in the middle ages as always. Some men were good farmers and some were bad. The bad ones sold their land to the good ones who added strip to strip. The twelfth century in particular was a time when many religious houses were founded and endowed with land. Many of the charters given to monks and nuns as evidence of their endowments have survived either in the original or in copies. This sort of evidence shows that the land of most villages was organized in two, rather than three, great open fields. Such phrases as 'ten acres on one side of the village and ten acres on the other side' are common and clearly show a two-field division of the village fields. One field was left fallow each year while the other was planted partly with autumn- and partly with spring-sown crops. To leave half the village land fallow each year seemed to many farmers an expensive way of securing the fertility of their fields, so that often individuals were tempted to snatch a crop from part of the fallow field. The three-field system was a natural development of the two-field system, for it seemed much more economical to let only a third of the land lie fallow, using half the remainder for autumn and half for spring sowings. A third field might occasionally arise from the common action of the village farmers in clearing and ploughing up part of the village waste. But common action must have been difficult to secure. All the evidence points to a conservative adherence to the two-field system, despite the obvious advantage of three fields. In the thirteenth century many tracts on agricultural practices were written, the most famous of 232 them by Walter of Henley in the middle years of the century. But practice lags after theory and in some parts of England, notably in Lincolnshire, the two-field system survived as long as medieval agriculture itself.

The open-field system meant that every operation must be conducted in common. No one could produce crops which would mature at a different time or want different treatment from the crops on his neighbour's strips. The village plough teams were made up of beasts supplied by the individual farmers. It was a rich man who owned a whole team himself. The fact that few villagers could produce a full team must have helped to keep the open fields in being. Each man had to put hurdles across the ends of his strips to prevent cattle straying from ways or commons to harm the corn or other growing crops. Each man must scour the portion of the ditches or drains which ran by his strips. Disciplinary measures against farmers who did not keep these rules, the decision about the actual moment at which a major agricultural operation should be begun, all these matters were the concern of all the farmers in the village.

After the harvest the animals of those who held strips in the open fields were turned on to them to eat what they could find. In summer the common waste land fed them. If the village had common woods as well as wastes the acorns and beech mast fattened the pigs for winter killing. The greatest problem which faced the farmer was the provision of winter food for man and beast. Swedes and turnips were still far in the future. The most valuable asset of the village was therefore its meadow. If any stream watered the village the village meadow lay near it. The meadow was shared among the farmers who held strips in the open fields. Sometimes individual farmers held scattered strips of meadow as they held scattered strips of arable land. Sometimes the meadows were divided up into equal areas and the farmers drew lots for them each year. Whichever way they were dealt with, mowing and haymaking was a common operation to be undertaken all over the meadow at the same time so that the village cattle might graze on the aftermath. The meadows were generally thrown open on 1 August. There was rarely enough grass to build up live-stock for good meat. When animals were killed off for lack of winter food and salted down they must have made but poor and stringy eating. Pigs, which fatten more quickly than other animals, formed the main source of the farmer's meat. Fattened on acorns and beech mast they were poor lean creatures in comparison with modern swill and skim milk fed animals. Poaching rabbits, hares, deer, and the rarer pheasants must have been of necessity a national occupation.

Even in those parts of England where the arable had been worked in open fields from a time beyond the memory of man there was an infinite variety of local custom in their lay-out and management. In many parts of England there were no open fields at all. The common fields have attracted an amount of attention perhaps disproportionate to their extent, very largely because they seem to offer examples of successful experiment in the communal life. In mountain, forest, or waste land open fields are not found. There are none in the Weald of Kent and Sussex, in the New Forest, in the Cornish upland. Dartmoor of necessity remained un-tilled but Mr Finberg has shown that in other parts of Devon 233 open-field cultivation was practised. Cheshire, Lancashire, Cumberland, and Westmorland lie outside the original open field area. The ancient forest land of Essex knew little of the system. Neither the records nor the present aspect of East Anglia suggest that the system flourished there. The small compact farms that the traveller in those parts passes as he drives along East Anglian roads remind the historian at least of the many grants of blocks of land in Norfolk and Suffolk villages which were made in the twelfth and thir-teenth centuries. Berkshire is a county divided into two parts; the east of the county, old forest slowly penetrated and subdued to the plough by individual effort, was still marked before the second world war by winding lanes and small hedged fields. Its open fields are insignificant. In the west of the county the Vale of the White Horse is classical open-field country. Everywhere all through this period the aspect of the country was slowly changing as the increasing population reduced more land to the plough. The open-field system might seem to clamp down the initiative of the individual, to tie men to the fields their fathers had laid out, but the village waste, and forests, whether they belonged to the king or to a great baron, were a continual challenge to a man of spirit.

Younger sons of farmers played a great part in the work of clearance which was going on continuously through this period. Land won in this way by an individual was often known by his name. 'All the assart of Ernwi in the southern part of the Holm next the way' is mentioned in a charter of 234 about 1150. Such clearances were enclosed, and worked as enclosed fields. If they were encompassed about by forest this was a necessity. Individuals who undertook this work for their own profit cannot have had an eight-ox plough-team to help them. In forest country the soil was often light enough for the work to be done by a couple of horses or oxen, or even with cows, once the preliminary felling and clearance had been done by human effort. But it was not only in forest country that men were supporting life on enclosed tenements. In the rich marshlands along the Lincolnshire coast they lived by a very different economy from that of the ancient open fields. The inhabitants lived not in village streets but in dispersed dwellings, supporting themselves on their small enclosures of meadow and marsh; 'nine acres and a rood and a half of arable between the lands of Walter Galle and Gilbert son of Alan, being the whole toft and croft where Reginald son of Grimkell died', 'eighteen acres where Robert son of Acke dwelt', and 'half an acre in the marsh of Holme where William Sitard dwelt' 235 are examples of such tenements.

In many parts of England the sheep and not the plough was the dominant interest and all over England throughout this period the pasture lands bore an ever-increasing sheep population. There is no sign as yet of ancient plough lands being laid down for sheep. The village wastes could still carry the number which were turned upon them, for the sheep is not hard to please. Twelfth- and thirteenth-century sheep grazed on the mountains as gladly as their present-day successors, and in those parts at least the aspect of the land has changed little. The sheep walks of the Cumberland hills are as they were when William I became king and as they had been from the remote past. But the modern sheep is a very different animal from his twelfth-century counterpart. Sheep were not primarily bred for meat in England in this period any more than cows and oxen. The twelfth-century sheep were hardworking animals, prized for their dung for tillage, the ewes' milk for cheese, their skin for parchment, and above all for their wool. The best evidence of their size is the width of the records and folios of this period into which their skins were turned.

Not very much is known about the medieval sheep, but there seem to have been two types. A small active sheep with short wool was bred on the poor mountain pastures, while the rich grasslands of fen and marsh fed a larger sheep which grew longer wool. The wide membranes of the Pipe 236 rolls must have come from the backs of the larger sheep, while the smaller supplied the rolls on which the records of the courts of justice were kept. Sheep undoubtedly helped to restore to prosperity the wasted lands of Yorkshire in the early part of the twelfth century. The Cistercian monasteries founded there in this age slowly built up their wealth on the wool of their increasing flocks. But this wealth was only built up slowly. When all the king's subjects were asked to contribute to Richard I's ransom in 1193 the two religious orders of Citeaux and Sempringham were allowed to give their wool for a year because they had no wealth in money. Most of the houses of the order of Sempringham were in Lincolnshire where through the twelfth century flocks of sheep seem to have been increasing. Twelfth-century charters, for example, speak of 'pastures for 300

sheep at Barnetby and Norton', for '500 sheep by the long
237 hundred at Swinethorpe'. There were great sheep runs in
the wolds. Flemish merchants were already familiar figures
in the markets of these wool-growing areas. The chattels of
the Flemings were seized by king John's order at the beginning of his reign and chance records that on this occasion 18
238 stones of wool were taken from Daniel the Fleming at Louth.

Throughout this period the market for agricultural produce was growing. The corn-growing districts of East
Anglia and Kent were exporting corn to the Flemish cities
239 in the closing years of the twelfth century. Both individuals
and the ports of those parts were fined by the king for doing
it because it was trading with the enemy without licence.
In the thirteenth century the rapid development of cloth
manufacture in Flanders encouraged the equally rapid
development of sheep farming in England. The two were
very largely interdependent. Both lay and ecclesiastical land-
holders increased their flocks of sheep through this period
and at the end of it were exporting large quantities of wool
each year. In 1275 Edward I won the wool merchants'
consent to a tax of 7 shillings and 6 pence on every sack
exported. So prosperous were the wool merchants that they
accepted this taxation without protest. It was different when
Edward's necessities in the last decade of the century forced
him to ask for more. His demand for 40 shillings a sack was
regarded as an 'evil exaction', but the fact that he could
make it illustrates the importance of the wool trade by this
date. The growth of sheep farming went with more care in
general arable farming. Great landlords, whether religious
houses or laymen, were able to treat their estates as a unit
and do something to raise the quality and amount of their
crops. They could marl and otherwise improve the substance of their land as the small farmer could not. They were
in a position to do whatever could be done in this age to
bring scattered blocks of land within a ring fence. Until this
was done no real advance could be made. The great land-
owner could drain his land, treating a wide area in a single
operation. Already before 1166 Nigel bishop of Ely had

reclaimed from the fens sufficient for 2½ knights' fees which
had never been cultivated before.   240

Village Communities and Manors

The economy of rural England in the twelfth and thirteenth
centuries cannot be brought into one description. Mountain and forest, arable and pasture, fen and marsh each
dictated to its inhabitants a distinctive way of life. The forest
hamlet, the nucleated village of arable country, the solitary
hut of the shepherd moulded the thought and feeling of those
who lived in them. Past history, too, still had its decisive
influence on the shape of rural life. The Danish wars
between the ninth and eleventh centuries had materially
hastened the tendency in rural society in southern England
from freedom towards subservience to a lord. Free peasants
who lost their stock and harvest through war were bound
to put themselves under the protection of some great man
and admit his lordship of themselves and their land. The
process was hastened by the harsh taxation the wars necessitated. In the country south and west of Watling Street
these forces, working in an ancient society under an
effectively centralized monarchy, had produced a complex
of personal relationships far different from the simple bond
of loyalty which held together the early generations of
Saxon and Anglian settlers. The Danish immigrants who
settled thickly among the Anglian population of the
northern midlands brought with them a more primitive
form of social organization. As free warriors they accompanied some man of position to England. When he settled
in the place of his choice his followers received land in his
neighbourhood. They still recognized his leadership by
paying him a money rent, by help at the busy seasons of the
agricultural year, by attendance at his court of justice, but
they kept their personal freedom and the right to deal as
they chose with their land. In the far north the English of
the border counties, out of effective reach of the West Saxon

131

kings, still lived a life nearer in social organization to the early days of the Anglian settlement. Much of the north was hill pasture dependent on an often distant settlement. At the beginning of this period the north was not yet laid out in counties with a royal officer in each as was the south. The 'shires' of the north were groups of villages or settlements which shared the hill pastures between them and managed the affairs of the shire. Men in the north were free, rendering food rents, help at busy seasons, and pasture rents, in Cumberland called 'cornage', for cattle grazing on the hills.

When William I's Norman clerks digested the information collected by the Domesday Inquest they inevitably found that they had much material which they could not easily understand. No attempt was made by the Domesday commissioners to visit the wild, primitive, and hostile north and the information that has come down to us in Domesday Book from other parts has suffered a simplification which hides much of its inconvenient complexity in a pattern the Normans could understand. Those who wrote in the Victorian age about medieval England set out a clear-cut and simple description of its rural society. They were unable to test Domesday Book by comparing it with the records of the succeeding generations because few of these records were as yet in print. Twelfth- and thirteenth-century England was to them a land divided up into 'manors', estates under a lord, whose tenants were mainly unfree 'villeins', who, week by week, did labour service on their lord's home farm, or demesne, in return for the land they held, and were tied by their servile state to the place in which they were born. These writers thought of the village and manor as roughly equivalent to one another in area, and saw in the Norman lords the ancestors of the benevolent squires of their own day.

The word manor was introduced into the English language by the Norman clerks of William I. When they noted the existence of a manor in a village as they wrote up Domesday Book they meant to imply that a man of local consequence lived there. The French word *manoir* meant no more than dwelling or residence. Many of the manors noted by the Domesday clerks, particularly in Lincolnshire, were very modest estates. Blancard, a man of Roger of Poitou, had a manor in Audleby, but he possessed only half a team of oxen. Outi's manor in Hibaldstow had only one 241 ox in its so-called team, and there were several other manors, equally meagre, in Hibaldstow as well. Even in the south, 242 where for generations society had been moving towards what can be called a manorial pattern, manor and village by no means always coincided. There was often more than one manor in a southern village, although the lords of most southern manors were better off than Outi or Blancard. It was only slowly that clerks extended the meaning of the word manor to include the whole estate of the lord. When king Stephen in 1139–40 granted to William earl of Lincoln an estate which would later have been called a manor he described it as 'the house of Walter de Amundeville in Kingerby and whatever belongs to it in Kingerby, in Osgodby and Owersby'. It was very convenient for clerks 243 when they drew up charters recording the gift or sale of an estate to be able to use a single word instead of a periphrase as king Stephen had done. The word manor had come before the end of this period to be almost a technical term. It meant an estate which was an economic unit, in which all the tenants were bound to the lord and his demesne farm, his free tenants paying him rent for their land and helping him at busy seasons; his unfree tenants doing weekly labour service; and all of them regularly attending his court of justice, his hall moot, for the settlement of their quarrels and for the regulation of communal affairs.

The knights to whom the king's tenants-in-chief gave land in the generations after 1066 aimed at creating estates of this sort and as the years passed the divergencies in social organization in different parts of England tended to be planed down. Increasing centralization, the constant demands of the central government for information about one aspect or another of local affairs made towards the same end. Nevertheless, the tendency towards normalization was not strong enough to rub out the peculiarities of Danish England. In every part of England where the Danes settled they impressed on rural society a mark which time has not erased. The free peasants who made up the Danish armies remained free when they became farmers. Their descendants were still free when the Domesday Survey was made. In East Anglia at that date there were many free peasants often holding minute fractions of land, but holding it so freely that 'they could go with their land to whatever lord they would'. They could sell their land, their sons could divide it, a practice which in part accounts for the small holdings characteristic of this country. The free peasants of East Anglia in 1086 were in social consciousness far nearer to the Danish armies of the ninth century than they were to the manorial peasants of the later middle ages. In the counties of Lincoln, Nottingham, and Leicester peasant society was a stage nearer the manorial type, but it still had a long way to go. There had been brought into being great complex estates called 'sokes', a name which the Soke of Peterborough still keeps on men's lips today. The free peasants of these parts can no longer take their holdings to another lord at their will. They are sokemen and they and their lands are attached to the lord of the soke. The head of the soke, the place where the lord of the soke had his demesne farm and house, often gave the soke its name, and the lands of which the soke was made up often lay scattered about in many villages, some of which might be far removed from the manorial centre.

The word soke means seeking, and stresses the fact that the sokeman must seek his lord's court of justice, must pay his lord a rent, and help him at moments of stress. But the sokeman was free; sokeland was not owned by its lord but by the man who held and farmed it. The sokeman could sell his land. The purchaser took over the seller's duties towards the lord of the soke. As in relation to his lord, so in relation to the king, the sokeman was free. He had the freeman's rights and obligations. Each became more clear and definite as the years passed. Despite the fact that portions of sokeland might lie at a distance from the lord's manor, a soke was not in itself a complicated form of social organization. The complication arose from the fact that in the Danelaw shires villages might contain portions of sokeland attached to more than one manor. More often than not, therefore, Danelaw villages were under divided lordship. The farmers in such villages had no single manorial court to which they could take their petty disputes. There was no single lord's court for the village to arrange such matters as the day when a start should be made on ploughing the arable fields, or the day when the meadows should be mown. More often than not manor and village in the south of England coincided in area, and the management of the village arable, meadow, and common could be discussed in the lord's hall moot. In villages under divided lordship such matters could be dealt with only in a general meeting of the village farmers.

All over England the manor as an organized estate was, throughout this period, secondary in men's thoughts to the village, the group of men of diverse wealth and status who lived together in a community. Where village and manor coincided in area the manor gained by that fact an added significance. The community might be a close-set village, complete with village street, church, and open arable fields, or it might be a hamlet in ancient forest country living by small 'intakes' of ancient forest land, a village in the making. In either case the community itself was the significant unit in the social structure of the twelfth and thirteenth centuries, for in the last resort it was only his fellows among whom he lived who could declare whether a man were of good repute or bad.

From an early time some responsibility imposed in the last resort by the king must have lain upon the little village communities of Saxon England. For the purpose of local government the land was divided into shires, each of which had its court of justice to which all men of any position in the shires were bound to go. They by long tradition formed the court and were the living repositories of customary law by which the suits that came before the courts were judged. They were the suitors of the court and they were the judges too, for they were bound to declare the law. The sheriff who presided over the court merely pronounced judgement in accordance with the verdict of the suitors. In some shires there are signs of a higher bench among the suitors called judges – the Latin word is *judicatores* or *judices*. The shires were divided into smaller units, called hundreds in the south and west and wapentakes in those parts in which the Danes had settled. Hundreds and wapentakes, too, had their courts, similarly constructed and held by the bailiff of the hundred in the absence of the sheriff. To these shire, hundred, and wapentake courts the law writers of Henry I's day state that the priest, the reeve, and the four best men must go if the village is not represented at the meeting by the lord or his steward.

The courts of shire and hundred met in early times in the open air arranged in the form of an open square; 'within the four benches of the hundred' is a contemporary description of such a court. The shire court of Berkshire had in Saxon times met at Scutchamore Knob on the Berkshire 244 Downs. In the twelfth century most shire courts sat in the county town, but hundred and wapentake courts still met in the open air. It is true that although proceedings began in the open air in this period the court generally adjourned to the nearest town if the weather were bad. Many hundred and wapentake sites can still be found, though not always very easily, today. A good example of a wapentake court site which can be seen from a main road is the dip on the left-hand side of the Fosse way going north-east just before the Fosse crosses the Grantham-Nottingham road by the Saxondale crossing. In a tilled field the sloping sides of this dip still retain something of the original rectangular form cut out of the hillside to give some protection to the men of Bingham wapentake when they met in their local court. Robert Thoroton writing his *History of Nottinghamshire* in Charles II's reign says of Bingham wapentake 'So called from the usual Place of Meeting, viz. a certain Pit on the

Top of the Hill on the contrary side of the Fosse Way, near the most westerly corner of Bingham Lordship, called Moot House Pit, where the Hundred Court is, or ought to be still kept, or called; though, I think, they usually remove to Crophill Butler, as the nearest Town for Shelter.'   245

Attendance at these courts was a burden which bore heavily on the men of shire and hundred. In 1217 Henry III's council in reissuing the Great Charter added a clause about the shire court. The king was made to promise that in future it should be held only once a month, and at less frequent intervals when it had been customary. A case in the king's court at Westminster gives a good illustration of the differences in point of view which might exist in regard to the shire in accordance with whether men were members of the court or wished to have a plea heard in it. Complaint had been made that two knights of Lincolnshire had obstructed the sheriff so that he could not hold his shire court, and four knights and the sheriff came, and they said that they 'were present in the shire court of Lincoln, where the sheriff held the pleas from dawn to vespers, and there stood over many pleas which could not be finished on that day because daylight failed, and when the parties asked the sheriff what they should do in their suits, the sheriff replied that they should come on the morrow at dawn and he would show them justice, and he told all the stewards and knights and others of the shire court to come at dawn and hear the suits and make the judgements. In the morning when they came, the sheriff sat and called for the suits and the plaintiffs and the judgements, and he ordered the knights and stewards who were outside the house to come in and hear the suits and make the judgements. And when they heard this, those that were in the house went out and those who were outside went away, saying that they ought not to hold the shire court for more than one day, wherefore because the sheriff could not alone hear the suits and make the judgements, he told the parties that they should come to the wapentake and he would do them justice there, and so they withdrew, and thus seven score cases stood over.'   246

The Villagers

It is true to say that throughout the period 1066–1307 by far the greater number of people living in rural England were personally unfree, people generally described throughout the middle ages as villeins. This is true even of the Danelaw, where the sokemen of Scandinavian descent formed a peasant aristocracy not found in other parts. But it is equally true to say that throughout the period there was a movement, slow perhaps, and to contemporaries not always perceptible, towards freedom. At the beginning of the period there were in the western and south-western shire people of even lower social status than the villein, so low that they are described in Domesday Book as slaves. There was a very real distinction between the unfree peasant farmer and the slave. Domesday Book notes the existence of these slaves and their numbers, but between Domesday Book and the records of the late twelfth century there stretches a long period illuminated by few contemporary records and by none general enough to show what was happening to the sons and grandsons of the Domesday slaves. Long before the thirteenth century they have disappeared. The lives they led and the place they filled in the society of their day can only be guessed at. Presumably they were the personal property of some greater man, passing their days in the routine labours of agriculture and husbandry or in personal service in the lord's house. In return for their labours they had the necessities of life. Their disappearance from the social scene can best be explained by the increasing power of the king and the law. Even the slave's life and limbs were his lord's, but for his crimes the lord would not wish to answer. With the good will of their lords the descendants of the Domesday slaves crept up into the lower ranks of the great villein class.

The Norman clerks who compiled Domesday Book did not find it easy to understand the subtle distinctions that might exist between different English villagers. Neither the free man nor the slave gave them any serious trouble. But in England in 1066 there were many gradations of tenure between the free man who could choose his own lord and the slave who was the property of another man. The sokeman the Normans could regard as a free rent-paying tenant of his lord. Apart from him in most counties they tended to group the inhabitants of a village under the simple headings villeins, cottars, and bordars. Cottars and bordars are easy to explain. They are cottagers. They held a few acres, sometimes no more than one, sometimes as much as five. Smallholders in an economy less intensive than today, they eked out their living by acting as labourers. The lord was always in need of extra labour on the home farm. Widows left to bring up a young family, villeins who had no sons to help them, would be glad to hire a neighbouring cottager's help. The village craftsmen, the smith, the miller, the wheelwright, and their like, were smallholders too. In Domesday Book the word *villanus*, villein, means little more than villager. It is a useful 'omnibus' word, implying that the men so described are neither free men nor slaves, neither sokemen nor cottagers. In the villein class is included by far the greatest number of English farmers in the middle ages.

The best way of finding out what sort of people lived in the twelfth-century English villages and the rents and services which they paid to their lords is to examine the surveys of villages made for the purpose of giving the lord just such information. Most twelfth-century surveys deal with lands owned by some ecclesiastical lord, for the lands of the church were more efficiently ordered at this early date than laymen's lands. This is not true of the thirteenth century, for by that time the lay lord could hire efficient clerks to keep his accounts. But it remains true that estates of which surveys were made were more efficiently run than many small manors of which little is known of their organization. A very early survey survives of the lands of Peterborough abbey. When abbot John died in 1125 the abbey property was taken into the king's hands. He entrusted it to Walter the archdeacon who rendered account of the revenue to the royal exchequer. In order that the king might get all he should from the lands a survey of them was made and 247 was copied into the Black Book of Peterborough. The abbey held many villages of which a compact group is still known as the Soke of Peterborough. Here it is possible to translate only that part of the survey which records the duties and payments of the men who lived in the village of Pytchley in Northamptonshire.

'There are there 9 full villeins and 9 half villeins and 5 cottagers. The full villeins work 3 days a week up to the feast of St Peter in August and thence up to Michaelmas every day by custom, and the half villeins in accordance with their tenures; and the cottagers one day a week and two in August. All together they have 8 plough teams. Each full villein ought to plough and harrow one acre at the winter ploughing and one at the spring, and winnow the seed in his lord's grange and sow it. The half villeins do as much as belongs to them. Beyond this they should lend their plough teams 3 times at the winter ploughing and 3 times at the spring ploughing and once for harrowing. And what they plough they reap and cart. And they render 5 shillings at Christmas and 5 shillings at Easter and 32 pence at St Peter's feast. And Agemund the miller renders 26 shillings for his mill and for one yardland. And all the villeins render 32 hens at Christmas. The full villeins render 20 eggs and the half villeins 10 eggs and the cottagers 5 eggs at Easter. Viel renders 3 shillings for one yardland and Aze 5; the priest, for the church and 2 yardlands, 5 shillings. Walter the free man pays 2 shillings for a half yardland. Leofric the smith pays 12 pence for one toft. Ægelric of Kettering pays 6 pence for the land he rents and Ægelric of Broughton 12 pence and Lambert 12 pence. And Ralf the sokeman lends his plough 3 times a year. Martin gives a penny and Azo a penny and Ulf and Lambert a penny. On the home farm there are 4 plough teams with 30 oxen and 8 oxherds who each hold a half yardland of the home farm. There are 2 draught horses, 220 sheep, 20 pigs, 248 and 10 old sheep in their second year.'

The yardland of which the survey speaks was the amount of land which a full villein held. It varied widely in acreage in accordance with local custom above or below a rough average of 30 acres scattered over the village arable fields. Sometimes it was as much as 40 acres, but often as little as 15. The half villein of the survey held a half yardland. The acreage of the Pytchley yardland is not given. The Pytchley villeins with their 3 days' work on the lord's land throughout the year and a full week's work during the six busy weeks of harvest were more hard pressed than villein tenants of the abbot in some other villages. At Cottingham in the north of the county the abbot received from his villeins only two days' work a week throughout the year and 3 in August. Week work sounds very much worse than it was in actual life. From each yardland only one man had to go to do the work, however many sons of working age a villein farmer might have living in his house. Naturally the villein did not send his most efficient son. Complaints about the work done by villeins are frequently found in thirteenth-century records. In his treatise on husbandry Walter of Henley more than once urges the need of watching the men who were doing their customary labour to see that they worked well. The 1125 survey says nothing of the length of the day's work or whether the lord gave food to his customary labourers. Ploughing in the old way with oxen or horses ceased at three o'clock. The villein probably had the rest of the day to himself. Sometimes the villein worked only to midday. If he worked all day the lord generally gave him food at midday, ale, or in some parts cider, bread and cheese, more occasionally meat or fish, or a sort of soup of which the main ingredients were beans and peas. This 1125 survey is very early indeed, too early to give the full details that the more practised clerks of the next century would include. All clerks left out much that would interest the historian but was irrelevant to the purpose of a survey of the lord's property. The animals mentioned in the account of Pytchley are the lord's stock on his demesne farm. The villein, too, had his pigs, his cow or two, and his sheep as

141

well as his plough-oxen. He had his common-rights to help him feed them, and his share of the meadow for winter fodder. That he had poultry is taken for granted. His payment of eggs to his lord at Easter is the origin of the modern Easter egg.

The men who are mentioned by name in this Pytchley survey are not villeins. They are rent-paying tenants, free of the burden of week work for the land they hold, able to hire themselves out as labourers if they wish or to make a better living by the practice of some craft. The four men who paid but a penny a year can have had but a minute piece of land, possibly an intake from the waste. The rest of the little group of rent-paying tenants seem to form a sort of rustic aristocracy in the village. They were probably all free; one of them is specifically called the free man, though he has only half a villein holding. The smith who had but a toft, that is a house and smithy, must have been dependent on his craft for a living. Apart from the priest, who had 2 yardlands, only one of these men had as much land as a villein. The amount of land that Ralf, the only sokeman in Pytchley, held is not given, but since he owned a whole plough team it may be assumed that he was better off than any other villager. Ralf was fortunate. This same survey records that at Collingham, Nottinghamshire, 50 sokemen had between them no more than the equivalent of 10 full villein holdings, while at Scotter in Lincolnshire the sokemen even did a day's work a week all through the year, a highly exceptional burden for a free man to bear. Any contemporary account of a set of villages shows how careful the historian should be in generalizing from isolated examples.

A little later in the twelfth century than the Peterborough document, two surveys were made of the lands of Shaftesbury abbey in Dorset. They are not dated, but it seems certain that the first was made about the end of Henry I's reign, that is, about 1130–35, and the second in the reign of his grandson, about 1170–80. They form a good contrast to the Peterborough document, for they relate to a part of England where the Danes never settled. Since they are a whole generation apart and relate to the same lands something can be gathered about what was happening in the remoter villages of Wessex in the middle of the twelfth century. The method adopted by the Shaftesbury clerks was to set out the names of the tenants in a list, adding to each name a note of what was paid to the lord. The village of Fontmell, Dorset, is a fair example to examine. The position of the village parson seems to have altered little between 1135 and 1180. Each survey records that he had two yardlands attached to the church, but in 1180 he had in addition one acre of the home farm. There is no hint that the parson of Fontmell had to pay anything to the lord. In the first survey, with hardly an exception the men of Fontmell bear Anglo-Saxon names. The priest is called Edwin. The exception is the most important man in the village after the priest, Richard son of Hugh, who had the same amount of land as the priest. His father must have been a Norman provided for in this English village. The earlier survey gives no hint of his services, but in the later survey his successor was obliged to attend the shire and hundred courts. For the rest there are in the earlier survey 65 tenants. It was a big village with 4 mills. One of the millers had as much as a yardland and a half and the others had respectively 5, 4, and 2 acres. There were 22 villeins each holding a yardland and 19 holding half a yardland. The rest were cottagers holding varying amounts of land, most of them 4 acres, but some two or less.

It is not easy to equate the two surveys, for there has been time for a whole generation to pass away. There were more households in Fontmell in Henry II's reign, 80 altogether, including the priest and the holder of two yardlands. Another man also has by this date acquired as much as two yardlands. There were still 4 mills in the village; one of them, to which 4 acres of land were attached, was at this date held by two sisters called Selivia and Edivia. There are some 28 villeins holding a full yardland and sometimes a little more, 27 holding half a yardland and, occasionally, a little more. The rest of them are cottagers, some holding four acres, some a 'curtilage', that is a house and enclosure around it, and one holding 'land not measured'. The impression the surveys give is of rising prosperity. It is clear that more land has been taken in from the waste. But the most significant information that a comparison of the two surveys gives is that between the first and the second the villein tenants have bargained with their lord to pay a rent instead of rendering week work. In Henry I's reign a villein in return for a yardland did 3 days' work a week, paid 7 pence halfpenny, ploughed an acre and a half and harrowed an acre, rendered a measure of corn and 10 pence for wood to repair his house and his fences. In Henry II's reign his successor paid a rent of either 15 pence, 2 shillings, or 2 shillings and 6 pence, helped his lord with mowing, reaping, and carting, did some other cartage duty for his lord, and paid either 20 pence or 10 pence for wood to repair his house and fences. Those who held less land paid proportionately less in rent.

How far such commutation was general in twelfth-century English villages it is impossible to say. The change from service to a money rent did not in itself make a man free, nor did twelfth-century commutation preclude the return to week work in the next century, when increasing population meant higher prices for agricultural products. The lord was often willing to give up the week work in return for a money payment, but he rarely wanted to let the villein off his help at haytime and harvest. Many free men had to do that. In 1202 Nicholas son of Norman brought an action against his lord's servants for evicting him from his free tenement in Mears Ashby, Northants. The jurors in their verdict said that both Nicholas and Norman his father held that tenement by servile customs 'at fork and flail' and they could not marry a daughter without payment, but Norman sought and obtained from his lord that his works and customs should be rendered in money as long as it pleased him – presumably it was the lord's pleasure, not Norman's. 'In such wise', continued the jurors, 'he held that land for twenty years.' The case was therefore dismissed, since

Nicholas was still a villein despite this commutation. 254
Nevertheless, the more closely the records of this period are
examined the more fluid does rural society seem. The
rigidity of the villein's position in law suggests a stability
that was far from the everyday facts of village life. In law the
villein was by his servitude bound to the soil of his native
manor. He could not leave his home to take up land elsewhere or earn a living by some craft in a town. However
much he might prosper as a farmer, even though he might
rent freehold land, all that he earned was in theory at least
his lord's. He must take his corn to be ground at his lord's
mill and pay for the grinding. He must have his loaves
baked in his lord's oven. He must pay 'tallage', a tax taken
at the will of his lord. When he sold a beast or married a
daughter he paid a fine to the lord. When he died his best
beast or chattel was taken by the lord. He himself and all
his family could be sold to another lord.

Many twelfth- and thirteenth-century charters recording
the gifts or sales of individual villeins or of villein families
survive to prove that this ultimate sign of servitude existed
in medieval England. That the sale meant the transfer of
an individual serf, separated from family, kin, and friends,
to a distant part is unlikely. Generally the transaction
meant little more than the substitution of one lord for
another. The words in which Robert de Sifrewast in the
latter part of the twelfth century expressed his sale of
'Wuluric the miller my man and all his issue, which has or
shall come from him' to the canons of Missenden in
Buckinghamshire, give the impression of utter servitude. 'I
grant this man to them, free and quit from all claim for
ever, so that they may do what they please with him as with
their own man; this stipulation being made, that if he shall
wish to go away, and desert at any time the demesne of the
canons, as my own man I shall take and seize him wherever
I shall find him. Know also that for this grant they have
given me 5 shillings.' When Isabella de Sifrewast, in the 255
next generation, gave a man and his land to Reading Abbey
her phrases are less austere, but equally definite – 'the half

virgate of land in Purley which Osbert son of Godwin the fisherman holds in villeinage with all its appurtenances for ever in pure and perpetual alms, free and quit from all custom and exaction and demand, and immune from all secular service. And so that the abbot and convent of Reading at their will and disposition may turn the aforesaid Osbert and his offspring either to the work of villeinage or 256 to an annual rent.'

Against these grants and sales of men must be set the many cases in the rolls of the royal courts of justice attesting the English peasant's tough resistance to servitude, his readiness to fight his case before the king's judges. The law of villein status might be harshly austere, but the king's judges were precise in their care that no man should lose his freedom unless his serfdom was adequately proved. At Lincoln in 1219 Adam son of Reginald of Stenwith claimed 2 bovates (the equivalent of the yardland of the south) as his inheritance against a widow who held the land as part of her dower. Her son, John of Stenwith, answered for her and said that Adam was his villein and therefore had no standing in the courts. To prove it he produced an uncle of Adam's who admitted that he was a villein. Adam replied that this uncle of his was his father's younger brother and he might well have sunk to servitude. The judges ordered the case to proceed to a jury. The jurors said that John of Stenwith's father had tried in vain to prove that Adam's father was a serf, 'but he never could convict him and 257 Reginald died a free man'. Adam therefore won his case and recovered his modest inheritance. Another Lincolnshire case of a slightly earlier date illustrates the same judicial care. In 1202 Robert Drop complained that Hawisa of Kyme had evicted him from his free tenement in Croft, a small tenement of 13 acres. Hawisa did not appear, but Simon of Kyme, her heir, answered for her. He was one of the most important country gentlemen in south Lincolnshire. He said that Robert 'was by origin a villein' and he produced kin of Robert's to prove it, 'namely Simon his brother, of one father and one mother who admits his villeinage, and Simon son of William, Robert's uncle, who likewise admits that he is a villein, and a certain Franc who says that the mother of his father was the sister of Robert's father and he admits that he is a villein. And Robert,' the record proceeds, 'admits that the aforesaid are his kin, as they say, except that Franc's grandmother was Robert's father's mother and not his sister, and Robert says that if they wish for a bribe or for any other reason to make villeins of themselves, he does not therefore wish to be a villein.' The case ends by Simon of Kyme offering the king 3 marks for licence to make an agreement with Robert, who recovered his land. This is a particularly significant 258 case, for Simon of Kyme had in fact satisfied the law by the production of so many villein kin. Clearly the judges believed Robert's story and, it may be presumed, brought pressure on Simon. The unusually large sum Simon paid for licence to come to terms with Robert suggests that the judges thought very ill of his attitude.

A villein who wished to sue another man for interfering with his property or preventing him entering into his father's land must take his complaint into the court of his lord. Hence the defendants in such cases in the royal courts often tried to prove that the man who was suing them was a villein. But occasionally the jurors themselves seem to have been uncertain whether a man were free or not. The men against whom Peter son of Ailwin brought an action for land in Thorney, Suffolk, in 1203 made no such exception against Peter, but when the jurors were asked if Peter had been evicted from his free tenement they replied that they were not certain if it were a free tenement or not, 'because as they heard say he could not marry his daughter outside his lord's land without his licence, so that a present was given to his lord for the marriage of his three sisters, and he makes his lord one work each year, so that last year he made fine with his lord for 20 pence for that work; and he ought to reap once a year for his lord, his lord feeding him, and give his lord a Christmas present, and he ought to harrow, so that if his lord feeds him he shall harrow till vespers, but if not until noon'. Peter thereupon denied that he owed these customs and said that he held freely for 9 shillings and 6 pence a year, one day's help in reaping and one in mowing and a Christmas present of 4 capons and 3 hens. The judges were somewhat at a loss at this verdict, for the defendants produced no proof of Peter's villein status. They therefore put off the case in order that the chief Justiciar might be 259 consulted. No record of a judgement has survived. But it is significant that the judges did not take the jurors' verdict as evidence that the case should not have come into the royal court.

It was not always easy for a plaintiff, charged in court with villein status, to prove his freedom. In 1219 a Lincoln-shire widow named Bela, seeking her dower from her husband's estate of 2 bovates (the equivalent of the usual villein holding) and 2 tofts, was faced by the reply that 'Simon her husband was a villein from his birth and a brother of his was sold for 10 marks and a sister for 20 shillings, and the land is villein land and Simon held it as a villein doing villein customs when it pleased his lord and sometimes rendering pence for those customs when there was no need of them'. Her opponent's attorney went on to say that he would have produced Simon's kin to prove villeinage adequately but he could not because they were under the power of another man. In reply to all this Bela said that her husband 'was a free man and held his land freely by 6 shillings and as a free man was on recognitions and assizes before the justices, and this is very evident for he was at one time on an assize when he was convicted of perjury and for that reason made compensation'. Both parties put themselves on a jury about Simon's freedom or servitude. When the day appointed came Bela appeared, 260 but her opponent withdrew. The fact that a compromise was ultimately reached suggests that Bela had proved her case.

It cannot have been easy to keep an adventurous young man of parts to his villein status, despite the harsh laws of servitude. Once he was away from his native village only successful action in the royal court could fetch him back. If he could get to a chartered borough and live there for a year and a day he was free. His lord had to be very sure it was worth his while to spend money on going to the court and very sure that he had adequate proof of villein origin before he took action. It can hardly have been worth the lord's while to try to find out where his villein had gone unless there were a possibility that the villein had prospered and become rich. If lords had thought it worthwhile to go to the courts whenever a villein strayed from their control the rolls would have been full of such pleas. There are some interesting cases. In 1202 the prior of Canons Ashby brought such an action to recover Stephen of Adstone as his villein 'whose father was sold to his church of Ashby'. Stephen replied by producing two of his brothers and a sister's son who all said that they were free men. The prior then produced the charter of Hugh Gulafre by which he granted Stephen's father, Wibert, to the church of Canons Ashby. He said also that two of Stephen's supposedly free men were the sons of his sister who was sold as a villein for 10 shillings. The proof of villeinage that the law demanded was not a charter of sale, but the production of villein kin, men ready to declare themselves villeins. This proof the prior did not offer against Stephen. Hence the case went to the next stage. Stephen put himself on the verdict of a jury as to whether he held freely of the prior and whether he was a villein or not. The prior agreed to the jury, and, indeed, gave half a mark to have it. The jurors said 'that Stephen is a villein and was, and his ancestors held and Stephen himself holds the tenement as a villein of the prior'. Stephen therefore remained in his villein status. 261 But he was not a runaway, merely a man who desired to be free.

Long before this period began the law of the land demanded that all men must be associated in groups of ten or twelve men of which the members were mutually responsible for each other's good behaviour. There were many exceptions to this rule. There was no frank pledge in 262

Shropshire. Lords lay or spiritual were by their position exempt. Members of their households and indeed of the households of any man of position were exempt, for their lords must produce them in court if need be. Men who held freehold land were exempt, for their land was their pledge.

The rule came to apply only to the unfree and in theory would seem to have strengthened the tie of the villein to his native manor. These groups were called tithings in some parts and frankpledges in others. All unfree men above the age of twelve were bound to be in tithing or frankpledge. Twice a year the sheriff visited the court of each hundred or wapentake to 'view' the frankpledges and tithings; to see, that is, that no one was living in the villages and hamlets outside a frankpledge. A village in which men were living who were not in one of these associations was fined. The king often granted to individual lords the right to hold the view of frankpledge within their lands, for it was a profitable process, and most lords to whom it had not been granted usurped the right. Many men for one reason or another were found to be 'outside frankpledge' when the periodical enquiries were held. It is safe to assume that many such men were villeins who had left their own parts to try their fortune in another place.

In days when accident or self-defence were not regarded as acceptable answers to a charge of murder or assault, many villeins had to flee because they had killed or maimed one of their fellows. Outlawed in due course, they could never return to their own parts, but must get a living as best they could by honest or dishonest means. The rolls of the king's court in the thirteenth century contain many cases of this sort. Robert the ditcher belonged to the household of Nicholas of Evenlode when he killed Henry of Evenlode in the village fields. He was not in frankpledge and he had no 263 chattels to keep him from flight. Nicholas le Mul of Ryall was living outside frankpledge in the village of Ryall when he struck Cecily his maidservant with a knife so that she died. Nicholas and his wife fled, leaving behind them 264 chattels worth 4 shillings. Both these cases and many like them came before the judges at Worcester in 1221. Who shall say what happened to such fugitives as these? They may have found another harbourage, but more probably they swelled the numbers of the malefactors who wandered the roads of England, lurked in the forests, and from time to time appear in the rolls as housebreakers, who have generally murdered the householder and his family. An example of this sort of case can be quoted from the same Worcester roll: 'Robbers came by night to Knightwick to the house of Alfred of Knightwick and killed him and Margaret and Maud daughters of Gunnild. It is not known who they were and no one is suspected . . . There is nothing to be done.' Strangers a few miles from their native village, 265 most of these fugitives must have found in the end an unknown wanderer's grave. Ralf son of John of Aston Tirrold was a more cheerful reprobate. He appears in a Berkshire roll of 1226. 'He behaved foolishly in inns and stole his neighbours' doves and when an enquiry was to be made about evil doers he took the cross and went away.' 266 As a Crusader he must have been a liability rather than an asset.

The villein of average ability can have had little expectation of securing his freedom. Perhaps in a good manor, with a just lord and honest bailiffs, he was not even very anxious for it. Many free sokemen of the Danelaw shires were far less well off than prosperous villeins. There is very little contemporary evidence to show how the villeins of the twelfth century were faring and whether they were nearer freedom as the years passed. In 1142 William de Roumara earl of Lincoln founded Revesby abbey in Lincolnshire. Since the land on which the abbey was to be founded was not the earl's own demesne land, but was held by his men, some free and some villeins, he felt himself bound to make provision for the men thus evicted from their tenements. The charter enumerates the free tenants and the amount of land they received in exchange. 'To all the rustics' (that is, villeins) 'living in Revesby I have given an exchange at their pleasure,' says the earl. 'All of them choosing and seeking the liberty of going with all their goods where they wish without any claim, as they chose and sought and of their free will desired I have sent away free, with their houses and all their belongings.' Thirty-one made use of this permission, enfranchised, with their possessions to help them towards a new start in life as free men. Seven chose to migrate to other villages on the earl's estate. He enumerates the services which they shall thenceforward render – identical to all appearances with those to which they had formerly been subject – but he grants that as compensation for disturbance they shall occupy their new holdings for a year free from all 267 service. Earl William of Lincoln appears in general history as one of the more aggressive magnates of king Stephen's unhappy reign, but he was clearly a considerate lord to his own tenants.

In medieval times when life was hard for most people it is unlikely that the average lord would be willing to free his villeins without some recompense for the loss of property. In theory the villein could not buy his own freedom, since all he had was his lord's. Practice was less strict and lords occasionally sold a man his freedom. The church was often the intermediary in such cases. In about 1170 Robert of Thurleigh in Bedfordshire 'quitclaimed and made free these three men, namely Ingeram, and Hugh, and Susanna their sister and their sons and daughters, so that they may go wherever they wish to choose a place and a lord for themselves. And I have done this,' he said, 'at the request of Alexander the prior and the canons of Ashby who have 268 given me 4 shillings that I should do it the more willingly.' It is a fair assumption that the 4 shillings were gathered together by the people concerned. The muniments of the Staunton family at Staunton in Nottinghamshire reveal most interesting information about the fate of a villein family between the end of the twelfth and the latter part of the fourteenth century. William of Staunton freed his villein, Hugh Travers, who lived at Alverton, and all his issue in order that Hugh should go on his lord's behalf to the Holy Land. Probably Hugh joined Richard I's expedition, although he may possibly have been one of those who obeyed the urgency of Innocent III in 1198. Hugh went and returned safely. When he came home again his lord issued another charter reiterating his grant of liberty and putting Hugh under the protection of God and St Mary and the rector of the church of Staunton. At the same time William of Staunton freed John, Hugh's brother and put him also under the protection of the church of Staunton and its rector. The fourth of this little group of documents is a notification by Richard the parson of Staunton that at the request of his patron William of Staunton he has granted to Hugh Travers 2 bovates in Alverton which William has given to God and the church of Staunton. Hugh is to render a pound of incense and a pound of cumin to the church in rent for his holding and the parson is to render a pound of cumin to William of Staunton. By this elaborate arrangement William of Staunton had, in fact converted a villein holding into free rent-paying tenure. It is particularly interesting to discover something of the fate of the Travers family. The enterprising spirit which won Hugh his freedom must have been a family trait, for they became prosperous, acquiring land in neighbouring villages. Hugh's descendants in the male line held land in Alverton until the end of the fourteenth century.   269

The increasing clarification of legal thought during this period meant that from one point of view the villein's position might seem to have hardened down more definitely to servitude. At the beginning of the period and until the king's judges had worked out the theory of villeinage many men in the land cannot have been at all certain whether they were free or unfree. When access to the king's courts depended on freedom, theories about the free and the unfree status were bound to be developed. Glanville's treatise written near the end of the twelfth century contains a brief discussion about how men may be freed, but he seems to think that a lord cannot free his villeins as against other people but only as against himself. He was troubled also by the problem of how a serf can buy his freedom since he has nothing of his own. He must, he thought, be bought by another, though he himself might find the money for the 270 purchase. By the time Bracton's book was written in the middle of the thirteenth century it was accepted by the lawyers that a villein might buy his freedom himself. The human element repeatedly confounded those who liked their social classes clean cut and easily understood. Glanville seems to have held that the children of a mixed marriage 271 are unfree, but Glanville's austerity was soon mitigated, and by Bracton's day the child of a mixed marriage is free unless 272 he was born in the villein tenement of the villein partner. Even at the end of this period these marriages still raised troublesome problems on which not all judges thought the same. Some thought that an unfree woman was freed by marriage with a free man while others thought that she was 273 freed only for her husband's lifetime.

It is possible that women in the higher ranks of society were relatively less free to order their own lives than the women members of the village families, free and unfree. The heirs, whether male or female, of sokemen were in the wardship of their kin, not of a lord who regarded them as in effect part of his saleable property. Marriages of sokemen and villeins were pretty much their own concern, though occasionally necessitated by the desire to forestall the arrival of the family. Even so, it was far better than being handed over to some elderly gentleman because he wanted the land that went with the marriage. Although a villein had to pay merchet, that is, a fine to the lord when he married his daughter, it was probably the general custom of most manors that the lord should not demand so much that the marriage was not made. The heir of a villein had to pay a heriot, generally his best beast, but that was relatively no worse than the feudal relief, which in the days before the Charter might be a crushing amount. The widow of a feudal tenant had her dower, but she had only a limited period in which she could enjoy her husband's home before she made way for his next heir. If the house were a castle she must leave it at once, though it is true that another suitable house must be provided for her. If her husband left an heir under age, her lord might well take over the upbringing of her child. How different was such a noble lady's state from that of the widows of Fleet in Lincolnshire. There, in Henry II's reign, Richard of Fleet, at the prayers and with the advice of Juliana his wife, released all the widows of Fleet for ever from paying 'the relief which in English is called heriot', and promised them that they should possess in peace the lands and houses of their husbands after their husbands' death as long as they could render the services and customs due from the land. ²⁷⁴

In later ages villein tenure gradually changed into copyhold tenure and the holder of such land, no longer regarded as a serf, could not be evicted from his tenement so long as he paid the rent and performed the services due therefrom. Only the first stages of this process can be seen in the thirteenth century. There was, however, one class of villein which during this period gradually established its right to protection in the king's courts. It comprised villein tenants on ancient demesne of the crown, estates which had been held by the king at the time of Domesday Book, even if they had since passed into other hands. The king's tenants, by the fact that they were immediately his men, were more easily able to appeal to his representatives, the justices itinerant, but since they were villeins these tenants had not the right to the free man's remedies in the courts of law. Nevertheless, the king, through his justices, showed that he was ready to see that justice was done. His villein tenants in return were ready to pay him for his protection. In the thirteenth century the royal courts were extending their tentacles over an ever-widening range of pleas, and it was easy for the chancery to devise writs which these royal villeins could buy. It was to the interest of both the seller and the purchaser of such writs that they should be made to serve tenants of land which at any time within memory had belonged to the crown. Domesday Book could be and was used as the test.

In Edward I's reign the tenants of the abbot of Reading

living in the ancient royal manor of Blewbury in Berkshire used this procedure to challenge the abbot's demands upon their money and services. They complained to the king that by the increase in the services which the abbot exacted from them they had suffered loss and damage to the amount of £300. This large amount is presumably the total of all that had been taken unjustly since these demands had first been made in the days of abbot Elias early in the century. The king instructed the sheriff of Berkshire to cause 4 lawful and discreet suitors, together with what the record calls 'a serjeant keeper', from every village in Berkshire which was royal demesne still in the king's hands to appear before the royal justices at Westminster to give evidence about the services they owed the crown. In addition to this considerable company the sheriff was to bring as well 18 men, as well knights as other free and lawful men, from Blewbury itself, through whom the truth of the matter could best be found out. It was pointed out that none of these 18 men must have any ties of kinship either with the abbot or with any of his recalcitrant tenants. The questions to be determined were the services which the men of Blewbury owed to the crown when the manor was first given to the abbot, and whether the abbot was trying to exact more from the men of Blewbury than they used and ought to give. It is hardly surprising to learn that the sheriff found some difficulty in gathering his little army at Westminster and the suit was adjourned to the bridge of Staines. There the parties appeared but the suit was again adjourned, probably because not all the men from the villages had turned up. The case was finally heard and determined on Caversham bridge beside Reading itself.

As might perhaps be expected the verdict of the knights and others showed that the abbot had been exacting more, and the tenants were trying to pay less, than ancient custom allowed. The whole story is too long to tell, but it appears that the men regarded 5 shillings as the appropriate rent for a yardland, while the abbot demanded 10 shillings, or more in some cases, and the jurors declared that 7 shillings was proper. The men particularly resented being amerced for their offences in the abbot's court at his will instead of 'by the judgement of their peers', and paying merchet for their daughters' marriages, and reliefs for entering their lands at the abbot's will instead of at a fixed amount. The jury declared that their amercements ought to be assessed in the full court by 4 suitors of the court; that the merchet paid for their daughters' marriages should not be so harsh that the marriage could not be made; that the relief for entering the inheritance should be at the abbot's will, but that he should not be so harsh that it kept a man out of his land. The men complained that the abbot tallaged them at his will and distrained them to pay hens and eggs, whereas they should be quit of these payments. The jury said that the men should be tallaged only when the king tallaged his demesnes through England and in accordance with the amount of land they held. The men complained that the abbot demanded rents of hens and eggs. The jury said that they should render hens but not eggs and that they should pay church scot. Many other interesting details of service are set down in this plea, of which the upshot was that both the abbot and the men of Blewbury were in the king's mercy, the abbot because he had exacted undue customs and the men because they had misrepresented their case. 275

Among their other grievances, the Blewbury farmers complained that the abbot compelled them to these contested services by distraint. They also complained that in the process of distraint he caused their beasts to be impounded in his court, whereas they were accustomed to have the pound in a known place in the middle of the village. Distraint was the recognized means of forcing men to pay their dues and perform their services. Royal officers 276 distrained men of all ranks to secure the payment of debts to the crown. Lords distrained their free tenants for rents and suit of court not rendered. Unfree tenants were forced to compliance by the same means. It meant the seizure of the chattels, generally the livestock of the debtor or withholder of service. These chattels were impounded, and in the early thirteenth century the debtor must pay his debt or do his service if he wished to recover his property. The lord could not sell the beasts, nor should he look after them. That must be done by their owner, who therefore had a real grievance if the pound were moved from its known place in the middle of the village. Much thirteenth-century legislation dealt with distraint as it affected the free population of the country. It was necessary to provide actions in the courts which would protect the free tenant from the misuse of distraint in order to exact new rents and services. It was equally necessary to provide actions in the courts which would protect the lord against tenants who might evade distraint for legitimate services by removing their goods out of the reach of his officers. Villeins who, unlike the men of Blewbury, could not claim that the manor to which they belonged had been ancient demesne of the Crown had no defence against a grasping lord, and could only put their trust in his adherence to the established customs of the manor.

While it is true that there were more serf than free in the English countryside there is a real danger that sympathy with a vanished social class may incline the historian to forget the existence of a steadily increasing number of free peasants side by side with the unfree. The historian is sometimes also inclined to forget not only that the unfree in considerable numbers won their way to freedom, but also that the free sometimes sank to servitude. The free peasant was in some ways worse off than the unfree, for his tenement could be divided by inheritance, while the villein tenement was preserved as a unit in the interest of the lord. Younger sons of villeins were stimulated by necessity to take up plots of waste or learn a trade or find their living as another man's labourers. Manorial extents give an entirely false impression of permanence and unchanging routine, in which son succeeded father in that state of life to which fate had called him. The reality is different. Human character was as infinitely varied as it is today. Villeins who prospered took up free land at a rent from other lords. Freemen agreed to hold villein tenements, so that their free status was jeopardized. Sons of villeins could somehow win an education and despite all difficulties become ordained as priests and occasionally climb high in their profession. Sokemen might sink to villein status, but they could also rise to knightly rank. English rural society was as fluid then as it has always been. 277

As a tailpiece to this account of English villagers, one aspect of their changing habits during this period may be illustrated. In 1066 and for a century afterwards the names which they gave to their children, both girls and boys, were predominantly English and, in the parts where Danes had settled, Scandinavian. Such names as Godiva, Ediva, Alfled for girls and Godwin, Godric, Alfred, Alfric, Leofgar, Leofwin, Leofstan, Wulfstan, and Wulfric for boys were very common as late as the early thirteenth century all over England. In the Anglo-Scandinavian northern midlands, in East Anglia, Lincolnshire, and Yorkshire a wide variety of interesting Scandinavian names are recorded from this period. Grim, Clac, Sandi, Unketil, Thurketil, Thurgar, Swein, Agmund, Kari, Besi are but a few examples. Such Danish names as these were borne by the ninth century invaders who settled in what became the Danelaw. Grimsby, Claxby, Saundby, Uncleby, Thurcaston, Thurgarton, Swainsthorpe, Amounderness, Careby, and Beesby still preserve their names. More rarely the memory of heroic stories is reflected in names found in records of the late twelfth century. Swanhild, Hengest, and Grettir are examples. Nevertheless, as the thirteenth century passes, these ancient habits cease to hold the English villager. By the end of this period there was little to show, as far as the names they bore went, that they looked back to a purely English or Anglo-Scandinavian past. Edward and Alfred were never to lose their power, but, for the rest, fashion had prevailed and William, Robert, Geoffrey, Rannulf, and their like dominated the cottage as well as the hall. 278

CHAPTER IV

CITIES, BOROUGHS, AND TOWNS

THE growth of towns in a rural society is inevitably slow and halting unless the king for his own purposes encourages the development of centres of population and trade. The early stages in the establishment of English boroughs had long been completed when William I became king. His Saxon predecessors had seen to it that in every shire there was at least one borough – a safe place for markets, a place where people could drive bargains before witnesses who would give evidence if the ownership of the goods were afterwards challenged, a place where money could be minted, and a place which could be a centre of defence and a place of refuge in time of war. Historians in the past have spilled much ink in argument whether trade or defence was the primary motive for urban development. Today, everyone would agree that both elements played their part in the movement which gave the land its towns. Another problem about town origins which has interested many people is why and how a particular site came to be chosen for a town. The lowest point at which a river could be forded and bridged, a point to which also sea-borne ships could come, was a predestined market, port, and borough. London is the pre-eminent example of the strength of these inevitable forces. Inevitable, again, was the growth of Southampton, product of the double tides of Southampton Water. Inevitable, too, was the appearance of Oxford, a natural meeting-place of roads from every quarter of the island. Many of our greatest cities were but rural manors in William I's day, for new discoveries and changing habits have necessitated new centres. But all our modern county towns and many others can look back over a long history to the Saxon past.

Some of them were built by Saxons on sites where the

Romans had in their day founded a settlement. Romans and Saxons alike had been attracted by the hot springs at Bath, by the gap in the Lincoln Edge at Lincoln, by the significance of the great confluence of rivers draining into the Humber by York, by the need for a fortress at Chester to protect the midlands from Welsh or Irish raiders. The barbarians' fear of cities and impressive buildings – the work of giants, a Saxon poet called them – meant that, deserted, they fell into ruin, so that the work of creating a town had all to be done again. If towns on sites once Roman were richer and larger than towns on newer sites, as York was richer than Norwich and Lincoln than Ipswich, it was because of present circumstances, not an inheritance from their remote past. When William I became king there were in England boroughs which would never develop into towns in the modern sense, places little more in size than villages, and there were villages that would in time become towns. Bedwyn in Wiltshire cannot now be called anything but a village, but it was a borough in 1086 when Domesday Book was compiled; so were Bruton and Langport in Somerset. It was not size or wealth that made a borough, but an act of royal will. The larger English boroughs at the beginning of this period had all grown up under royal protection and control as an integral part of the royal policy for the development of national resources and national defence.

The Danish invasions of the ninth century drove home the lesson that the land must be set about with strong defensive posts. At the same time, increasing trade already meant a growing need for secure markets and places for the storage of merchandise. The older trading centres in Saxon England were newly fortified, and, in the land re-conquered from the Danes, those places which the Danes had made the headquarters of their armies, Cambridge, Nottingham, Northampton, Huntingdon, Leicester, and Derby, for example, were continued as boroughs. The Anglo-Saxon genius for local government showed itself in the development of these new boroughs as county towns, centres for the local government of a newly laid-out shire. This arrangement of county town and shire attained a precision of organization outside the old Wessex which had never been necessary within its borders. There, the royal power was securely based on ancient loyalties in a land where royal manors were numerous. But in the old Wessex as in other parts, the kings on their own lands founded many new boroughs in the last generations of the old English state.

There is no better evidence of the economic importance of towns in these early days than the fact that the Saxon kings deliberately decentralized the actual coining of money and decreed that every borough should be a minting place. That meant that in every borough there was an exchange to which bullion could be brought for sale. And every borough was a centre from which coined money went out to help the circulation of goods in its neighbourhood and so to filter into remote parts within and without the kingdom. When he made this enactment with regard to moneyers in boroughs, king Athelstan, grandson of Alfred, enumerated some of the more important boroughs and noted how many moneyers each should have, concluding that every borough must have one man occupied in this task. In London the king declared that there should be 8 moneyers. In days when there were no banks and no operations by which credit could be arranged local exchanges and mints were an efficient substitute. The Saxon kings maintained a close control over these men although they worked in small boroughs remote from the court. Domesday book records that they all had to go to London to get the dies for the coins which they were to strike and they had to make a payment to the king when the pattern was changed and a new coinage issued. Athelstan decreed that a moneyer who was convicted of striking bad money should be punished by having his hand cut off and pinned up on the smithy of his mint; a savage punishment, but moneyers were royal agents who must be made to realize their responsibility.

Check could be kept on the moneyers because the silver penny, the universal coin throughout the period of this book and afterwards, bore on one side of it the king's image and his name and on the other the name of the moneyer and the place where he worked. Silver pennies in great number have survived from the late Saxon age and from the period with which this book is concerned. Men buried hoards of coins when danger approached and often did not live to dig them up again. The type of silver penny issued by Henry II before his great recoinage of 1180 is known as the 'Tealby type' because an immense hoard of these pennies was found at that otherwise unremarkable Lincolnshire village. A vast hoard of 'short cross pennies', so called from the fact that the cross on the reverse of the coin is confined to the inner circle within the legend, was found early in the present century in Brussels. These pennies must have been hidden there when the coin was in current use early in the thirteenth century. The volume of money current at once in this period was very large and it is quite impossible to make any estimate of the amount that was turned out from the mints year by year. It is found all over Europe where it wandered with contemporary traders. The coins that have come down to the present day are, it should be stressed, merely the drippings of the medieval sacks and barrels of pennies. It was in sacks and barrels that they were sent about England in the early thirteenth century to be laid up in local treasuries ready against the king's need as he moved about the land. In barrels they were exported to him when he went abroad on his military adventures.

280
281

Much of this vast quantity of medieval coinage was melted down within a few generations. An appreciable amount was formally melted every year in the king's treasury to test the fineness of the pennies with which the sheriff paid the debts he owed the king. From each separate account due in tested money two pounds of counted pennies plus some extra pence were taken. Then, 240 pennies were melted down to test its fineness. If any contention arose between the accountant and the officials responsible for the assay another 240 pennies were also melted down and a second test was made. When king John issued a new coinage in 1205 he declared that money which did not lack more than 2 shillings and 6 pence in the pound's weight should remain current, but that all money below this standard should be bored through and returned to its owners. The evil practices of clippers of money tended to reduce its weight and all clipped money was to be bored through. In every borough or castle or market town the sheriff was instructed to appoint 4 lawful men to whom the owners could pay in this clipped and bored money. They then 282 placed it under seal in a box for the king's use. Presumably it was ultimately recoined into the new fat pennies. Despite all this destruction, museums are full of these pennies and dealers' shops can still supply the curious with specimens at a very reasonable price. A country with a sufficiency of boroughs and markets for a lively national and international trade, with a well organized currency of good silver pennies, lay at the Conqueror's feet in 1066.

He made no attempt to change the good and tested methods by which the English coinage was ordered. The dies for all England continued to be made in London and at regular intervals when the type of the English money was changed the local moneyers went to London to obtain their dies. The designing and cutting of the dies was a skilled operation and the workmen deserve admiration for their ability to turn out with elementary tools a series of portraits, all recognizable as the same man, and one who 283 had earned the title of 'Conqueror'. English and Scandinavian names on the pennies of William I and his sons show that the Norman kings made no attempt to evict native moneyers from office. The continental names which gradually appear upon the coins merely show that English moneyers in the twelfth century were adopting the new foreign fashions in naming their children. The moneyers were not mere workmen, themselves hammering out coins at the forges. They were leading members of the merchant communities, who employed 'hammermen' to work for them. For the quality of the coin the moneyer whose name appeared on it was responsible.

The extremely high standards of William I's days resulted

in the appearance by the year 1087 of the word 'sterling' as a new name for the English penny. It means 'tough' or 'strong' and seems to have been adopted because each type of William I's pennies was of the same weight. This was not so in the Anglo-Saxon times. Domesday Book itself recognizes that pennies of two different weights had been current before 1066 and the coins which have survived bear this out. After the Conquest the higher weight was enjoined on all moneyers. All through the middle ages English coins deserved the title of 'sterling' for their uniform weight and the high quality of their metal. When Henry I found that 284 his moneyers were becoming careless about the quality of their coins he summoned them to Winchester at Christmas, 1125, and, one by one, they were deprived of their right hands and emasculated. The Anglo-Saxon Chronicle records that this dour business was completed by Twelfth Night. As far as design and portraiture went the latest types of penny issued by Henry I were fully equal to those of his father's day, but careless workmanship at the forges more often than not spoiled the appearance of the coins.

The death of Henry I without a son to follow him meant that new dies must be cut for a new ruler before there was any assurance who that ruler would be. The simple, though temporary, solution that was found for this difficulty – a meaningless run of letters, P E R E R I C, instead of a monarch's name – has given coin collectors many a happy hour of speculation. Stephen soon issued coins in his own name, but he was not strong enough to prevent his great nobles from embarking on the profitable business of issuing money. Baronial pennies were generally rough and ready in design and workmanship. While Maud was in England trying to win the throne she, too, issued pennies, which were little if at all better in workmanship than those of the great nobles. Save for Maud's brief moment of triumph in 1141, London, where the king's dies were cut, supported Stephen throughout the reign. Perhaps the best evidence that the king was gradually strengthening royal control over the realm in his last years can be seen in the last type of pennies put out in his name. The so-called 'Awbridge type' of penny, coined all over England, was clearly the product of 285 a centralized financial organization.

The best way to judge the comparative wealth of English towns is to count the number of moneyers at work in them at the same time. By this test London, York, Winchester, Lincoln, and Norwich stand out as busy commercial centres, but surprising results appear from a comparison of this sort. One is that Thetford in this age ranks with Ipswich and Norwich. There is no doubt about the weight of trade which flowed through the eastern counties in the eleventh and twelfth centuries. It may be due to changing patterns of trade that the tiny south-western boroughs, such as Bruton and Langport, cease to be minting towns after the Norman Conquest and that no moneyers were working at Maldon or Malmesbury after William I's death, but it was clearly the building of a castle at Marlborough which caused the transfer to that place of the moneyer who had previously been working at Bedwyn.

The process of reducing the number of mints was never consistently followed in the twelfth century. Richard fitz Nigel in writing of the exchequer in Henry II's reign says that some counties from Henry I's days were allowed to pay their dues in pennies of any sort of money provided it was silver and of a lawful weight, because by ancient arrangement not having moneyers they had to seek their money where they could get it. The counties he names specifically were Northumberland and Cumberland. No coins were struck for the English king at Newcastle before Henry II's reign, for Scottish influence penetrated the north during the uncertain days of Stephen. Cumberland was not included in the English kingdom until its conquest by William II in 1092 and no coins appear to have been struck at the newly-fortified castle and town of Carlisle until about 1136. Henry I's active policy of founding towns in south Wales is illustrated by pennies minted at Pembroke by a moneyer called Gillepatric. At Reading where a single moneyer had been working at least intermittently, under the Confessor, Henry I allowed his new abbey the possession of a moneyer either there or at London. Later the abbot preferred to exercise his rights in London rather than Reading, for the abbot and monks were given the use of one of the London moneyers. Through all these changes the metallic content of the English coinage, variable before the Conquest, became stabilized at a standard which by 1163 closely corresponded to that of sterling silver.

As the year passed and the Angevin administrative machine was elaborated, the old connexion between the boroughs and the coinage became an anachronism. Already at the beginning of Henry II's reign the sheriff of Norfolk and Suffolk was allowed £6 off his annual payment to the crown from those shires because there were fewer moneyers working at Ipswich and Thetford. Early in Richard I's reign there were 5 fewer moneyers working at Winchester than there were when the annual payment to the crown was fixed. But at the same time there was no attempt to break the tradition of decentralization. Henry II's first coinage was minted at 30 places. At some of them, Carlisle, Launceston, Lewes, Newcastle, Shrewsbury, Wallingford, and Worcester, only one moneyer is known to have worked; at Bristol, Chester, Leicester, Salisbury, and Stafford, two. Some of the local mints, however, still had a considerable number of moneyers in these years; Canterbury had 9, Lincoln 6, Northampton 7 and both Norwich and York 8. London with 18 far outran them all.

Although John issued a new coinage in 1205 he did not change the type of penny. The short cross on the reverse of the coins remained a dominant feature of the English coinage until 1247. More remarkable is the fact that neither Richard I nor John put his own name on his English pennies. All their English coins have HENRICVS REX on the obverse, but in the middle of his reign John issued portrait coins bearing his own name, from the Dublin mint. When he issued his new English coinage in 1205 he declared that all coins must be of proper weight and fineness and that all must have an outer circle. For a little time there was an improvement, but moneyers soon lapsed into bad ways again. None of the coins issued between 1180 and 1247 will bear comparison in workmanship with those of the late Saxon or the first three Norman kings. Commonplace in design and lettering, they suggest that wholesale manufacture has replaced the craftsmanship of an earlier age. The number of towns with working moneyers dwindled during this period still further. At one time or another during these years moneyers were working at 21 towns, but several of these places were newcomers and temporary additions to the list of minting towns. The 3 moneyers who worked at the bishop of Norwich's town of Lynn in John's reign illustrate the success of that newly-enfranchised town in drawing trade from the older market of Norwich, but its mint was only a temporary acquisition. It reflects the friendship between the king and the bishop, his minister, whom he would have liked to see archbishop of Canterbury. The solitary moneyer at Lichfield early in Richard I's reign, the 4 moneyers at Chichester and 3 at Rochester in John's reign worked for only a short time. When Henry III began his reign only 6 mints were still working, London, Canterbury, Winchester, Durham, York, and Bury St Edmunds. Even the mints of Winchester and York were closed for a time and only the mints of London and Canterbury and Bury St Edmunds were in operation in 1247.

In that year a new coinage was issued. Like the preceding coins these are also named from the size of the cross on their reverse. In order to make clipping less profitable it was ordered that the cross should be continued to the outer edge of the coin and that no coin should be valid if the ends of the cross had been clipped off. To the king's name, III or Tercius was added. When this coinage began only London, Canterbury, and Bury St Edmunds had mints, but they did not produce enough currency to meet the demands of trade and for a short time 16 other mints were opened. The king's brother shared in the profits of this recoinage in return for financial aid to the crown. He therefore issued coins at Wallingford, the old shire town of Berkshire and head of one of the great honors of which the earl was lord. The most interesting experiment made in this period was the attempt to initiate a gold coinage in 1257 after the style of the gold florin struck at Florence in 1252. Henry III's gold penny is a very beautiful coin, of which few examples are known. When one comes into the market it fetches a very high price. The ratio which should be established between gold and silver was never at any period easy to determine, and in 1257 too low a value was set for gold. The coin was therefore not popular in England. The issue was never large and after a time the project was dropped. It is probable that many of these beautiful coins went out of the country and were melted down abroad.

The long cross pennies of Henry III were continued into his son's reign. It was not until 1279 that Edward I issued a new coinage bearing his own name. In this reign the mints were put under a new organization directed by a central official who was to become Master of the Mint. Responsibility for the coins was laid on him instead of being distributed among the individual moneyers working in different towns. This new arrangement meant that it was neither necessary nor desirable to put the moneyers' names on the coins, although one issue from the abbot of Bury's mint bore the name of Robert of Hadley, the abbot's moneyer. The other coins simply bear on their reverse the name of the mint. Along with this departure from ancient tradition went the coinage of money of new values. The groat worth 4 pence makes a temporary appearance in this reign, together with the round halfpenny and farthing. Hitherto when change was wanted for a penny it had been necessary to cut the penny into halves and quarters. The Edwardian money proclaims by its appearance that it is the product of a highly centralized administration. Here as in other departments of his government Edward I initiated vital reforms. But the unrelieved competence of the coinage takes away something of its interest. Coins were issued from London, where as many as 30 furnaces were in operation, Canterbury, Bristol, Exeter, Hull, Newcastle, Chester,

Lincoln, and York, as well as Bury St Edmunds and Durham. The mint at Durham was the bishop's, and bishop Anthony Bek was the first subject to put his private mark on the coins made at his mint. The need of supplying a currency for the English soldiers and officials in Scotland produced a temporary mint at Berwick-on-Tweed. Even when the high middle ages have set their seal on the English currency and established the form and style which English coins shall follow until the reign of Henry VII these kings of all England are still obliged, like the Saxon kings before them, to have their coins minted in leading cities and towns about their land.

In early days every borough, whether it were an ancient centre newly fortified or a new settlement of royal land, was 286 in a peculiar sense the king's. It was his because he had chosen to make it a borough and set it about with walls or earthworks. He wished it to prosper and he expected to share in its prosperity. Its mint was a privilege. Its market, also, was a privilege granted and protected by the king. The foundation by the king on his own land of a borough, its defence by walls or ramparts, was accompanied by the settlement within the walls of men who were willing to hire plots from the king for purposes of trade. The king was the lord of every town of any consequence, but many men who were not his immediate tenants had plots or houses within the walls of every town. In almost every borough, from the largest down to the smallest, it was customary for individual houses to be annexed to individual manors in the neighbouring countryside. Houses thus acquired by gift or purchase were regarded as most valuable property by their lords. A house in a borough gave a lord access to the borough market both to buy and to sell, and a share in the burghal privileges. It gave him a place to live in when business or his feudal duty took him to the town. The great men of a shire had to go to the county town on many occasions through the year. Monthly meetings of the shire court came to be held there. In the Norman age a castle to which magnates owed castle guard was built there. In times of danger a house behind the town walls was a refuge. London shared in this development. Property in London was eagerly sought after and already in the eleventh century the estates which great men held in London had developed into 'sokes', that is, properties over which their lords had rights of justice.   287

When John Speed published his maps of English counties in the reign of James I he decked out the corners of the pages with little plans of the boroughs within the county displayed upon the page. These plans, drawn in the early years of the seventeenth century, still show in many cases the plans that the founders of the towns had had in mind. It is clear that sites had been chosen carefully to make full use, for example, of the protection an encircling river could give. Sometimes the lie of the streets shows clearly the result 288 of careful town-planning. When a borough was laid out the individual plots seem to have been broad-fronted on the road. The early burgesses were farmers as well as traders and their houses were farm houses which needed ample space about them for stock and the implements and processes of husbandry. With very few exceptions every town had open arable fields and pasture-lands around it. The citizens or burgesses had their share in the open fields and pasture like the inhabitants of villages. Town dwellers still lived close to the land. Their houses had broad gates for waggons. The broad frontages of early days made it easy at first to increase the number of houses within a town. A site big enough for a farmhouse and yard could easily accommodate at least one or two more houses. The town fields, too, provided room for suburbs as trade rather than agriculture became the primary interest of urban dwellers. Long before the end of the Saxon period Oxford had spilt over into suburbs and by the end of the twelfth century no ancient town of any note can have found room enough within its walls.

The Saxon kings made every effort to encourage the growth and wealth of the boroughs and to make the men who dwelt in them proud of their status. The men they settled in boroughs were free men, and freedom came to be especially associated with life within the walls of a town. Through the middle ages, a serf who escaped to a town, was accepted, and lived unchallenged within its walls for a year and a day, could claim to be regarded as a free man. The importance of the part that the king intended the towns to play demanded that their inhabitants should have the dignity and responsibility of free men. In London from early days an even higher claim than mere freedom was made by its citizens. The leading men of London were recognized as barons and were so addressed by both William I and Henry I. They even claimed the right to play an especial part in the making of the king. The title 'barons' was claimed, too, by the men of the Kent and Sussex harbours known collectively as the Cinque Ports. On them had been laid the responsibility of finding ships and sailors when the king needed them. Early in his reign Henry II gave a charter to the 'barons' of Hastings and by John's reign the other members of the group were being addressed by the same title.

The Norman conquest and the troubles of the years that followed it meant bad times for the towns as for many parts of the countryside. Norman markets were open to traders from England, but William I's relations with France and Flanders were uneasy. The threatening attitude of Denmark, whose king still hoped to win the English crown, must have hindered trade with the north and east. That the year 1066 marked a break in trade with the Scandinavian countries is borne out by the fact that there are few coins of William I found in any of the three northern kingdoms. Far from making English trade with the continent more free and rapid, the conquest must for a time have contracted its volume. William I, moreover, could not trust the towns, centres where people could talk and plan treason against the new king. He caused castles to be built in almost every county town and to make room for them houses were laid waste. When Domesday Book was compiled a description of most towns was included in it. Unfortunately neither

London nor Winchester is described, but so many towns are dealt with that it is possible to gather an impression of the immediate results of the conquest on the thriving communities of Saxon days. Most towns seem to have declined in population since the Conquest. It was a passing phase, for the world was forced to accept the Conquest and make the best of it. Trade revived and towns with it. But in 1086 most towns had many waste dwellings. At Lincoln there were 240, of which 166 had been 'destroyed on account of the castle. The remaining 74 are waste outside the castle boundary, not because of the oppression of the sheriffs and officers, but by reason of misfortune and poverty and the ravage of fires'. In the ancient borough of Torksey, a dependent borough of Lincoln, the Survey states that 'there are 102 burgesses living there, but 111 messuages are waste'. At Shrewsbury the Survey describes how the English burgesses of the town took it very hard that they had to pay as much to the king in taxation as was paid from the whole town in king Edward's day, 'although the earl's castle occupies the site of 51 dwellings and another 50 are waste, and the French burgesses', who apparently did not pay anything, 'hold dwellings that used to pay in the old days, and the earl has given 39 burgesses, whose predecessors used to share in the payment, to the abbey he has founded'. At Oxford there were, the Survey states, 478 houses so wasted and destroyed that they could not share in the payment due to the king.

The mention of French burgesses in the Domesday account of Shrewsbury gives early evidence about one of the communities of Frenchmen which were settled in many ancient boroughs in the years after the Conquest. The reason for these settlements is not far to seek. An unadulterated English borough might be a dangerous knot of disaffection to a Conqueror's new régime. Frenchmen, too, were very ready to take their share in the profits of a burghal market. In the early days of the Conquest it is unlikely that individual Frenchmen would have been very welcome members of an ancient English borough. Frenchmen were therefore established as separate communities. Each of these communities had its own court parallel to the portmoot of the English borough, as at Nottingham, where the common assembly of the French borough was itself known by the English name 'portmannemot'. At York, as at Shrewsbury, the Frenchmen were allowed exemption from the payment of dues exacted from English burgesses. The French burgesses had their own customs, particularly with regard to inheritance. Although in process of time these communities became assimilated into the common life of the borough, traditions of their separate origin survived.

Despite the apparent concision of the Domesday figures it is not easy to make a definite statement about the population of English towns at the end of the eleventh century. The population of Lincoln was much larger than the apparently candid opening of the Domesday account of the city suggests. 'In the city of Lincoln there were in king Edward's day 970 inhabited messuages. This number is reckoned according to the English method, 100 counting 120.' The clerks were interested only in messuages which contributed to the payment due to the king. These messuages were the original areas into which the king divided a newly fortified borough. They were therefore big enough for a number of individual dwellings. By this date full advantage of these sites must have been taken and these city messuages must have accommodated several houses. The number of people who made up one household can be only most roughly guessed. A household must have numbered many individuals in days when employees as well as domestic servants lived in. At least 6,000 people and in all probability many more than that must have lived in the Lincoln of this age. Norwich was of much the same size as Lincoln. Thetford probably contained about 5,000 inhabitants and Ipswich about 3,000. York outnumbered them all. It must have exceeded 8,000. These figures are based on the 289 number of messuages in Edward the Confessor's day. They are large enough to make the walled heart of the borough or city seem a genuine urban centre and small enough to make the bad times of the Conquest evident to all.

Towns were in a sense anomalies in the Anglo-Saxon arrangements for local government. Townsmen could hardly be expected to go to the shire court, which might be held at a distance, and Saxon kings solved the problem by treating the town as a unit, giving it a court of its own. But it was not put completely outside the shire in which it lay. The sheriff collected the rents and other payments due to the king in the town as in the shire, and with them the profits of the town court. The earl had his third penny, that is a third part of the profits of the shire court; often also he had the third penny of the profits of the town court too. The earl's share in the profits of justice within a borough was something of an anachronism at the date of Domesday Book, but it was the relic of an association between borough and shire which had once been intimate.

There is evidence that in towns where Danish influence was strong there existed a class of hereditary lawmen, generally 12 in number, who were in an especial sense the custodians and expounders of the law. Their knowledge of the complicated processes of customary law was passed from father to son. In the time of Domesday Book these hereditary experts were still functioning at Lincoln and Stamford. A solitary lawman, holding his office by hereditary right, was still functioning at York in the reign of Henry I. The name existed as a surname at Northampton in Henry II's reign, but changing times had made the office obsolete long before the end of the twelfth century.

In function, though not in origin, the aldermen of London had much in common with the lawmen of Lincoln and Stamford. The office of alderman was generally hereditary and its holders were regarded as having an especial knowledge of the law and a duty to declare it. The division of London into wards goes back to an early date and is associated with the office of alderman, for each alderman was in charge of a ward which originally seems to have borne his name. Even in Saxon times London was a formidable city; so important were its barons that their city was treated almost as a shire. Its folkmoot, which met in the open air outside St Paul's church, had the power of out-292 lawry, as the shire courts had. All Londoners were bound to attend this meeting and no other summons to it was made than the tolling of the great bell of St Paul's. A meeting so miscellaneous in character, and one which met only three times a year, was not the place for the complicated suits inevitable in a place of international trade. Such business belonged to the Hustings, which met every Monday in the Guildhall. There the aldermen formed a bench of experts in the law. The conduct of their wards was managed in wardmoots, which may be compared with the hundred courts in the countryside. No other town had, or needed, so elaborate an organization for the settlement of suits between its citizens and others.

The first signs that the English boroughs desired to be free of control by the officers of the shire in which the borough lay, and, particularly, free to pay their dues themselves to the Exchequer appeared in 1130, when London and Lincoln made offers to the king to secure the privilege of direct access to the Crown. The burgesses of Lincoln offered 200 marks of silver and 4 marks of gold 'that they might 293 hold their city of the king in chief'. The men of London offered 100 marks of silver 'that they might have a sheriff 294 of their own choice'. Henry I's charter to London gave them control not only of the dues from their own city, but of the county of Middlesex in which it lay. They could also choose the Justiciar who tried the pleas of the Crown in London. The Lincoln men chose their own reeves to collect their dues and take them to Westminster. Henry II was mistrustful of his towns, but he allowed Wallingford to account for its own farm for a time because of his gratitude to the burgesses for the help they had given him in securing his kingdom. Wallingford under Brian fitz Count had stood by Maud all 295 through Stephen's reign, and it was at Wallingford that Henry II and Stephen came to terms. At the end of Henry II's reign only 5 English boroughs apart from London were responsible directly to the Crown for their own dues and in no case was a town sure of keeping the privilege. Richard I's need for money in his first year, when he was about to go on crusade, gave several towns the opportunity of securing by charter freedom to conduct their own affairs and collect and pay their own dues. Thenceforward town after town bar- 296 gained with the king and no town which could afford it failed to get a charter. John needed money as much as his brother and there was nothing to prevent an ancient town from acquiring its desired liberty save inability to pay the sum the king demanded.

Henry II's dislike of burghal independence arose from his observation of the activities of towns on the continent. In France desire for freedom from the control of a lord created in many towns a desire for complete independence. The idea of a town as a sovereign state was abhorrent to the auto- cratic Anglo-Norman monarchy. In France the outcome of 297 this desire for independence had led to the creation of many communes, sworn associations of burgesses or citizens, who claimed to exclude all outside interference and to rule their town as a sovereign body, maintaining a force capable of defending the town walls. London was the only town in England large enough and cosmopolitan enough to hope for any success in going along this road. Many foreigners had settled in London for trading purposes and their pre- sence encouraged the development of ideas about civic government strange to English towns. It was not until Stephen's reign that London could make any move towards attaining independence of the Crown. William I had built the Tower of London on the east of the city by the Thames. He had balanced the Tower on the west by two castles – Baynard's Castle where the Fleet flows into the Thames and Montfichet's Tower not far from it. The Norman kings fully 298 appreciated the strength of London. In his charter to the Londoners, William I said that he would be a good lord to them, but he gave them no chance to resist him.

In Stephen's reign the Londoners seized the opportunity of a civil war to form themselves into a commune, but it was 299 short-lived and in Henry II's reign they had no chance to experiment again. Throughout his reign Londoners had cause to regret that they had driven out the king's mother from their city when she was attempting to win the crown from Stephen. Their annual rent to the Crown, reduced to £300 by Henry I, was raised again to the much heavier figure at which it had stood at the beginning of the twelfth century, and the citizens were asked for frequent aids and gifts. Attempts were made at Gloucester and York to form communes in Henry II's reign, but were sternly repressed 300 by the king. At the beginning of Richard I's reign the citizens of London were conciliated by a return to the conditions established by their charter from Henry I. They could choose their own sheriffs again and their farm was reduced to £300. When trouble broke out in England between Richard I's unpopular Chancellor and John, the king's brother, while Richard was on crusade, the Londoners took the opportunity to acquire more power. To win their support, John and the other magnates swore to support the commune which the Londoners had set up. Again, their commune had but a short life. Nevertheless, from this abortive effort to secure complete freedom from control the Londoners rescued something. They preserved the communal chief officer known as the mayor. The first mayor of London was named Henry fitz Ailwin, and he is described as mayor in 1193. Other towns soon followed the London practice, and the word mayor became accepted generally in England as the proper description of the first officer of a town.

The constitution of London was of necessity much more complex than that of any other English town. The 24 aldermen of London were an inevitable body of city fathers, who in association with the mayor looked after the city's affairs. The poor men of London were not always content with their rule. In 1196 armed revolt against them had to be suppressed by the king's Justiciar. John tried to provide for an elected council of 24 persons who need not be aldermen, but in Henry III's reign the aldermen were again in control. In an attempt to win the support of the Londoners John in

1215 gave them a charter granting the citizens the right of electing their mayor annually. Until this date in London, and still later in other towns, the mayor seems to have held office for life. During the thirteenth century other towns followed the pattern of London and set up councils to advise the mayor. More often than not these councils, like that of London, consisted of 24 members. All through this period, as through all other periods of English history, London was a community so rich and so strong that kings were bound to deal cautiously with it. Its support of the barons in their revolt against the king in 1215 and again in 1258 secured the success of the rebels. 301

A description of London in the days of Henry II was written down by William fitz Stephen as a preface to a biography of Thomas Becket, who was a Londoner by birth. 302 William describes himself as the fellow citizen of the archbishop, 'his clerk, and a member of his household . . . I was his draughtsman in his chancery, subdeacon in his chapel when he celebrated, reader of letters and instruments when he sat to hear suits, and in some of these, when he himself so ordered, advocate'. William was proud of his native city, with its 'Palatine Citadel' on the east 'exceeding great and strong, whose walls and bailey rise from very deep foundations, their mortar being mixed with the blood of beasts. On the west are two strongly fortified castles, while thence there runs continuously a great wall and high, with seven double gates, and with towers along the North at intervals.' He describes the Thames as 'teeming with fish'. Already populous suburbs connected the city with the king's royal palace at Westminster 'a building beyond compare'. The suburban houses had their gardens, 'planted with trees, spacious and fair, adjoining one another'. Near the city on the north William describes the great forest with its lairs of wild beasts, the fertile fields, and the wells where students from the schools and young men from the city go out in the evening to take the air. 'In truth,' says William, 'a good city when it has a good lord,' the nearest he dare come to criticism of Henry II.

The feature of the city which perhaps more than any other impressed the author of this description was the public cook-shop 'upon the river bank amid the wine that is sold from ships and wine cellars'. 'There daily according to the season, you may find viands, dishes roast, fried and boiled, fish great and small, the coarser food for the poor, the more delicate for the rich, such as venison and birds both big and little. If friends, weary with travel, should of a sudden come to any of the citizens . . . they hasten to the river bank, and there all things desirable are ready to their hand.' The population of the city was so great that it could send forth 20,000 armed horsemen and 60,000 foot-soldiers to the wars of Stephen's reign. These numbers must be regarded as apocryphal, for no medieval writer seems to have been able to count a crowd of men. The London schoolboys enjoyed cock fighting and ball games. Young men engaged in sports very like a more mild form of tournament, riding on horseback with a lance and shield. 'To this sport many courtiers come, too, when the king is in London and young men not yet knights from the households of the earls and barons.' On winter feast days boar, or bull, or bear baiting provided amusement. The marshes outside the north wall froze over in the winter and provided a playground for the young. 'The citizens have the special privilege of hunting in Middlesex, Hertfordshire and all Chiltern, and in Kent as far as the river Cray.' 'The only plagues of London are the immoderate drinking of fools and the frequency of fires.'

London never possessed an important institution which appears in most other towns of note in the generations after the conquest, the gild merchant. The idea behind all gilds was simply association for mutual profit, both spiritual and secular, in a difficult world. In Anglo-Saxon days there had appeared in Canterbury, Winchester and London, if not in other centres, an institution known as a *cnihtena gild*. In origin these gilds were most probably associations of the cnihts, or servants of great men settled by their lords in a town to look after their interests and provide them with goods. If this is the origin of the *cnihtena gild* of London it

303

must soon have had a far wider membership than this. By the time of the Conquest this gild was very wealthy and leading citizens belonged to it. But there is no evidence that the gild, as a gild, had any responsibility for the affairs of the city.

In all probability London did not acquire a gild merchant because it did not need one to foster its sense of civic unity. In other towns the growth of the town as a community which could act as a corporate unit would have been far slower had it not been for the gild merchant. The ancient borough court, the portmoot, was presided over by the reeve who was a royal officer though he was also a member of the burgess body. The reeve saw that the king's commands were carried out and his dues collected, although it was the sheriff of the shire in which the town lay who was responsible for taking the money to the Exchequer and accounting for it. The portmoot was an ancient court of justice, but it could not easily adapt itself even with the king's approval to the business of organizing the common life of the town. It had no means of raising money for necessary works. It was bound by the traditions of its origin. But the gild merchant was allowed to charge an entrance fee, so that it had a common purse. The two bodies, the burgesses of the town and the brethren of the gild merchant, who were after all very largely the same people, came to be identified in thought in most towns. Under their chief officers, known as aldermen, the merchant gilds in English towns during the twelfth century helped the towns to draw nearer the conception of a corporation. During the last twenty years of the twelfth century many of the more important towns had won a degree of independence assured to them by royal charter and had acquired a common seal for the common business of the town.

Every medieval town was intensely individualistic and the gild system increased this tendency. The primary aim of the merchant gild was to further the mercantile interests of its members and to exclude strangers from a share in the benefits that gild association gave. The records of the

Leicester gild merchant are more complete than those of any other town and they show how tight a hold this associa-
304 tion had over the trade of the town. The wool trade in Leicester as in most other centres in this age was the dominant trading force. It was impossible to prosper in this trade in Leicester and to remain outside the gild. Only gildsmen could buy and sell wool wholesale to whom they pleased and gildsmen must not sell it retail to strangers. Only they might wash their fells in the waters within the town jurisdiction, and only for them might the Leicester wool packers and washers work. Strangers who brought wool to Leicester for sale could sell only to gildsmen. Certain properties essential to the manufacture of wool were maintained for the use of gild members, who also seem to have had their wool weighed free on the gild wool-beam. Against these advantages a prospective gildsman had to set the many obligations which he must undertake when he swore the gildsman's oath. He had to pay an entrance fee and subject himself to the judgement of the gild. He must not go into partnership with a man outside the gild. It was the gild that fixed wages. In 1281 the whole community of the Leicester gild merchants determined that wool wrappers should be paid both winter and summer a penny a day with food, and flock pullers three halfpence without food and a halfpenny with food. If any employer was found to have paid more, he was to give 6 shillings and 8 pence to the 'community of Leicester'. The gild forbade the use of false weights and measures and the production of shoddy goods. The gild enforced its rules against its own members in the gild court. It could impose a fine or forbid men to follow their trade for a year.

The advantages of membership of the gild extended further than profit in the wool trade. Members were free altogether or in part from the tolls that strangers paid, and the gild made every effort to see that strangers paid their tolls in full. Gildsmen alone were free to sell certain goods retail. Gildsmen, too, had the right to share in any bargain made in the presence of a gildsman, whether the transaction took place in Leicester or in a distant market. The mayor had the special privilege that his bargains alone were free of this tax. In the general interest the gild forbade middlemen to profit at the expense of the public. The practice of 'regrating', as it was called, was constantly attacked by those who suffered from it, and the gilds always tried to check it. At Leicester butchers' wives were forbidden to buy meat to sell again in the same market unless they cooked it. In 1221 the Worcester citizens complained that the men of Droitwich used to come to Worcester market early while the Worcester people were all at church and buy up the food, so that when the knights of the shire and the other Worcester people got to the market there was nothing to buy, because the Droitwich men were holding it all to sell at a higher price. 305

In order to eliminate competition from outsiders as far as possible the gild limited the hours at which goods could be exposed for sale in the market. 'Forestalling' goes with 'regrating'. The Droitwich men complained that the Worcester men injured them by refusing to let them buy food in Worcester market before the third hour. Gildsmen 306 feasted in common and they supplemented the feasts by the barrels of ale which, in Leicester at least, were a common fine laid on offenders. The accounts show frequent payments for a bull, required it may be assumed in early days for bull baiting. When men who were not natives of Leicester joined the gild they paid an entrance fee of 20 shillings and a bull. In the latter part of this period newcomers no longer supplied the bull itself, but paid a sum of money varying from 6 shillings and 8 pence to 12 shillings and 6 pence instead of the actual animal. 307

The gild merchant generally came to be associated with the governing body of the town. Its jurisdiction was general and its members followed many trades. At an early date the men following individual crafts began to form associations with the object of furthering the interests of the suppliers and consumers of their own particular commodity. There was no point in members of a trade organizing themselves in a gild if there were not enough of them in the town to make their gild effective. They must, in fact, be well enough off to secure from entrance fees and other sources enough money to purchase the right to association and all that association entailed. Common feasts, a regular meeting at which rules could be made and breaches of them dealt with, and ultimately a place to meet, both on social and business occasions, were necessary. The trades associated with wool were possibly the first to organize themselves in this way. Gilds of weavers and fullers appeared during the twelfth century in most important centres. Early in his reign Henry II confirmed to the weavers of London their gild as they had had it in his grandfather's day and forbade that anyone not of their company should practice their craft in London, Southwark, and the places dependent on London, except in accordance with the custom of Henry I's day. In return for this charter the weavers agreed to pay the king 2 gold marks a year, that is, 1,440 silver pennies, a large sum which even the weavers occasionally found it hard to meet. The weavers' gild of London became so important that the city was jealous of it and tried to bribe the king to dissolve the gild. The city, however, did not pay the bribe they had offered the king and the weavers increased their annual payment. Instead of paying 2 gold, or 18 silver marks, they agreed to pay 20 silver marks in future; 1,600 silver pennies instead of 1,440.

Although the king's consent was in theory necessary before a gild could lawfully be established, in many towns gilds arose naturally and the necessity of royal consent was overlooked. The idea of association was not a new one. The legislators of Anglo-Saxon days assumed that men would form gilds to help them bear the misfortune of life. The merchant gilds and craft gilds of the post-Conquest period are simply the extension of an ancient habit. If gilds did not obtain the royal consent and pay the king an annual sum there is not likely to be much twelfth-century evidence of their existence. In 1180 Henry II, conscious that many gilds were making no payment to him, seems to have made a special effort to find out these unlicensed associations in order to fine them. In the Pipe roll of that year the result of this activity is shown in debts charged for gilds without warrant, although the nature of the gild is often omitted from the entry recording the debt. Three gilds at York, the sadlers, the glovers, and the hosiers, were charged respectively 20 shillings, 2 marks, and one mark. The borough of Barnstaple 309 paid one mark and the burgesses of Totnes paid 3 of the 5 marks they were charged for a gild without warrant. At 310 Lydford, now a place of little note, Ralf the Rich was fined 5 marks for the same reason, one other man was fined 5 marks, two were fined 3 marks, and a clerk one mark. The 311 burgesses of Launceston paid 3 marks. The borough of 312 Wareham paid 3 of the 6 marks with which it was charged. 313 Axbridge paid 20 shillings and Langport half a mark. The 314 burgesses of Ilchester owed 20 shillings. Bridport paid half a mark and Dorchester 3 marks. The citizens of Exeter accounted for £40 'for a fine of a plea touching gilds'. They paid £20 of their debt. It seems as though there must have 315 been several unlicensed gilds in Exeter and the citizens compounded in a lump sum. At London no less than 19 of these bodies, described as 'adulterine' gilds, were reported and charged with a fine. Unlike the gilds in the other towns, 316 the Londoners made no attempt to pay their debts and in the middle of John's reign, 1208, they still owed the whole of the £120 with which they were burdened in 1180. 317

The London list is particularly interesting. Each of the gilds had an alderman as its chief officer and his name is given. Occasionally the gild is distinguished merely by his name – the gild of which Goscelin is alderman. There was a butchers' gild and a pepperers' gild. The goldsmiths' company makes its first appearance as a unit on this occasion, although it is highly probable that the London goldsmiths had some form of association in Henry I's reign. More interesting, because unconnected with trade and therefore suggesting a survival of the Anglo-Saxon conception of a gild, are the gild of St Lazarus and the Pilgrims' gild. The former was probably some sort of leper charity and the latter a club to help its members who wished to go on pilgrimage.

There were four bridge gilds, each with its own alderman. Presumably their purpose was to keep London Bridge in repair. In discussions of medieval merchant and craft gilds there is always so much to say about the organization of medieval trade that the 'burial and benefit' aspect of the medieval gild is sometimes overlooked and always understressed. The gilds are the direct ancestors in spirit of the working men's clubs, and the Freemasons.

Towns did not fit neatly into the pattern into which William I's clerks tried to shape all English land holding. They could not be entered in Domesday Book as part of the king's land, for men who did not hold of him were members of every borough community. It was inevitable that the town should be regarded as a unit and it was taxed as such when the king took a tallage from his demesne manors and boroughs. The fact that the towns are tallaged is an illustration of the anomalous position they hold. Tallage was a form of taxation which came to be associated particularly with the unfree. A lord could 'tallage' his villeins. He took an 'aid' from his free tenants. The boroughs were put in a position analogous to that of the tenants on the king's demesne manors. No one would have claimed that burgesses were unfree, and there was an element of bargaining in the tallage they paid. In 1206 the mayor of Lincoln had a sworn agreement about the tallage taken in Lincoln in 318 that year. It was agreed that the city should pay £400 in two instalments of £200 each. Henry II's wide empire enabled the English merchants to grow rich on a protected trade. The Pipe rolls show that in the latter part of Henry II's reign he took more tallages from the towns than had been done before. Both Richard I and John tallaged the towns as often as they could. In this as in other matters London stood alone. It was not tallaged, but paid aids or gifts. In 1208 it paid most of a debt of £1,000 charged in 1204 as a fine to exempt the city from service with the king's army abroad. The citizens were barons and collectively 319 they paid baronial taxation.

It was rarely that ancient boroughs founded in the past

by Saxon kings came under the direct lordship of anyone other than the king himself. Leicester is an exception to this rule, for in the first half of the twelfth century the earl of Leicester obtained the lordship of the town and his successors retained it. Bath was given to its bishop by William II and Reading to its abbot by Henry I, but neither was a county town. Northampton and Warwick for a time fell under the lordship of the earls of their counties. Many 320 English towns of varying importance were founded by local magnates anxious to develop the resources of their estates. The process began immediately after the Norman Conquest when many foreigners were faced with the problem of impressing their authority on a hostile or indifferent tenantry. The new towns thus established in early days were often planted beneath a castle, for defence was still important. A new town was generally given a charter by its lord in which the burgesses' privileges were set out. Rather than write out these privileges in detail many lords gave their newly-founded boroughs the same customs that some other town enjoyed. At this date the most popular set of privileges was that enjoyed by the town of Breteuil in Normandy. Its lord, William fitz Osbern, a close friend of William I, became earl of Hereford and lord of much English land. His estates lay largely in the west along the Welsh border, where unconquered Wales was a perpetual danger. He founded many boroughs, as centres of defence and trade, and gave them the customs of Breteuil. These customs were so popular that other magnates followed William's example and gave their new boroughs the same privileges. As the lords of the Welsh march won lands from their Welsh neighbours they secured them by building castles, beneath which more often than not they planted a town. 321

Towns thus set up during this period in Wales and Ireland became centres from which civilization could spread into the surrounding districts. They were settled with Englishmen, Normans, or Flemings who were glad to take up holdings and enjoy the townsmen's privileges. The great towns of Wales, Swansea and Cardiff, to name only two, were in origin alien centres in a conquered land. The little village of New Radnor, with a present population of about 200, offers concrete evidence of the way in which these towns were planned and laid out. It lies beneath an impressive castle mound, all that remains of the castle held by successive members of the Braiose family, who conquered those parts from the Welsh. An earthen grass-covered bank is all that now remains of the wall that once surrounded the town. The main street runs up to what was once the market cross and parallel to it on either side is another street. One street runs at right angles across the town. Radnor never developed into a commercial centre and it remains today, crystallized in its decay, an example of the careful symmetry with which the Norman barons laid out their towns.

The founding of boroughs by magnates was by no means confined to danger points like this. All through this period magnates were endeavouring to increase the financial capacity of their tenants by raising existing villages or towns to burghal status. Occasionally the burgesses of a borough created by a magnate obtained a charter from the king as well. The borough of Wells was created by bishop Robert of Bath and Wells between 1136 and 1166. John issued a charter for Wells in 1201. John's trusted minister William Briwerre made Chesterfield in Derbyshire and Bridgwater in Somerset into boroughs. The king gave him a charter for each of them. Chesterfield was given the customs of the town of Nottingham. These places were all made 'free boroughs', that is, they were given the liberties and customs which free boroughs had. The borough of Lynn in Norfolk, mentioned earlier in this chapter as a minting place in John's reign, owed its charter to its lord, the bishop of Norwich, who was allowed by the king to choose the customs of whichever town he wished for his new borough. He chose those of Oxford – a good choice, for Oxford enjoyed the customs of London. In the king's charter to Lynn the burgesses are told that they may refer to Oxford in case of any doubt about what their customs should be. The abbot of Burton founded Burton-on-Trent early in the thirteenth century and in 1222 a later abbot of Burton founded Abbots Bromley, giving to their foundations, with the king's approval, the liberties of the men of Lichfield. All over England charters were being granted to make little communities into boroughs. 322

The status of a borough was no assurance of prosperity and it was easy even for an ancient borough to lose ground to a new competitor. When late in the middle ages a bridge was built over the Thames at Abingdon it diverted the London to Gloucester road and drew trade from the borough of Wallingford, in early days the chief borough of Berkshire. But long before this, between Abingdon on the one hand and Reading on the other, where Henry I's new abbey brought trade to the town, Wallingford was losing ground. Even today it has spread little beyond its Anglo-Saxon defences. Many of the boroughs founded by magnates did not prosper, either because of too close competition or because the site was unsuitable to a town. In Lancashire only 4 of the 23 boroughs founded there between 1066 and 1372 survived the middle ages as boroughs. Even Manchester and Warrington failed to keep their burghal status continuously into the modern age. Magnates might found boroughs because they wished to draw wealth by trade into their own sphere of influence, but if a borough showed signs of becoming too independent its lord might well try to push it back into the position of a manor. Burgesses were free men. Their court, even if the range of cases they might deal with was limited, was their own court. In 1300 the lord of Warrington forced the men of Warrington to attend his manor court and abandon their own borough court, so that their town became 'a sort of urban manor'. Something of 323 the same thing happened, though at a much later date, to the borough of Burford in Oxfordshire. 324

Between the metropolitan wealth of London and small stagnant communities like New Radnor there lay a vast number of boroughs with an infinite diversity in wealth. Some of the privileges which the ancient boroughs cherished most could be granted only by the king. If the lord did not already enjoy in the manor court the right of trying thieves and enforcing the assize of bread and ale, and if he had not already the right of holding a market and a fair he could not himself give his new borough those rights. All that he could then do was convert villein tenure, that is, unfree tenure, into burgage tenure, that is, free rentpaying tenure. Any group of villagers would have been glad enough to get such a concession. But often the lord already had the right to a market and a fair and a court competent to try thieves. Then the new borough could start its career well equipped for economic advance. Every borough was jealous of its neighbours and grimly set on the preservation of its liberties, on the watch all the time lest a new market should be established so close that it might be to the prejudice of its own market. For this reason market days must not be changed, and if they were changed, the fact must be reported to the king's judges when they came round. Eustace abbot of Flaye toured England in 1201 preaching against Sunday markets and in response many places changed their market day without licence from the king. At Oundle, Rothwell, and Peterborough, for example, the 325 day had been changed from Sunday to Saturday. The chronicler Roger of Howden says that people soon went back to their Sunday markets again 'like dogs to their 326 vomit'. Sunday was a good day for a market, for customers were free of other occupations and could enjoy looking at and sometimes buying the goods displayed.

There was an element of unreality in classing together under the same descriptive title of 'borough' places like Oxford or Northampton with a long urban history behind them, lying in the heart of England on a nexus of ancient roads, and such modest towns as Clifton-on-Teme, chartered in 1270 but having no genuine court of its own, or Higham Ferrars, enfranchised by its lord in 1251. From at least 1166 onwards, boroughs were expected to send 12 men to meet the king's judges when they came round, but the smaller ones were generally glad to be let off with 4 or 6 representatives. In 1252 boroughs were ordered to set a watch of 12 men every night from Ascension to Michaelmas for the apprehension of malefactors. In villages, according to their size, a watch of 4 or 6 was held to be sufficient. The smaller boroughs again were probably glad to be let off with the smaller number of watchmen. These smaller boroughs came in Henry III's reign to be called 'market towns' or more accurately 'merchant towns' to distinguish them from the village on the one hand and the borough on the other. But in Edward I's reign boroughs were taxed at 327 a higher rate than the counties so that Exchequer officials tended to class even small market towns as boroughs, while the local officers tended to depress even ancient boroughs into the class of market towns. The title by which a place was called had a real significance when Edward I made it a permanent part of his policy to summon burgesses from the boroughs together with knights of the shire to meet in Parliament to hear his intentions and promise him financial aid to carry them out. The question whether a particular town was for this purpose a borough or not, originally in the sheriff's discretion, was in the last resort settled by the practical issue – could it afford to send representatives to the king's Parliaments? 328

In many towns the market was held not in a market square but in the open street. Anyone driving through Leighton Buzzard today on a Tuesday can still see a market held in this fashion, the stalls being set up in the gutter along the edge of the pavement. Oxford's market was held in the middle ages in High Street and the street now called Cornmarket, for corn was sold in the middle of the street on market day. The width of High Street and Corn- 329 market is due to this ancient practice. Broad Street, so wide that a car park can be made in the middle, owes its width to the fact that horses were sold there in this period. It is possible, though there is no evidence about it, that the width of St Giles, outside the city walls, is due to the sale of cattle and sheep there in the middle ages. Oxford market at the beginning of this period served a very wide area indeed.

Abingdon had only recently acquired its Monday market from Edward the Confessor, but Eynsham did not get its Sunday market until Stephen's reign, or Woodstock its Tuesday market until Henry II's reign. Bampton's market was mentioned in Domesday Book, but Burford had not acquired its Saturday market by that date. Charlbury did not get its Monday market until 1256. It may be that this increase in the number of markets had something to do with the decline in wealth in many towns in the latter part of this period. Unless there was a marked increase in the volume of goods and money in circulation more markets could only spread the national wealth more thinly. From about 1250 Oxford steadily declined in wealth all through the medieval period. Lincoln was at its most prosperous in the twelfth century.

Market means little to the average citizen today, but in this period it was the centre of his week, the day he could take his goods to sell and buy himself what the market could provide. Retail trade was conducted very largely in the market, for the medieval shop was less a store than a workshop. Traders kept no stocks of made-up goods, but sat in their shops and made what was ordered of them. Shops were generally very small, often no more than 6 feet wide. Oseney abbey built the Golden Cross Inn towards the end of the twelfth century. It sold the inn, but kept the ground floor, consisting of 4 shops, each measuring about 6 by 15 feet. Very often, although there seems to have been no compulsion, men who followed the same trade lived in the same street. At the end of this period part of the High Street in Oxford was called the spicery because men who sold spices had their shops there. Another part was called the place of the goldsmiths. In York the street known as the Shambles still had 26 butchers' shops in 1892 though changing times have reduced that number to 5.

The streets of a medieval town were generally narrow. Steep Hill at Lincoln, too steep and too narrow for anything but foot traffic, gives a good idea of a medieval street. The men who laid out the ancient English towns were practical

men with a good eye for the lie of the land and a keen sense
of the importance of siting a town so that its streets drained
off into a watercourse. The only drains of the town ran down
its streets, which sloped towards the middle where the open
drain or gulley ran. Hence streets were paved with stones
or cobbles as the neighbourhood provided them, and there
were no paths for walkers. Footpaths were necessary only
long after this period, when streets were made up in the
middle and drained to the side. Buildings, houses, and
shops, although their posts might be tough beams of oak,
were very vulnerable. All through this period there was
constant anxiety about fire. The name of one of the Lincoln
churches, St Peter Stanthaket, that is, stone thatched,
suggests that even churches were thatched with reeds or
straw. Richer men built stone houses, but they were
remarkable enough even at the end of the twelfth century
to be described as such when they are mentioned in a deed.
Steep Hill, Lincoln, can still show two of its fine twelfth-
century houses standing and in use today. One of them was
described in the thirteenth century as 'the great hall of
Peter of Legbourne and Joan his wife'. It is an impressive
and substantial house of two stories looking out over the
city below. It must have been the town house of some
Lincolnshire magnate of those days.

It is often said that the first people to build stone houses
in England were Jews anxious to protect themselves from
their debtors. The hall of Peter of Legbourne used to be
ascribed, without evidence, to the famous Jew, Aaron of
Lincoln, whose financial dealings stretched over a great
part of England. He died in 1186, and must certainly have
known both Peter of Legbourne's hall and the other
twelfth-century house which is still standing on Steep Hill
in Lincoln. Next door to it is another stone building which
dates from the twelfth century. It seems to have been the
synagogue of the Lincoln Jewry in that age. The period of
this book covers the whole history of the Jews in medieval
England, for they gradually drifted here in the wake of the
Norman conquerors, were already flourishing in Stephen's

reign, enjoyed their greatest prosperity under Henry II, were persistently mulcted of their profits by his successors, and were finally expelled from the country in 1290 by Edward I, when their wealth was practically exhausted. Most of the county towns, all those that were important trading centres, had a settlement of Jews. If Jews wished for any reason to live in the country or in a place where a Jewry had not been established, they were expected to obtain royal permission. In many old towns today the memory of the medieval Jews is perpetuated by the survival of the name Jewry, marking their former homes. In York there was no separate Jewry. There Jews lived, as a royal decree of 1278 declares, 'among the Christians as they were wont to do in times past'. Leake and Thorpe's shop in Coney Street stands on the site of the stone house built by Josce of York, who was killed in the riots of 1190, and of his son, Aaron, whose financial operations were as extensive as those of his twelfth-century namesake in Lincoln.

Christians were forbidden by the Church to engage in usury, that is to lend money for interest. In an age of expanding trade, increasing wealth, and great building activity there was a constant call for capital, which the Jews were able to satisfy. The princes of the Church who wished to beautify their cathedrals or monasteries found Jewish moneylenders ready to help them. Men temporarily embarrassed borrowed both large and small sums freely. The rate of interest was high, for there was no other source from which money could easily be obtained. A few Christians defied the Church and engaged in the trade, but they were not to be found, like the Jews, in every town. Even in small towns, like Windsor, where there was no permanent Jewry, individual Jews attended for business. It has been reckoned that the average rate of interest they charged was 43 per cent, but it was often higher than this. When Richard of Anstey early in Henry II's reign was trying to get his case heard by the courts, he was constantly in need of small sums of money and always seems to have found a Jewish moneylender at hand to help him. 'When,' he says, 'I sent my brother over sea for the king's writ I borrowed 40 shillings from Vives the Jew of Cambridge, paying in interest 4 pence a pound a week, and I kept the money 14 months and paid 37 shillings and 4 pence in interest.' The following Easter Vives lent him 60 shillings at the same rate. He kept it 6 months and paid 24 shillings in interest. When he went abroad himself to get the king's writ he borrowed £4 10s. from Comitissa of Cambridge at the same rate, kept it 9 months and paid in interest £2 14s. When he was pleading at Canterbury at Whitsun he borrowed £2 at the same rate from Deulecresse the Jew, kept it 2 months and paid in interest 5 shillings and 4 pence. When he went abroad he borrowed £3 from Jacob the Jew of Newport at the same rate, kept it 13 months and paid £2 12s. interest. When he sent his clerks to Rome Hakelot the Jew lent him £10 at 3 pence a pound a week. He kept it 7 months and paid £3 0s. 10d. interest. After Michaelmas Hakelot lent him another £3 at the same rate. He kept it 3 months and paid 9 shillings interest. In November Jacob of Newport lent him £3 10s. at the higher rate. He kept it 8 months and paid 37 shillings and 4 pence interest. At the same time Benedict the Jew of London lent him 10 shillings for 2 pence a week. He kept it 3 years and paid £1 6s. in interest. When he took his writ to be sealed to the bishop of Chichester Jacob the Jew lent him £5 at 3 pence a pound a week. He kept it 10 months and paid in interest £2 10s. When he sent his clerks to the Pope he borrowed £4 from Hakelot the Jew for 3 pence a pound a week, kept it 6 months and paid 24 shillings interest. When he went to plead at Windsor Deulecresse the Jew lent him £2 at the same rate. He kept it 4 months and paid 8 shillings in interest. On the same occasion because his money ran out at Windsor Brun the Jew lent him half a mark (6 shillings and 8 pence) for three halfpence a week. He kept it 10 weeks and paid 15 pence interest. On the same occasion at Reading, Hakelot the Jew, whom he found there, lent him 30 shillings for 3 pence a week a pound. He kept it 5 months and paid 7 shillings and 6 pence for it. At Woodstock, when he won his case, he borrowed £4 10s. from Mirabelle the Jewess of Newport at the higher rate of interest, kept it a year, and paid her £3 18 shillings interest. This was not the full extent of his borrowings. When it came to paying what he owed the king he had to go to the Jews again. Hakelot obliged him with three separate sums of £20, £7, and £2 all at the lower rate of 2 pence a week a pound. Nevertheless as he sadly says 'I 333 still owe the principal and all the interest.'

These high rates of interest meant that the Jews gathered great wealth but were hated by those who went to them for help. They always felt themselves to be in danger of attack from their embittered debtors. Moreover, they were strange and alien to the people among whom they lived. Some of them were men of great learning in their own law. Besides the English and French they spoke in their daily life they knew Hebrew and Latin. Some of them collected books. The great moneylenders were international figures, with a know-ledge of the world far greater than that of the dwellers in English provincial towns. They represented an ancient civilization which the average man of the day did not under-stand and instinctively mistrusted, a mistrust which religious prejudice turned into a virtuous hatred. Hence the Jews were suspected of the most revolting crimes. In 1130 the Jews of London were charged with a debt of £2,000 'for a sick man 334 whom they killed'. A Jewish doctor must have failed to save his patient's life and the whole community was punished. Already in 1144 Jews were accused in Norwich of the ritual murder of a Christian boy named William, whose story was told within a few years of his death by Thomas of Mon-mouth, a Norwich monk. William was about 12 when he was found dead in Thorpe Wood near the city. His father, a farmer named Wenstan, was already dead, but his mother Elviva was alive and had been offered for William a post in the kitchen of the archdeacon of Norwich. The man who made the offer took William away with him and called on William's aunt to tell her about it. She told her daughter to follow and see where William was taken. The child said that he was taken into a Jew's house. William was next seen dead in Thorpe Wood. The credulity of the populace and their readiness to suspect the Jews made William a miracle worker and consequently a saint. Between 1144 and 1172 his body was four times translated, each time to a place of higher honour. It lay at last in a chapel on the north side of the High Altar of the cathedral church. William was only 335 the first of a series of English boys whose unexplained deaths were attributed to the Jews.

With the tightening of royal control over the resources of the land in Henry II's reign the place of the Jews in the national economy was clearly defined. Henry II protected them from the hatred of their debtors because he regarded them as instruments for the collection of money for the Crown. As usurers they followed a profession which the Church condemned so that their goods and chattels were forfeited to the Crown on their death. The son of a Jew who wished to acquire his father's estate must purchase it from the king. Aaron of Lincoln's affairs were so complicated and his debtors so widespread over England that when he died in 1186 a special department with two clerks was set up to deal with them. It took the 'exchequer of Aaron', as it was called, some time to sort out the debtors into their appropriate counties, so that they could be summoned to pay their debts at the royal Exchequer. By 1191 the work was finished and the debtors appear on the Pipe roll. From Cumberland 336 and Northumberland down to Kent men had been going to Aaron for help. Among his debtors were many of his own race, moneylenders themselves on a smaller scale. Twenty years after Aaron's death many of these debts were still owing. Some of them had been extinguished by the payment of a sum down, smaller than that owed to Aaron; some were being slowly paid off by small instalments; others were recognized as bad debts. In 1208 Aaron's son Elias offered the king 200 marks for '£400 worth of the worst of the charters of Aaron his father which are not paid off and are worth little to the lord king'. Elias was too optimistic about these debts, for a little later in the same year he offered the king an additional 3 marks of gold 'to have charters such as

337 may bear fruit to him and whence he can have some advantage'. The capacity for resistance to demands for payment was one of the reasons for the excessive rate of interest.

In 1187 Jerusalem fell to the Saracens and in England as elsewhere in western Europe a new zeal was stirred up for the Crusading cause. Henry II from his Christian subjects took a tenth, and from his Jews a fourth of their chattels for the Crusade. This renewed enthusiasm for the war against the infidel roused the ever-present hatred of the Jews. The death of Henry II, whose favour the Jews had enjoyed, encouraged outbreaks against them in many parts. Richard I's coronation was marked by a rising of the London populace, swelled by visitors for the occasion, against the London Jewry. The rioters were encouraged in their work by the pleasing rumour that the new king had ordered that all Jews should be exterminated. The example of the Londoners was followed in the spring by many other towns. At Bury St Edmunds, Thetford, Norwich, and King's Lynn, at Stamford, Lincoln, and York in greater or less degree the same trouble broke out. At Lynn and Stamford much of the trouble was attributed to young men, anxious to go on crusade, who had collected together from various parts of the country. They resented the wealth of the Jews while they themselves had not the money necessary for their journey. A young man called John who acquired much booty in the Stamford riots deposited it with someone at Northampton and was slain by his host in the night and his body was cast outside the town walls. The slaughter in this manner of a crusader encouraged the common people to regard him as a martyr and to honour his grave with solemn watches. The bishop heard that his grave was being turned into a place of pilgrimage and hastened to forbid the 338 veneration of so false a prophet.

The riots in York were the more dangerous in that men of position led the rioters, anxious to destroy the record of their indebtedness to the Jews. To make such destruction more difficult, provision was made in 1194 for the establishment in six or seven towns where there were important

Jewries, of chests with triple locks for the storage of the Jews' bonds. All loans were to be made in the presence of the officials in charge of the chests and for the greater security a copy of all Jewish transactions was to be enrolled. This 339 organization soon developed into the Exchequer of the Jews, a court at which all Jewish affairs could be dealt with and litigation which concerned them conducted. The king won a firmer hold than ever on all Jewish financial transactions. One of the Justices of the Jews was himself a Jew, who bore the title of Arch-Presbyter of all the Jews in England. Despite the title, the Arch-Presbyter was a lay official. He 340 was chosen because of his position, for he was always the Jewish financier who was at the time of his appointment the richest and best regarded among his fellows. He had to act as the liaison officer between them and the king. He presided with his fellow Justices of the Jews, Englishmen and lawyers, over the Jewish Exchequer, hearing suits and arranging tallages when they were demanded by the crown. It was a thankless office. As the needs of the king increased, so his demands on the Jews grew. In the thirteenth century no considerations of economic theory troubled the minds of kings or ministers. On the one hand Englishmen hated the Jews and demanded protection from the consequences of borrowing at a high rate of interest more money than they could ever repay. They also demanded that the king should not insist on the payment of interest and principal if the debt came into his hands and the debtor fell on evil days or died. On the other hand the king treated the Jews as though they commanded illimitable stores of wealth which could be tapped at his will.

In the first part of the thirteenth century Jewish wealth could still be built up within a few years as it was in the York Jewry after the disasters of 1190. Josce of York, the richest man in the York community, was slain in 1190 and his debts were collected for the king. By 1219 his son Aaron was one of the twelve leading Jews in the land. Aaron rebuilt his father's house in Coney Street, York, and maintained an office in London. He lived in great splendour, riding about on a black palfrey of particular beauty. His financial transactions rivalled those of Aaron of Lincoln a generation earlier. Aaron of York was Arch-Presbyter for seven years, 1236–43, a time when the king's demands for money from all his subjects were growing. The purses of the Jews were raided again and again. Every social and political occasion – the king's marriage, the marriage of Richard earl of Cornwall, his brother, Earl Richard's crusade – was an excuse for the exaction of money from the Jews. In 1241 at Worcester 106 representatives of Jewry were brought together in a 'Parliament' to discuss how they could raise among themselves a tallage of 20,000 marks to pay the king's debts. Irresponsible accusations against the Jews of coin-clipping or of ritual murder were made the pretexts of extortion. Even wealth built up on the rates of interest current in the early thirteenth century could not sustain the royal demands. When Aaron of York died in 1286 he was a ruined man. Edward I expelled the Jews in 1290 because 341 their days of usefulness were over.

It is inevitable that in any discussion of the place of Jews in medieval English society the limelight should fall on the great money lenders whose names recur in every record of those days. It is inevitable, too, that the stress should be laid on the hatred which broke out again and again in riots and bloodshed. When Henry III was passing through Norwich in March 1235 the citizens came to him and complained that a greater number of Jews than usual lived in their city and that Jews who were of ill fame elsewhere came to their 342 city to dwell to the harm of the city. During the Barons' War the rebels sacked the Jewries in many towns. Their object was always to get possession of the chest of bonds in order that they might destroy all evidence of debts. Nevertheless, there is another side to the story. Not all Jews were international or even national moneylenders. There were many humble Jews, who earned a living so modestly that history ignores them. Many Jews were learned men, particularly in matters of Jewish law and practice. An outstanding example of the learned Jew was Master Elias of London, who died in

1284. He was the direct descendant of a learned Jew who lived in Mainz about the year 1000. The first of the family to come to England was Elias's great grandfather, who settled in Bristol. His son, Yom Tob, Elias's grandfather, cared more for learning than business and wrote a book in Hebrew of which only the title has survived. Master Moses of London, son of Yom Tob, was also a scholar and writer as well as a moneylender. His work on biblical punctuation has been published many times. Five books are attributed to Master Elias, the son of master Moses, and his reputation as a scholar and a doctor was as high on the continent as it was in England itself.   343

Not everyone hated the Jews. One man even was burned to death for love of a Jewess. He was a deacon who abandoned for love's sake the Christian for the Jewish faith, was brought to trial before the archbishop in a council held at Osney by Oxford in 1222, and condemned to death by burning. The sentence was carried out by the lay power. In Henry II's reign the wealthy Jurnet of Norwich married a Christian heiress and for his presumption was fined 6,000 marks. His wife became a Jewess and was deprived of her lands. The whole Jewish community of England was charged with Jurnet's fine. He and his wife fled abroad, but were back in business in England before the end of Henry II's reign. Both their sons became moneylenders. All 344 through the history of the medieval English Jewry, too, there was a welcome to the Jew who became converted to Christianity. Already in 1154 there existed a school for converts in Bristol. The Church taught that converts should be in better circumstances after their conversion than before. 'Let no poverty or any other cause which we can avert make him regret leaving his kin and his Law for Christ's sake,' wrote Anselm at the beginning of the twelfth century. Hence Henry III, impecunious though he was, founded a home for converted Jews where today the Public Record Office stands at the end of Chancery Lane. Converts gave up their property and men received from the king three halfpence a day, and women 8 pence a week.

Occasionally converts were planted out in religious houses about the country if accommodation in London was insufficient. When Jews were converted they took a Christian name, often that of their patron, who stood godfather to them.

The presence of Jews in every English town – the outstanding figures among them, with their houses in the Jewry of their birth or choice, and their offices in London or Paris – is striking evidence of the elaborate financial transactions arranged in this period. Behind the international trade of the twelfth and thirteenth centuries stood the Jewish moneylender, ready with capital to enable men to undertake far-reaching trading adventures. When in the last half of the thirteenth century royal extortion was rapidly ruining the Jews, Italian moneylenders had appeared to succeed them, until they, too, failed. Isolated Italians were engaged in the business in England at the end of the twelfth century. By the middle of the thirteenth century there were many Italians in the field.

The men who lived in the walled towns of medieval England were anything but cloistral in their outlook. Their walls, with the gates locked nightly at sundown, protected the town's heart in time of trouble, but were never intended to bar the foreign trader. Even in the very beginning of this period, when there were few, if any, Jewish moneylenders to provide capital for trade, English traders did very well without it and moved freely about the known world. When Alexius Emperor of Constantinople wished to send his greetings to Henry I and his queen there was an Englishman at Constantinople by whom he could send letters and gifts. He was Wulfric, an Englishman from Lincoln, who brought back with him to Abingdon the arm of St John Chrysostom which he had begged the Emperor to give him.

The men of Lincoln and York may have inherited with their Danish blood something of the Viking restlessness. They were both great cities with stiff-necked inhabitants, conscious of their past. William I had to build two castles before York could be repressed, and Lincoln maintained that ill-luck threatened a king who wore his crown within its walls. Trade with the north must have been the basis of their wealth. The story of Magnus Barefoot's treasure illustrates this close kinship between the men of the English Danelaw and the Scandinavian homeland. Magnus was king of Norway and is said to have deposited a great treasure with a citizen of Lincoln before going on an expedition to Ireland. The Lincoln citizen had supplied the king with arms and plate, ornaments and all the miscellaneous equipment a king required. When the king died his agent returned to Lincoln and grew rich trading with the treasure. Henry I demanded that Magnus' treasure should be surrendered to himself and, when the Lincoln man denied its existence, convicted him of lying and extorted from him more than £20,000. Despite this act of extortion 347 Henry I did much for the prosperity of the city by reopening the Fossdyke, a waterway made by the Romans, connecting Brayford Pool at Lincoln with the Trent at Torksey. This 348 gave Lincoln double access to the sea, from the Wash by way of the Witham and to the Humber by way of the Trent and Fossdyke.

But in 1204 when the taxable capacity of English ports can for the first time be compared Lincoln and York were losing ground. The Witham was silting up so that sea-going ships were content to tie up at Boston. In 1204 the merchants of Boston paid £780 against £556 from the merchants of Lincoln. Boston paid more than any other English port, apart from London. York, too, was yielding place to Hull, a port first mentioned in 1193. In 1204 the merchants of Hull paid £344 against £175 paid by the merchants of York. The same process was going on in East Anglia, where the list shows that while Ipswich and Norwich paid approximately £7 apiece the bishop of Norwich's new foundation of Lynn, later called King's Lynn, paid £651. Yarmouth was charged with £54. When Norwegian piracy was 349 quelled and a monarchy capable of protecting the coasts ruled all England, merchants could safely lay up their goods in places with immediate access to the sea. The much-prized Norway hawks came in from the far north by all these ports. In John's reign Nicholas the Dane offered the king one or two hawks a year that he might trade freely 350 through all England. Henry II established his falconer on estates both in south Lincolnshire and in Norfolk so that he should have ready access to the fairs of Boston, Lynn, and 351 Yarmouth. Goods drifted into England along the northern route, from Russia by way of the Baltic, even from the Far East. Lincolnshire was well abreast of the news and stories of the world. In 1207 and again in 1219 a man called Prestre Johan (Presterjohn), can be seen acting as the legal agent of the Lincolnshire prior of Thornholm. His parents evidently named him after the great priest king of the legend current 352 in Europe in the mid twelfth century.

Yorkshire and Lincolnshire were great wool-growing shires. Lincolnshire wool in particular was very fine, so that foreign traders were drawn to the northern markets by whatever route they came to England. The great emporia in the towns of the lower Rhine, in particular Cologne, were the immediate jumping-off ground for the merchants who had brought goods from the east by the southerly route, along the Danube or through Italy and down the Rhine. These traders would most easily approach the Sandwich, Rye, and Dover group of ports if they did not come direct to London. The trade from the Bay of Biscay brought wine to all the southern ports; even Fowey in Cornwall was charged with £48 in 1204, but Southampton with a tax of £712 was the principal harbour on the south coast. In this generation Manasser of Winchelsea drove a flourishing trade in wine with ramifications in various parts of England from the town by which he was known. The Winchelsea tax in 1204 was nearly double that of Dover; £62 against Dover's £32. No west-coast port appears in the 1204 list, for there was little regular Irish trade. The £836 paid by London puts it above all other towns, but hardly illustrates 353 its actual supremacy. There were other ways of taxing London merchants.

To trace the ups and downs of economic life during this period is impossible, but certain facts and tendencies seem to appear from the thinning mists of the past. The lively trade of Saxon times was interrupted by the disorders of the Conquest, and the political situation which followed did not make for its immediate revival. But the energy of the Norman kings and the long peace of Henry I's reign encouraged a prosperity which even the distress of Stephen's reign could not entirely destroy. The most prosperous time for the ancient centres, the county towns which had their origin in the Saxon past, was probably the reign of Henry II, before the vast expansion in the number of chartered boroughs of the late twelfth and thirteenth centuries. In trade as in every other department of national life Henry II's reign meant stimulus, activity, an incitement to effort. New markets, arising everywhere, vied with the ancient centres for local economic leadership. Charters of privilege, granted in great numbers, often conflicted with one another. The right to exact toll was opposed by the right of exemption from toll and many fierce quarrels between town and town brought actions in the king's courts which could be settled only by compromise. At the end of this period the conception of free trade over all the land was still far from the men of English boroughs, and there is nothing they would have wished for less.

CHAPTER V

CHURCH AND PEOPLE

THE hard-headed practicality of the medieval people is nowhere more clearly shown than in their attitude to God and religion. They lived in a small world and knew nothing of its place in the universe. The conception of a globe revolving in space in a determinable relationship to other bodies had not dawned upon even the most advanced thinkers. Beyond the limits of their known world lay an unknown fringe of incalculable depth, sea or land, equally remote and full of perils. Their lives within the little medieval world were hard and brief and they accepted unquestioningly a religion that offered to the poor and hungry an eternity of satisfaction. Since so much of the world about them was unknown the invisibility of the next world did not trouble them. It was as real to them as remote lands tòday are real to the untravelled. They were equally assured of its existence. For this reason there was no questioning of the articles of the Christian belief, nor was their acceptance the result of a deliberate and considered act of faith. Heaven, purgatory, or hell ranked equally with the world around them as the unavoidable experience of man.

This complete acceptance of the inevitability of the after life, together with the literal interpretation of Christ's promise of pardon to the repentant sinner, no matter how many times he had fallen back again into sin, accounts for much in the medieval attitude to the Church and religion that is alien to modern thought. Even death-bed repentance could snatch a soul from immediate peril of hell and in purgatory souls not yet fit for perpetual bliss could spend a time of waiting which earnest supplication offered for them on earth might shorten or end. From one point of view the whole vast organization of the medieval Christian church can be regarded as the result of man's fear of eternal damnation and his desire for eternal bliss. It was for this that rich men gave land to the religious, who paid for it by prayer on behalf of their patrons. There was a direct simplicity about the relationship of God and man, an element of bargain, a hint of the market place. But in England at least there was neither doubt nor questioning of the beliefs and practices of the Catholic church.

The Christian faith had been brought to England by monastic missionaries sent by the Pope, and throughout the Anglo-Saxon period the Pope had no firmer supporters than English churchmen. From England missionaries went to preach Christianity to heathen Germany and Scandinavia and in England the lay power accepted full responsibility for the support of the Church. Saxon kings had been accustomed to send to Rome a contribution known as Peter's Pence, and it was still being collected and sent through this period. The Anglo-Saxon state insisted that the Church's demands should be met by laymen; that plough-alms, soul-scot, and church-scot should be paid. 'Plough-alms' was the penny paid within a fortnight of Easter for each working plough team in the parish; 'soul-scot' was the chattel devoted to the church for the benefit of the dead man's soul; 'church-scot' was the portion of grain, varying in different parts of the country, which was paid to churches founded in early missionary days. From the tenth century the payment of tithe by the laity was enforced by the law of the land, but it was only slowly that tithe became part of the endowment of the parish priest. In early days the poor and pilgrims had, if anything, a greater claim to a share in the tithe which it was a Christian duty to devote to religious purposes.

Most of the churches founded in the early missionary days were built by kings or bishops and they often housed a community of clerks whose duty it was to convert and minister to the inhabitants of the large area dependent on the church. 354 The group of clergy who served an early church lived at first as a community and their church was often described as a minster. The Latin word was *monasterium*, the word which described a community of monks, but these clergy were not monks. These ancient minsters were missionary churches which passed naturally into parish churches. Some of them retained their collegiate character into the twelfth century and later, but they were anomalies in an age which expected a parish church to be served by a single priest, who might or might not have an assistant priest to help him. The churches of the late Anglo-Saxon period could be classified under three headings, the ancient minster, the ordinary church with a graveyard, and the field-church. The ordinary church with a graveyard was a parish church, usually built within the boundaries of the territory originally served by an ancient minster. Very often the priest of such a church was bound to pay a pension to the rector of the ancient minster. The field-church had no graveyard. It was put up to serve new settlements which were too far from the parish church to attend its services. It was, in fact, a chapel rather than a church and the parish church retained the burial fees of its parishioners.

It is impossible to bring the history of the foundation of English parish churches under a single simple formula. Political circumstances vitally affected the development of smaller parishes within the lands of the ancient minsters. In the English south, where, despite periodical devastations of raiding armies, there was no break in the continuity of political life, the establishment of churches with graveyards and of field-churches or chapels proceeded throughout the Old English period. But in the uncertain conditions of the far north not even the Norman Conquest did much to hasten the subdivision of the ancient parochial areas. In the Dane-law the settlement of a heathen race destroyed the organization of the Christian church so that it was not until after the Norman Conquest that conditions were favourable to a general movement for the building of parish churches. One generalization can, however, be made; for there cannot be any question that the overwhelming majority of English parish churches were built by laymen and that the layman 355 who built a church regarded it as his own property. Every man of position desired to have his own church and to appoint his own parson. Hence where a village had more than one lord it more often than not had more than one church. If it had but one church, that church was often owned by more than one lord, who shared the right of presenting the parson. The church of Brocklesby in Lincolnshire is a good example of one of these divided churches, for, as a late medieval document states, 'it was divided before the union into six parts corresponding to the estates of the lords and the patrons'. 356

Neither the ecclesiastical nor the lay power interfered to control the building of churches. The only check on church building came from the fact that every new foundation infringed existing rights. If a chapel was built to serve a remote hamlet the tithes, fees, and offerings of the parish church would be diminished. Throughout at least the early middle ages there was litigation, generally ended by formal agreement, because the foundation of a new church or chapel threatened to take something from the income of an older church. The men of Hutthorpe in Northamptonshire desired to build a chapel for themselves in Henry II's reign. Since Hutthorpe belonged to the parish of Theddingworth in Leicestershire the men of Hutthorpe gave to Theddingworth church for the support of their chapel one acre in each of the two village fields from every yardland in the village. But the land was given to Theddingworth church. It was for the rector of Theddingworth to pay what he liked to the incumbent of Hutthorpe. The haphazard way in which the 357 land was provided with churches meant that some parts had too many churches and other parts had too few. There are 39 churches marked on Sir Francis Hill's map of Lincoln in about the year 1100, and it is true to say that in every medieval county town there were far more churches than can ever have been necessary for worship.

All through this period every man was conscious that the peace of the land was uncertain and might be broken in a moment. As he went about his work he carried his horn slung on his shoulder so that he could at once send out a warning to his fellow-villagers or call them to join in chasing a criminal. In a society thus poised precariously on the edge of war the sanctuary of the parish church and churchyard gave a steadying sense of security. The churchyard was a refuge to which in bad times men took their few poor household goods and drove their stock. In remote parts even today an old churchyard with its curving boundary hedge or wall and funereal ancient yews still carries the marks of the days when it could be fortified with a stockade. The first surviving roll of pleas of the Crown for Yorkshire after the war between king John and his barons contains a number of cases which well illustrate the use of the churchyard as a sanctuary in times of war. Brian de L'Isle's corn laid up in the churchyard of Laughton en le Morthen was carried off by the constable of Tickhill castle and Brian's men were chased away. Another man falsely accused a neighbour of robbing him of two marks of silver and a silver seal in the graveyard of Weaverthorpe. From Thirsk churchyard armed serjeants who came from the Moor carried off a man's horses. That there were not many recorded genuine infringements of the law of sanctuary was probably due to its stern enforcement. In answering an accusation of maiming the accused replied that his accuser had lost his hand in the war by judgement of the marshal of the army for 358 stealing a cow in a churchyard.

From the last years of Stephen's reign there survive two documents which show two of the most efficient and disinterested bishops of that age intervening to secure the making of graveyards to serve as sanctuaries for the people. Gilbert Foliot, bishop of Hereford from 1148 to 1163, informed all sons of holy mother Church that at the request of Robert of Hampton and with the assent of the monks of Leominster he has consecrated the graveyard at Hampton as a place of refuge for Robert and his men. In return for the monks' consent, Robert has given them his own demesne tithe and the tithe of the men of his fee and 30 acres of land. He has also promised that he and his heirs will pay without any failure the half a mark he owes yearly to the church of Leominster. This complicated arrangement by which the mother church of Leominster, the old minster, allowed its daughter church of Hampton to have a grave-yard was made in the presence of the bishop, his archdeacon of Shrewsbury, his chaplain, his nephew, and many others. 359 Robert de Chesney, bishop of Lincoln from 1148 to 1166, made a very similar arrangement for the benefit of the men of Essendine in Rutland. In this case the memorandum states that 'the men of Essendine were placed in grave danger not having whither they can safely flee if the attacks of robbers shall fall upon them'. Essendine already had a chapel, which Anglo-Saxon law would have called a 'field-church', but it was a dependency of the church of Ryhall. A third of the church of Ryhall with the chapel of Essendine had previously been given to the monks of Northampton. According to the memorandum it was in return for the confirmation of these gifts that the monks were brought to agree that a graveyard should be made at Essendine 'not that the chapel should be made a mother-church,' they are careful to stipulate, 'since it is a member of the church of Ryhall, but so that, if by chance the need suddenly rushes on them they can have a safe refuge close at hand, whither betaking themselves, they may save both themselves and their goods from attack, the chapel remaining, as before, a chapel'. The agreement was made before the bishop, the archdeacon of Oxford, a number of clerks, and others. Each 360 of these documents has the appearance of a record made by the bishop's authority in a local synod.

Throughout the period covered by this book and for long afterwards no use was made of the parish as such for the purpose of lay administration. It was to the group of men among whom an accused man lived that the courts of justice looked for evidence as to his repute. Village and parish might coincide, as they often did in the south of England, but records never call on the parish or the parishioners as such to testify to any point at issue. It is all the more remark-able that innumerable parish boundaries have been pre-served unchanged throughout the centuries. Even today it is often possible, by following the line of a parish boundary, to trace the outline of an Anglo-Saxon estate as it is recorded in a tenth-century charter. Ancient thorns and old apple trees may no longer be growing on their old sites, but roads still follow their ancient course, although they may have been reduced to a green path between two hedgerows or a line of tree-stubs. There is no evidence that the parish beat the bounds on Easter Monday in this period, but some such ceremony must have been necessary in days when no maps could be made to help oral testimony to preserve the ancient boundaries. To the historically minded, a country walk can be given a purpose if it is directed along a parish boundary; for it is unlikely that the pedestrian will not find something which shows the intelligent care with which medieval Englishmen kept their parish bounds. Three ancient yew trees known as the Three Shepherds on Offa's Dyke still mark the point where the boundaries of three border parishes meet high on the Herefordshire hills. They can be seen from miles around. The Dyke itself was often used as a parish boundary. In less spectacular country great sarsen stones frequently remain to mark the ancient lines.

In Anglo-Saxon days the devotion of English kings and the ability of English churchmen had meant that the Church had in some sense dominated the state. Churchmen were the leaders in the king's council and there was no feeling that the affairs of the Church were exclusively for churchmen to consider. As churchmen and laymen sat together in the king's council, so in the courts of shire and hundred the bishop, the earl, and the sheriff sat together, and together dealt with the cases that came before them, whether they concerned laymen or clerks. A new era began with the Conquest in this as in other matters. William I was a devout son of the Church, but he was also an autocrat. The traditional ties between English churchmen and the Pope, the free coming and going between Rome and England by letter and by personal intercourse, seemed to him to threaten the royal control over the church of his conquest. In Lanfranc, an Italian scholar who had migrated in youth to Normandy, William found an archbishop who was both prepared to support the king in controlling relations between the English Church and the Pope, and also able to revise the organization of the English Church and bring it into line with the best continental practice. By royal decree suits which concerned the cure of souls were transferred to the bishop's exclusive hearing in accordance with the law of the Church, and the bishop ceased to sit in the local courts of justice. The attempt of William I to exclude the Pope from direct uncensored intercourse with the English Church inevitably failed in the days of William's successors, but William I took the first step to the establishment in England of the hierarchy of ecclesiastical courts. Despite the continental influences which played upon the English Church, its organization preserved throughout the middle ages innumerable features which had arisen in the period before the Norman Conquest.

In particular, the Anglo-Saxon tradition that the right of presenting the parson belonged to the man who had put up the church and endowed it with its glebe preserved for the lay courts the jurisdiction over cases concerning the advowsons of churches. Even the murder of archbishop Becket, which enabled the Pope to break down the restrictions of the Conqueror, failed to force Henry II to retreat from the position he had taken up in the Constitutions of Clarendon in 1164 – 'If controversy shall arise between laymen, laymen and clerks, or clerks concerning the advowson and presentation of churches, the matter shall be discussed and terminated in the king's court.' Patronage remained property 361 which a layman could hold, buy and sell, or give away. The quality and status of the parish priest depended on the goodwill of the patron and public opinion of the age. Between the years 1066 and 1307 many changes took place which vitally affected the men who served the country churches. Successive archbishops, following the trend of ecclesiastical opinion, tried to raise their standard of life and to improve their education. It is always much easier to find evidence about the abuses of patronage than about the virtues of medieval parish priests.

For this reason the twelfth-century life of Wulfric of Haselbury by John abbot of Ford is of peculiar value, for it takes the modern reader into the life of a village church in 362 the first half of the twelfth century. John of Ford wrote the *Life* between 1180 and 1186. He had known men who had known the saint well. He checked his evidence and gave the source of all his tales. Wulfric was an Englishman of modest birth who about 1125 settled as an anchorite beside the church of Haselbury. His holiness, his miracles, and his accurate prophecies made him famous. He was visited by king Henry I and by king Stephen and his queen. St Bernard is said to have asked for his prayers. When Wulfric first sat at Haselbury the priest who served the church was a certain Brictric, who was married to a woman called Godida, and had a son, Osbern, who succeeded his father as parish priest. The new rules against clerical marriage laid down by post-Conquest councils of the Church had been no more successful than the preaching of Anglo-Saxon reformers in persuading the English clergy to adopt celibacy. Neither the saint nor his biographer of the late twelfth century saw anything amiss in the household of Brictric. John of Ford describes how Brictric spent day and night in psalms and prayer in church so far as his ministry allowed him. He rode home to his dinner from the church and back again as soon 363 as he had finished it. From the lips of William, a lay brother of Ford, who, as guest master, frequently had occasion to pass by Haselbury and had become a close friend of Wulfric, John heard a good story about Brictric which he enjoyed telling.

On one occasion when William visited the saint and asked him, as usual, how he was, the saint replied that he was well enough except that 'our priest Brictric' had spent the day trying to quarrel with him. William asked why so modest a man as Brictric should be driven to anger, especially with Wulfric. He replied that a dumb man had been brought to him and when he prayed and laid hands on him the dumb man began 'to speak accurately and readily, not only in English, but also in French. When Brictric saw this, he blamed me bitterly saying, "Lo, I have served you so many years, but today I have proved that it is in vain, for to a stranger for whom it would have been quite sufficient for you to have loosed his tongue, you have devoutly ministered the use of two languages, and to me, who when I come before the bishop and archdeacon am compelled to be silent like a dumb man, you have not given the use of French".' 364

An anchorite was bound to have a servant who could run errands for him and keep him in touch with the world. Wulfric's boy was constantly kept on the run because the master through his miraculous power saw something happening in the neighbourhood which needed his attention. Godida, Brictric's wife, was making an alb for the church from some linen given to Wulfric. She made a false stitch and the saint sent off his boy to tell her to work more carefully. Osbern son of Brictric began life as Wulfric's 365 attendant and his acolyte when he served at the altar. When he had succeeded his father as parish priest Osbern usually slept in the church. It seems as though Osbern was not married. He was alive fifteen years after the saint had died, but was dead before 1174. Another priest lived close 366 at hand named Segar, evidently also English by birth. The saint confessed to Segar a divine revelation and John of Ford takes the opportunity to record that Segar had four sons who had all entered religion at Ford, three of them monks and the fourth a lay brother. The priests of Haselbury, 367 although they were married, seem to have lived very near to God. They were fortunate in that they had at hand an example of holiness in Wulfric and that the saint was a man of learning. He trained a boy who lived at Haselbury to write so that he became first a scribe at Ford abbey, and later a monk there. He, too, had married and his son, likewise, became a monk at Ford. 368

The *Life of St Wulfric*, too, provides a few revealing sidelights on one of those patrons who so often appear in the retrospect of history as greedy consumers of the poor priest's tithe. William fitz Walter was lord of Wulfric's birthplace, Compton Martin, and when he heard of Wulfric's holiness as a young priest he invited him 'to a priest's work in his native place'. There Wulfric lived in his household and 369 'obediently ate at his table'. When Wulfric felt an overpowering desire for the austere life of an anchorite his lord helped him to find the cell at Haselbury, of which he was 370 also the lord. He also provided Wulfric with a coat of mail which he assumed to mortify his flesh. The coat was too long to kneel in and Wulfric sent to tell William fitz Walter, who hastened to the cell to suggest sending the coat to London to be trimmed down. Wulfric said that would take too long. 'Exeter is nearer,' said the lord, but that also seemed to Wulfric too far away. Then Wulfric told William to take the shears and cut the coat while he himself prayed, and so the coat was cut down to the right length. The work was only hindered for a time when Wulfric stopped praying to see 371 how it was getting on and as a result the shears stopped too. William fitz Walter and his family move in and out of the story of Wulfric's life at Haselbury. One of William's sons, Walter, was once left in London by his father as security for a debt and the boy wrote to Wulfric to ask for his prayers. Later, this same boy became a monk at Glastonbury abbey, 372 of which his father held five knights' fees. The lord's daughter, Beatrice, came to the cell for holy water when her 373 mother was ill.

Rumours of Wulfric's powers of prophecy, his capacity to know what was happening far off, and his readiness to speak his mind gave him more than a local reputation. Henry I visited him at the queen's request. One of the courtiers, a certain Drogo de Munci, suggested that the king should search the anchorite's cell for money. Drogo was at once struck with paralysis. The queen suggested that Henry I should ask the saint to cure the unfortunate man and St 374 Wulfric at once obliged him. Henry I's death was miraculously known to Wulfric the day after it had happened and he advised his lord to consider what he ought to do. Although the saint had foretold in Henry I's reign that

Stephen would become king, William fitz Walter found it difficult to make up his mind whether to support the side of Stephen or that of his rival, Maud, daughter of Henry I. Before William had made up his mind Stephen's queen visited Corfe castle and all the local ladies went to see her. Since William had not yet given his allegiance to Stephen the queen ignored William's wife, showing that she was as haughty as her husband's rival. Before she left those parts the queen visited the anchorite, only to be upbraided for 'disdaining to greet a faithful and holy woman and refusing her the kiss of peace. Behold,' he prophesied, 'the days will come when you will be glad to kiss poor and ignoble persons nor will you repel any mouth which you can kiss with yours.' 375

It is worth while to dwell on the simple lives of Wulfric's circle, for information about the life of the parish priest in the Norman age is very hard to find. Indeed there is little concrete information for the whole century. The priest was a free man. Both pope and king agreed that the sons of villeins should not be admitted to holy orders. But it does not seem to have been difficult to obtain admission to minor orders. In the days before bishop's registers were kept it must have been difficult to prove that a man who shaved his head and claimed to be in orders was an impostor. Throughout this period a distinction must be made between the beneficed priest and the unbeneficed clerk who can be hired as an assistant priest for a small stipend. The quarrel between Henry II and Becket about the punishment of criminous clerks has focused attention unfairly on the crimes of the clergy. It is worth noting that the men who in the earliest assize rolls seek the benefit of clergy and are handed over to the church for trial and punishment are not parish priests. Sometimes they are deacons, often they are simply called clerks or acolytes. It is true that the parish priest of Desborough in Northamptonshire in 1202 was charged with going with others to the lodging of their accusers and breaking the windows and throwing out their chattels, but when the judge sent knights to see if an

offence had been committed they came back and said that
376 they found no fault there. The parish priests who appear in
the earliest assize rolls are actively engaged in farming their
glebe, like Robert of Blyborough in Lincolnshire, who in
1202 was convicted of dispossessing one of his parishioners
of a headland, and of digging a ditch which hindered his
377 mill from working. The undistinguished record of the
anonymous parson of Stain in Lincolnshire is worth remembering, for in 1202 the jurors said that he was so old that no
378 one could say who presented him.

By the time that episcopal registers were kept and other
records survive which tell more of the state of the country
churches, conditions had changed radically from the days
of Henry I and Stephen. The new activity of the archbishop, spurred by the zeal of the Pope, was bound to have
its effect on the village church. Remote as Haselbury was,
Brictric its priest had clearly experienced the embarrass-
ment of appearing before the bishop and the archdeacon.
Already in Saxon days the bishop seems to have had his
archdeacon to help him supervise his diocese, but after the
379 Conquest the archdeacon had much more work to do. The
new church courts increased his responsibilities. The stricter
control of the bishops over their dioceses was maintained
largely through the labours of their archdeacons who visited
the parishes to see that the churches were properly equipped
with books and vestments and that the property of the
church was well looked after. In Henry II's reign the
organization of the Church was becoming even more
elaborate, for the office of rural dean had appeared before
the middle of the century. For rural deaneries the Church
seems generally to have adopted the same boundaries as
the hundreds or wapentakes, and in such cases the court of
the rural dean was the ecclesiastical parallel of the hundred
court of secular jurisdiction.

The Conquest itself was not immediately followed by any
particular signs of increasing religious zeal. Norman bishops
and secular lords began the building up and down the
country of many cathedral and parish churches, but rather

to expiate the sin of an aggressive war and to use some of the new wealth that war had given them than to express a genuine love of God. But in the uneasy times of Stephen's reign a real religious revival took place. It was given a firm background by the more highly organized Church of the new régime. This new zeal expressed itself largely in the establishment of monastic foundations which were endowed with land, tithes, and churches. It is one of the signs of the new spirit that so many men, feeling that the choice of a priest was in some sense a religious office, gave churches to a religious house. Sometimes, like William II when in 1095 he gave a number of East Anglian churches to Battle abbey, the donor stipulated that the sitting parson should be undisturbed in his possession for life. These particular parsons were to pay a pension to the abbey and entertain the abbot for two nights when he visited them.

In the early years of this period a religious house which had received the gift of a church was free to dispose of its income, making what provision seemed suitable to the head of the house and was acceptable to the parson. The income of a church in this period consisted of the greater tithe, that is, the tithe of crops and stock; the lesser tithe, that is, the tithe of hens and such-like things; the fees coming from baptisms, marriages, and burials; the offerings to the altar, among which must be counted mortuaries, the medieval successor of the soul-scot of earlier days. There seems no reason to believe that at any period in the twelfth century there was any strong ecclesiastical feeling that all these should by right go to the parson of the church himself. But there was a strong body of opinion that the parson who served the church should be adequately provided with a living. Far back in the twelfth century bishops were making it a part of their duty to see that the owner of a church made proper provision for the priest.

In his survey of the present state of the Church made by Innocent III in the Lateran Council of 1215 to an assembly of princes, magnates, and prelates from the whole Christian world, the Pope pointed out that it was often impossible to find an educated man to serve a church where the owner allowed him but a meagre subsistence, while the revenues of the church were kept in his own hand. He declared that in future the parish priest must be given a reasonable living 384 and security of tenure. It was for the diocesan bishops to put this decree into operation by instituting vicarages, which should be the freehold of the priest who served the church. Hugh of Wells, bishop of Lincoln from 1209 to 1235, instituted more than 300 vicarages in his great diocese and his record of his institutions shows with what scrupulous care the work was carried through. Some of the vicarages which Hugh instituted were assessed as low as 3 marks, but many of them stood at between 5 and 6 marks and some still higher. These values were lower than the actual worth of the vicarage to its holder, for a precise estimate of an income from tithes and offerings can hardly be given. The bishop seems to have been guided by the working rule that the value of the vicarage should be roughly a third of the full value of the church. The vicarages were not all to one pattern, for occasionally, as in regard to the churches belonging to Oseney abbey, the vicar was put in a very intimate relation with his patron. The vicars of St Mary Magdalene at Oxford, of Cowley, Foresthill, Kidlington, Hampton Gay, Weston, Watlington, Hook Norton, Chastleton, and Waterperry each had 2 marks a year for clothes, all mortuaries up to 6 pence and half those worth more, mass penny and offerings when a vicar celebrated mass, a horse, if necessary for visiting the sick and attending councils, a key to the abbey, security of tenure, and a sufficiency of food sent from the monastery if the vicar could not feed at the canons' table. Each vicar was also to be provided with a clerk for his 385 church and a boy to wait upon him. Most of the vicars whose churches were near the abbey which owned them were put in what must have been a tedious subordination and dependence on their patron. Although they had their own house they must eat with the monks, as at Breedon in 386 Leicestershire. Where no house for the vicar was already in existence it was expressly stated that one should be provided.

Where the patron of the church was a layman, the vicar often received the whole income of the church subject to a pension to a man the patron had appointed as parson, or rector.

Bishop Hugh was the first bishop of Lincoln and probably the first bishop in England to keep a register of his acts. His rolls show how complicated the administration of the diocese had become. The bishop's official, the archdeacons, and the rural deans all appear in the elaborate routine of assisting their lord to govern his diocese in accordance with the rules laid down by councils of the Church. There is some evidence that the bishop tried to enforce the rule about clerical celibacy. The parson of Little Dalby, presented by the prioress and convent of Langley, was admitted to the cure of his church provided he first put away his concubine whom he confessed publicly he had kept, and on condition that he lost his church if he co-habited with her again. 387 Alan vicar of Ashwell, Herts, who had been presented by a lay patron, was obliged to execute a bond undertaking to pay 30 marks if he again co-habited with his former mistress, Annora. The archdeacon had the bond. There are 388 other cases of stern action against incontinency, but there are far too few to suggest that the bishop went out of his way to eradicate clerical marriage. There is much more evidence about the bishop's attempts to secure a more learned clergy. William Malebisse presented his son Robert to the church of Mavis Enderby, Lincolnshire. Robert was to have charge of the church and to be instituted by the bishop if he proved, on examination and after attending the schools for reading and singing, to be sufficiently learned. If not the patron was to be informed that he was unsuitable and another clerk was 389 to be presented. Many of the men presented to the bishop for institution were ordered to attend the schools. Geoffrey of Cropredy, presented to half the church of Heyford, was instructed to spend three years at the schools studying the 390 holy scriptures and the canons. The necessity for the priest to learn singing and music is often stressed. Richard of Farlesthorpe, the clerk, was refused institution to the church

391 of Bilsby, Lincolnshire, because he was almost illiterate. Hugh of Wells took care to see that when the incumbent was absent at the schools his church was not neglected. When Stephen de Holewell was admitted to the church of Caldecote, Huntingdonshire, and enjoined to study in the schools and learn singing, he was also instructed to appoint a suitable chaplain and threatened with deprivation if he 392 did not. The duty of serving the church personally was often mentioned at the time of institution. Many of the men who were nominated by patrons to be parsons or vicars were styled clerks, but had not yet been admitted to the diaconate. Ralf of Owmby, the clerk, was instituted to the church of Dunsthorpe, Lincolnshire, on condition that he was ordained deacon at the next ordination and then proceeded to full orders, took up residence, and personally served the 393 office of priest. The contemporaries of Hugh of Wells in other English bishoprics were doing the same sort of work, but there is less evidence about it. Their successors throughout the century continued the struggle to provide the parishes of England with priests, ordained, sufficiently learned, and leading a celibate life. Cardinal Otto, sent by the Pope to visit the English church in 1237, and Cardinal Ottobon, sent in 1268, put out constitutions which regulated the rights of patrons and vindicated the rights of the parochial vicars. They set standards from which human frailty often fell short.

It was inevitable that monks and diocesan bishops should take divergent views of the problem of apportioning the parochial income. In the thirteenth century it was no longer possible for a lay patron by his own mere motion to give his church to a religious house, and for the religious house to appropriate the revenue to its own uses and appoint a clerk to serve the church without secure provision for his maintenance. All such transactions now came under the purview of the bishop, who was slow to allow further appropriations by monasteries. The chronicler Matthew Paris, himself a monk at St Albans, complained about the damage and loss inflicted on the religious by bishop Robert Grosseteste of

Lincoln, who pursued Hugh's policy of instituting vicarages in appropriated churches. Bishop Robert found himself in 394 conflict with the Pope also over the question of parish churches. Since Innocent III had forced king John into the 395 position of a papal feudatory, popes had been able freely to exercise their undoubted right to provide incumbents to English benefices, overriding even the rights of the patrons. The quarrel over papal provisions grew more bitter after this period ended, but already in the early thirteenth century there were complaints that English money was going abroad to support papal nominees who might never visit the churches to which they had been appointed. Nevertheless, provided a vicarage had been established in the parish church and a worthy vicar instituted to serve there, it was not unreasonable that a certain amount of money should go from local churches to maintain the supreme court of ecclesiastical justice to which English churchmen, like those of every land in Europe, were only too ready to appeal.

The king, too, expected that the riches of the Church should be available for the reward of his clerks. Kings would have been less generous to the Church had they not expected to appoint deserving royal servants to benefices. Great laymen who owned many churches expected to reward their clerks or provide for their younger sons in the same way. The Pope was very willing to sell dispensations to individual clerks allowing them to hold benefices in plurality, sometimes up to a stated annual value. The system of vicarages and the fact that, despite papal rulings, many men were ordained to the priesthood without any adequate title so that they could be hired for a few marks a year to serve a church made the practice possible and, perhaps, less harmful than at first sight it seems.

When all the difficulties of transport are taken into account it is clear that the parish priest was kept in reasonably close touch with the men who ruled the church in England. The bishop held synods of his diocese attended in the twelfth century by the leading laymen of the shires as well as the clergy. In the thirteenth century their composition was more narrowly ecclesiastical. Confirmations then as now took the bishop about the country, and the archdeacon was bound to make his regular visitations of the parishes. From the latter part of the twelfth century the rural dean was holding chapters of his deanery and moving about in it. To a poor priest living in the meagre farmhouse of the period, a hall and a chamber, with livestock in adjoining buildings, the prospect of an episcopal visit must have been intimidating. But the bishop would probably have been just as alarmed as the priest at the prospect of lodging in a rural vicarage. Most parishes came to terms with the bishop or archdeacon and paid a small annual sum, known as 'procuration', to exempt them from this burden of hospitality. The Pope, concerned that the higher clergy should not exploit the parish priests, issued rules for the guidance of visiting officials. An archbishop must not be attended by more than 40 or 50 men, a bishop by more than 20 or 30, an archdeacon by more than 5 or 7, while a rural dean must be content with 2 horses only. Nor must these visitors take with them their hounds and hawks. Archbishop Hubert Walter repeated these rules in his council at 396 London in 1200.

From early times bishops had compelled not only the clergy but also the laity to keep in touch with the mother church of the diocese. At Whitsuntide from long custom processions of clergy and laymen had come with offerings to the cathedral, taking back the consecrated oil needed in each parish during the following year. In the later middle ages the offerings were frequently called smoke-farthings, a name which indicates that originally the amount was governed by the number of houses in the parish. It was very early assessed as a small annual sum to be paid by each 397 parish. The early twelfth-century charters which mention this custom show that the bishop expected to receive not only the regular smoke-farthings, but also offerings from the faithful, which might take the form of gold, silver, or vestments, or hangings for the church. About 1138 bishop

Alexander of Lincoln granted that Oxfordshire folk should go to Eynsham abbey instead of Lincoln, because Lincoln was so far away. Nevertheless, he adds, penitents and others who so desire ought to visit their mother church. There are 398 signs that Alexander's successors regretted his generosity to Eynsham. Bishop Robert in 1154 wrote to his dean and chapter informing them that he had caused the processions from the rural deaneries of Fritwell, Hanwell, and Norton to go to Banbury for this purpose. The reason for this was 399 the bishop's desire that his fair at Banbury should have the profits from these religious holiday-makers. Ten years later both bishop Robert and the dean of Lincoln confirmed the right of Eynsham to the processions, but reserved to the church of Lincoln two-thirds of the special offerings. 400

Between 1109 and 1114 archbishop Thomas II of York granted that the men of Nottinghamshire who had previously gone to York for their processions should go thenceforward to his cathedral minster of Southwell. He was then engaged in building the great nave of Southwell. The offerings of Nottinghamshire men were needed for the work. Southwell never seems to have obtained a Whitsun fair to increase the profits of these processions. In making his grant to Southwell minster archbishop Thomas promised that the Nottinghamshire men who went to Southwell should have the same pardon which they had previously enjoyed at York. These Whitsun processions therefore take their place 401 as modest pilgrimages which brought their appropriate reward. From early Christian days pilgrims had ranked with the poor as worthy objects of Christian charity and from the time of the conversion the roads to Rome had been continually worn by English pilgrims' feet. All great churches tried to acquire relics of some famous saint and to encourage people to honour the saint by visiting the church on the day sacred to his memory. Reading abbey, founded by Henry I, was fortunate in obtaining among other relics a fragment of the true cross and of the hand of St James the apostle. This last relic was brought back from Germany by the Empress Maud and laid up by her in her father's

foundation. Archbishop Theobald of Canterbury promised
to all who visited Reading to honour the wood of the cross
on the day of its finding or exaltation the remission of
402 twenty days enjoined penance. To those who visited Reading with due devotion on the day of the apostle whose hand
lay there he promised the remission of forty days enjoined
403 penance.

Very many other bishops of the twelfth century rewarded
the hospitality of Reading abbey by issuing indulgences
similar to those which Theobald had granted. Most of them
gave a remission of twenty days of enjoined penance,
404 although Hilary bishop of Chichester granted only fifteen.
Archbishop Thomas Becket who consecrated the abbey
405 church was among them. In the last years of the twelfth
century successive popes tried by promising indulgences to
spur more men to undertake a crusade for the salvation of
the Holy Land. Innocent III in 1201 promised remission
to those who did not go in person but merely provided
406 money to support others in the field. Many men yearned to
undertake the supreme pilgrimage of the crusade and took
the cross but failed to get a passage to the east for lack of
money. All through this period there was a large floating
population, some drifting from shrine to shrine seeking the
cure for the incurable disease, others satisfying their uncon-
trollable urge for change of scene by incessant pilgrimage.
Long before the twelfth century was ended the tomb of
archbishop Thomas himself at Canterbury was drawing a
host of pilgrims, and its fame has survived all changes of faith
and the world. In the middle ages this habit of pilgrimage,
whether it was made to the mother church of the diocese,
to the hand of St James at Reading, to the tomb of St James
at Compostella, to the tomb of St Thomas at Canterbury, to
Rome or to Jerusalem itself, brought the dwellers in
remote country parishes into touch with the great world
outside.

In the Norman age the cathedral churches attained a new
importance, for the new spirit of discipline affected the
church no less than the state. Up to the generation before

the Conquest it is true to say that traditions of the missionary days still hung about the organization of the English church. It was only in the reign of the Confessor that men were beginning to feel that the bishop's seat should be in the largest centre of population in his diocese. The first sign of this feeling was a move to Exeter by the bishop of Crediton. Archbishop Lanfranc encouraged similar migrations from what bishop Stubbs called 'places of retreat' to centres of activity. His council at London in 1075 provided that the bishops of Lichfield, Selsey, and Sherborne should move their seats to Chester, Chichester, and Salisbury. Even earlier the first Norman bishop of Dorchester had begun the removal of his seat to Lincoln. The establishment of the cathedral church of East Anglia at Norwich was the result of a double move from North Elmham by way of the once populous town of Thetford. The transference of the bishop's seat involved the building of a new cathedral or the enlarging and rebuilding of an already existing church. It also enabled the bishop to organize a new chapter for his new cathedral.

At Canterbury and Rochester, Winchester and Worcester, where no suggestion of removal to another site could possibly be made, the chapter which served the cathedral church and acted as the council of the prelate was monastic. At Durham, where the tradition of St Cuthbert was still strong, a monastic chapter was established in the first generation of the Conquest. At Norwich the bishop founded a new monastic church. But the Normans who were appointed to English bishoprics preferred to work with the type of chapter to which they were accustomed in Normandy and the newly organized chapters of this age were generally made up of secular clergy or canons. In the highly organized Church of the twelfth century the maintenance of the elaborate and ordered routine of the cathedral church belonged to the dean and chapter, while the conduct of the purely diocesan work fell on the archdeacons and rural deans under the supervision of the bishop. This division of labour meant that the administration of the diocese was unaffected by the existence of a monastic chapter, since the maintenance of cathedral services was fully provided for by the discipline of the monastic community.

At York, Lincoln, Lichfield, and Salisbury new chapters were established at about the same time and organized on lines with which the Norman bishops were familiar in 407 Normandy. There were generally four chief dignitaries of the chapter, the Dean, the Precentor, the Chancellor, and the Treasurer. The Precentor was responsible for the conduct of the service and the singing. Lesser in dignity was the Subdean. The Precentor, too, at Salisbury had a dignitary subordinate to his own office, the Succentor. The archdeacons were also members of the chapter, five at York, seven at Lincoln, and four at Salisbury, these numbers being determined by the geographical divisions of the sees. For the rest the chapter was composed of canons for whose maintenance a common fund was set up from some of the endowments of the cathedral church. This organization could be perfected only slowly, and without many fresh gifts the bishops of the post-Conquest age could not have set up so large a group of men to serve their cathedral churches. In developing their chapters the Norman bishops employed a method already used by their Saxon predecessors, by which definite estates and churches were assigned as 'prebends' to the support of individual canons. But the creation of prebends was a slow process, depending on the grants of kings and laymen. The great collection of charters at Lincoln shows how all through this period bishops were concerned to acquire lands and churches which would be appropriated either to the common fund of the canons or 408 to particular prebends. Evidence of their success can still be seen today in cathedrals such as Lincoln, where above the stalls of each canon are set up the names of the prebends, thus slowly built up during the early middle ages.

The Norman kings expected their bishops to be great feudal magnates. Like lay nobles, they owed knight-service to the king for their lands. They were expected to attend the king's court and council, to aid him with advice, to act as ambassadors to other kings or to the pope, to share in the government of the land in whatever way their help was needed. The bishop of Lincoln, whose diocese stretched from the Humber to the Thames, who owed the king the service of sixty knights, held as great a position in the land as any but the greatest earls. Bishop Robert II in 1166 reported to the king that his tenants owed him the service of no less than 104 knights. His predecessors had found it hard 409 to obtain a fitting habitation in Lincoln itself. Bishop Robert I had obtained leave from king Henry I to use one of the city gates as a residence. But the bishops possessed 410 many large manors scattered over the Midlands, and before 1135 they had built three castles within their barony – at Banbury and Sleaford and in their borough of Newark-on-Trent, where a strong twelfth-century tower still attests their feudal greatness. It was inevitable that magnates with such vast and varied responsibilities should depute the charge of their cathedral church and its services to the dignitaries they had appointed for the purpose. Very early in the history of cathedral chapters in England many bishops had transferred to their chapters not only control over the services of the cathedral church, but also spiritual jurisdiction over all the lands of all its prebends. In the thirteenth century and later there was frequent tension between bishops, who regretted this loss of jurisdiction, and deans and chapters determined to retain the privileges which their predecessors had acquired.

The cathedral clergy lived around the church in an area which throughout the period of this book was constantly expanding to accommodate new ministers to the services of the Church or to improve the dwelling places of its dignitaries. The acquisition of the lands around the cathedral went side by side with the building-up of the prebends, and towards the end of this period the process was more or less complete in most cathedral cities. At Lincoln the earliest settlement of the cathedral clergy was within the Bail, the area included within the Roman wall which marked the boundaries of the original Roman town. Before the end of 411 the twelfth century many of the cathedral clergy were living also outside the bail, and when the cathedral was enlarged in the thirteenth the extension was built across the town ditch. In 1285 the dean and chapter were complaining that they were liable to attack as they went from their houses to their church and asked for permission to enclose 412 their precinct. The wall was completed in 1327.

If the cathedral chapter became a close corporation jealous of its rights and privileges, each individual member of the chapter was equally tenacious both of the rights of his own prebend and of the rights of the canons in relation to both bishop and dean. Canons were appointed by the bishop, but when the see was vacant the king claimed the appointment to vacant canonries as well as to the chief offices in the chapter. The canons claimed to elect their own dean, but had to assert and maintain their right against both bishop and king. When Geoffrey, the illegitimate son of Henry II, was archbishop of York he maintained a running quarrel with the chapter, with its individual members, and with the king over the question of appointments to the chief offices in the chapter. At one point in the quarrel, which went on throughout Geoffrey's tenure of the see, the chapter suspended the services of the church, preventing the ringing of the bells, and locked the door of the archbishop's stall in the church and the door by which he entered the church from his palace. On that occasion the citizens took the arch- 413 bishop's side and a riot broke out. The quarrel cost both sides large sums of money in appeals to Rome, for Geoffrey never hesitated to excommunicate his enemies. The quarrel at York was particularly virulent, but at one time or another similar quarrels broke out in almost every cathedral served by a secular chapter. The peace of the cathedral close could be maintained only by a tactful bishop who was prepared to allow his chapter a high degree of independence.

The chapter was equally jealous of its rights in matters of secular jurisdiction. At Lincoln the dean and chapter claimed civil and criminal jurisdiction over all the tenants living on their land, whether they belonged to the common fund of the chapter or to any individual prebend. A test case was heard there in 1219 when the dean and chapter claimed that 'all pleas as well of the Crown as other pleas of assize and other writs belonging to the lord king . . . ought to be heard at the door of the great church of Lincoln, so that the justices shall send there a discreet knight on behalf of the lord king who shall be present there and hear that those pleas shall be reasonably treated and brought to a due end'. Judgement was given for the dean and chapter. 414 The same rights belonged to the chapter of York and to the canons of the three other churches in which the archbishop of York had his archiepiscopal throne, Southwell, Beverley, and Ripon. At Southwell the king's judges held pleas at the south door of the church, hearing criminal cases outside the Minster yard in one of the canons' houses. A solemn inquest was held at York in 1106 by royal judges when Osbert the sheriff was trying to infringe the liberties of the chapter. Its findings, which applied also to the archbishop's churches of Beverley, Hexham, Ripon, and Southwell, were set out and confirmed by the king. 415

When cathedral chapters were established in the first generation after the Norman Conquest their founders realized that to enforce continuous residence on the whole chapter would be impossible. The statutes which bishop Osmund drew up for his cathedral at Salisbury in 1091 provided that the principal dignitaries should always be in residence, 'putting away all thought of absence'. He also 416 laid down that no canon who was not resident should share in the common fund of the chapter. But Osmund, who had been the Conqueror's chancellor, was prepared to allow his canons to be absent 'in the schools'. He provided that one of his canons might be serving in the king's chapel, that the archbishop might have one, and that he himself might have three in his service. If a canon should hold it to be necessary for the common good of the church and his prebend, and the necessity were manifest, he might absent himself for a third of the year. Henry of Huntingdon's account of the chapter of Lincoln as he knew it in the first half of the twelfth century suggests that the principle of residence was 417 still in operation there. But it could not be enforced perpetually. Regular participation in the routine of services for the maintenance of which the chapter had been set up was an exacting task. The work began at five o'clock with matins and continued with very little pause until noon. In the afternoon and evening came vespers and compline. Moreover, it was impossible for a canon who had been instituted to a prebend to serve both in the cathedral church and the church of his prebend. Men marked out by their ability for the service of the state and rewarded for that service by institution into a rich prebend were not easily brought to see that they must undertake a reasonable period of residence in which the services of the cathedral church must be their first charge.

Just as the problem of the necessary absence of an incumbent was met in the prebendal churches by the appointment of vicars, so in the cathedral church the work of absent canons was performed by singing vicars, vicars choral. They were all fully-ordained priests and before the end of the twelfth century they had become a recognized part of the organization of most if not all cathedral churches. At Lincoln at this period they lived a collegiate life and were receiving grants of land for their maintenance. Before 1236 418 statutes were governing their appointment and their duties. At Exeter the vicars choral were given a separate endowment in the early thirteenth century. At Chichester in 1197 they were given threepence a week for attendance at matins 419 and vespers.

The essentials of cathedral organization can be understood today more easily by a visit to a small place like Southwell than by studying a great cathedral in a large town. At Southwell the framework of the medieval system remains in an eighteenth-century guise. The place is little more than a large village. The minster stands in a churchyard, which until the present generation was the burial-ground of the inhabitants of Southwell. Close to the boundary on the south stand the ruins of the archbishop's palace.

Close to the church on the east, standing on what was once part of the churchyard, is the Vicars' Court, two pairs of rose-coloured eighteenth-century brick houses facing each other across a court at the end of which stands the Residence, where, in later centuries, the canons lived in turn for their statutory period of service in the church. Each of the canons of Southwell had his prebendal house in the town, and his separate cellar in the Residence. Most of these houses survive today, known by the names of the prebend to which they belonged. But the canons rarely lived in their prebendal houses, for most of them were flagrantly non-resident and their houses were let, while a parochial vicar looked after their prebendal churches. Southwell was unique in that the chapter had no dean or provost at its head. The senior canon in residence presided over the chapter, but often at the end of this period no canon resided at all and the work of the chapter was performed by 'churchwardens' who were themselves no more than vicars choral. No cathedral close grew up at Southwell. It lay off the main roads, safe in a little town where everyone was the tenant either of the archbishop or of the canons themselves.

*

In Anglo-Saxon days Englishmen had regarded the monastic life as that which most nearly approached the perfect expression of the worship of God. Monks had brought 420 Christianity to England and the foundation of monasteries had always been regarded as the duty of Christian princes. Evidence of the learning of the great monasteries of the north had survived their destruction by the Danes. The works of Bede were its living memorial. The revival of religious life and order in the tenth century had been the work of monks influenced, although not inspired, by the rebirth of monastic enthusiasm on the continent. But political disunion and the unwillingness of great landlords to accept monastic rivals had prevented any general restoration throughout the land of religious foundations in which men could lead the monastic life. At the beginning of this period Burton was the only monastery north of the Trent and the only house in Lincolnshire was the small abbey of Crowland. No attempt had been made to rebuild the ruins of St Hild's house at Whitby or Bede's monasteries at Jarrow and Wearmouth. There were in England about thirty-five monasteries, all of the Benedictine order, all of them independent houses, without ties of affiliation with one another or with any continental house. Despite the rich endowments of the fenland abbeys of Peterborough, Ely, and Ramsey, and the long history of Abingdon or Glastonbury, the living heart of English monasticism in 1066 lay in the Severn valley, where Wulfstan, the saintly monastic bishop of Worcester, and Æthelwig abbot of Evesham ruled and inspired houses where the religious life was followed as strictly as the most earnest reformer could desire. But in 1066 the monastic habit, so familiar in the social scene of the thirteenth century, in the north of England had fallen out of use.

In the generation of the Norman Conquest the monasteries of Normandy itself were flourishing in the shadow of a fortunate ruler who was prepared to concern himself with every aspect of his duchy's life. Scholars were attracted to the Norman houses and their schools were becoming famous. The new prosperity showed itself in an effloresence of building. The best testimony to the quality of the Norman monasticism is the number of competent abbots who were drawn from Norman houses to bring the old English abbeys into the new order of the Conqueror. Lanfranc, himself a monk, a scholar, and a statesman, regarded the monastery less as a retreat from the world's problems to the security of religious observance than as a training ground for scholars, bishops, and statesmen. It was not men from Normandy sent by Lanfranc who restored monastic life in the far north, but a Norman knight named Reinfrid, moved by the ruins of the northern monasteries, and two Englishmen, Ealdwine, a monk from Winchcombe, and Ælfwig, a monk of Evesham, who with the blessing of abbot Æthelwig of Evesham set out on foot from that house bearing their vestments and books upon an ass. The desolation of the north which attracted these men made their task difficult and the unwillingness of the north to submit to Norman control meant that it was not until 1083 that the bishop of Durham could establish monks again in his cathedral church. Some years before this, probably about 1078, a group of monks from the newly-restored abbey of Whitby had founded the great abbey of St Mary at York.

On the site of the battle which had won him his kingdom William I founded Battle abbey as a daughter house of the abbey of Marmoutier. But he made no great effort to found new religious houses in England nor did he incite his barons to do so. Many of them gave land to Norman houses and little groups of foreign monks were generally established to look after the new property. The prosperous Norman houses produced many suitable candidates whom William I could promote to the rule of English abbeys. He is said to have asked the famous abbot of Cluny for twelve of his monks, whom he undertook to place in high office in England, but the abbot was uninterested in sending his monks across the sea to a land whose king kept so tight a hold over the affairs of the Church. Nor had he monks to spare from the continuous chanting of the services which the Cluniac ritual demanded. Only one house of the Cluniac order was established in England during the Conqueror's reign, the priory of Lewes in Sussex, founded by William de Warenne. To Lewes the abbot of Cluny sent only three monks, one of whom he recalled after a short time. It was only with difficulty that William de Warenne secured the abbot's interest and his promise always to send to Lewes as prior the holiest and wisest monk that could be spared.

Lewes in time became a rich and important house, founding daughter houses, dependent like itself upon the mother house of Cluny and contributing an agreed sum each year towards its support. Before the end of the century other Cluniac houses had been established; Bermondsey, founded by an Englishman, a Londoner; Wenlock, Castle

Acre, and Pontefract. The elaborate ritual of Cluny appealed to those who wished to found a monastery, but made it difficult to maintain an adequate supply of suitable men to fill the Cluniac houses and implement all the beginnings of the early twelfth century. All the Cluniac houses began modestly with the settlement of a few monks, often less than six. Whether they acquired the full status of a priory depended on the support they received. By 1160 there were about thirty-six Cluniac houses in England, but only about a third of them were full-scale priories. The rest were small cells, where two or three monks led very lonely lives. The great abbey of Reading was founded by Henry I as a Cluniac house and seven monks from Cluny formed the nucleus from which it grew. The connexion between Reading and Cluny was maintained throughout this period, but Reading was an independent abbey, as befitted a royal foundation.

The wave of enthusiasm which filled England with religious houses did not fully break until the twelfth century was well advanced. It was roused not by contemplation of the old religious houses or the important new foundations of black monks like Lewes or Reading, but by the desire for a simple life of self-denial and the service of God in some remote valley or wood. It was this desire which created the orders of Citeaux, Tiron, and Savigny in France in the first twenty years of the twelfth century, and it was through these orders that much of contemporary English zeal found expression. The first foundations in England were made in places so remote that they had little chance of development. The abbey of St Dogmael in Cardiganshire was founded by the brown monks of Tiron about 1115, while grey monks from Savigny were settled at Tulket in Lancashire in 1124 and three years later at remote Furness, remote even today. By 1147, when the abbey of Savigny submitted itself to the rule of the abbot of Citeaux, there were already eleven houses of the order established in England.

It was the Cistercian order which flourished above all others in England in this age and it is worth remembering that the real founder of that order was an Englishman from Sherborne in Dorset, Stephen Harding. After making a pilgrimage to Rome, Stephen joined the little community of hermits at Molesme from which the Cistercian order grew. He was sub-prior at Molesme when in 1098 part of the community moved into the woods of Citeaux. He was prior of the new community from 1099 to 1109 and abbot from 1109 to 1122. He was the author of the *Carta Caritatis* which sets out the rules which governed the order. It was he who insisted on that isolation from the world which later in the century caused English benefactors to root out whole villages so that their monks could have their desired solitude. Stephen Harding planned for an organization of daughter houses, retaining their close connexion with their mother house at Citeaux, but without the fire and eloquence of St Bernard, who brought 30 companions to Citeaux in 1112, the conception of Stephen Harding would have been still-born. The first Cistercian house in this country was established at Waverley in Surrey by the bishop of Winchester in 1128, but Yorkshire, where the dales, still suffering from the devastation of the Conqueror, were awaiting resettlement, became the home of the most famous Cistercian abbeys. The white monks of Citeaux planted the abbey of Rievaulx in 1132, and, just as the example of Bernard and his monks at Citeaux's first daughter, Clairvaux, stirred questionings among the black monks of the continent, so the harsh poverty of Rievaulx stimulated an exodus from the abbey of St Mary of York. Archbishop Thurstan and Bernard himself supported the party which demanded a return to the pure rule of St Benedict. They were settled by the archbishop on waste land in Skeldale, where from modest beginnings in huts beneath an elm tree grew up the most famous of all the Cistercian houses of Yorkshire, the abbey of St Mary of Fountains.

Many factors contributed to the astounding success of the Cistercian order. Not the least of them was the rule that the site of an abbey must be far from the habitation of man, that the land must be tilled mainly by the labour of the monks themselves, that the entangling problems of dependent villagers should be avoided. An abbey often had lands outside the main site of the abbey property, but any such dependency was run as a grange, staffed by lay brothers. The Cistercian monks therefore welcomed the illiterate and humble, who became the field workers on whose labours the material prosperity of the house depended. In Cistercian abbeys there were no children being trained to sing the service and become monks themselves. Hence there were no schools and in early days the writing of books was not regarded as a proper function for a monk. The elaborate ritual of the black monks was abandoned for a much simpler routine and all, even choir monks, were bound to work with their hands. The absence of lay servants, the abandonment of the school, the choice of a remote site, all made for a simplicity and austerity which satisfied the needs of its generation.

These characteristics also made for the economic success of the Cistercian abbeys. Although they were set in remote and often waste places, yet their land could always be made to blossom into wealth by the devoted labour of dedicated men. Unlike most of the older Benedictine abbeys they were free from the burden of providing knights to serve the king. It was with great difficulty that the state could tax them in early years. When Richard I's ransom had to be found and free-will offerings were asked from all, the Cistercians were asked for their wool for a year as their contribution. They resisted the demands of John, pleading the liberty of their Order, but in 1210 they were forced to pay. By this date their years of poverty were over and their buildings were beginning to give evidence of wealth. Gone, too, was the early stress upon the avoidance of learning, which, indeed, could not be maintained when some of the leaders of the Cistercian movement, like Bernard himself, and in England Ailred of Rievaulx, were natural writers. By the early thirteenth century abbots were collecting libraries and in many individual houses chronicles were being kept which are of the first importance for the history of their time. The Cistercian houses were members of a close-knit organization which gave them many opportunities for collecting news. Each year the abbots met in the general chapter of the order at Citeaux and each year the abbots of the houses which had founded daughter abbeys visited their daughters to ensure the maintenance of discipline. Citeaux was itself visited by the abbots of the four first houses it had itself established.

Even the new orders of Savigny and Citeaux did not entirely satisfy the needs of some Englishmen who craved for the life of isolated service and prayer. Wulfric of Haselbury, in his cell beside the parish church, was outstanding only by the force of his personality, not by his mode of life. The names of five enclosed women and one other man are mentioned in the Life of Wulfric by John of Ford. One of these anchoresses was still living in John's day. Early in the twelfth century a monk of St Albans named Roger left his monastery to settle in a cell on the Dunstable road, where he was joined by five other men. All through this period retreat of this nature was possible, although as the authority of the bishop became more effective most bishops were inclined to question the establishment of new anchor houses. Perhaps the most distinguished anchoress of the period, at least socially, was the widow of the last earl of Leicester of the Norman line. She lived in retreat for many years and was asked by Simon de Montfort for information about the rights of the earl of Leicester as high steward of England. To women the appeal of the life of an anchoress must have been powerful in days which offered them no career other than marriage, and that a marriage arranged by parents or the overlord. There must have been many girls like Christina of Huntingdon, who, forced into a distasteful marriage, left home to live in a cell beside an anchorite on the Dunstable road. When he died she took over his cell and other women came to join her. Abbot Geoffrey of St Albans (1119–46) founded the nunnery of Markyate for Christina and her companions, who seem to have spent much time doing fine needlework on vestments for the church.

It was in answer to the needs of women that the only order of purely English origin was founded by Gilbert of Sempringham about 1130. Gilbert was the son of a Norman honorial baron. Unsuited physically to a knightly career, he became a clerk, studied abroad, and returned to Lincolnshire where his father presented him to two churches. As parish priest his teaching was probably much more inspiring than that of most of his fellow-parsons. He found himself forced to make provision for a number of women who wished to enter the life of religion. To the original group of nuns at Sempringham, he added lay sisters, so that the nuns might be free for their spiritual meditations. As gifts of land came in lay brothers were needed to till and cultivate the nuns' property. Gilbert himself remained responsible for the rule of the order, but by 1147 he felt that some more regular provision for the spiritual needs of the nuns should be made. He failed to persuade the Cistercians to take up the rule of houses for women, but was himself confirmed in his rule by Pope Eugenius III. The popularity of this order in Lincolnshire and the rapid increase in the number of houses under Gilbert's direction meant that he was bound to provide chaplains to serve the nuns' churches. He therefore added canons as a fourth member of his order and finally founded houses of canons, as at Old Malton in Yorkshire, where his nuns' priests could go for training or a period of retreat. Gilbert himself lived until 1189, when he was over a hundred, and his fourteen houses together accommodated a large number of men and women. The limit of numbers had previously been set at 960 nuns and 496 lay brothers, without counting the lay sisters and the canons, but it seems probable that in the twelfth century, at least, these figures
421 were exceeded.

No such numbers were drawn to the order which was from its foundation the most austere of all the new forms of the religious life. The Carthusians after hesitant beginnings were established as an order by their fifth prior between 1110 and 1136. He founded six houses, each of which took the name of the original community at Chartreuse, which itself became the Grande Chartreuse. The Carthusians were unique in that each brother had a private cell. Only a portion of the daily services was held in the church and recited by all the monks together. The rest, each monk recited in his cell. There he lived alone in meditation and prayer. His diet was spare and he wore the hair shirt of the hermit. On certain days the monks met for common meals and conversation, but the private cell where a life of solitary worship and contemplation was passed was the essential feature of each house. Lay brethren protected the seclusion of the monks. They tilled the land and performed the manual tasks, but they were never allowed to take any share in the administration of the monastery. This form of the religious life had only a limited appeal for Englishmen, and Witham, founded by Henry II in 1180, for long remained the only Charterhouse in England. But the order can never be ignored in the history of English monasticism, for it brought to this country Hugh of Avalon, who became prior of Witham in 1180 and in 1186 was elected bishop of Lincoln. He was bishop for fifteen years, but he always maintained his close connexion with Witham, often visiting it in the autumn and allowing his servants to go home to help in the harvest. His memory is kept green by the choir he built at Lincoln.

By the end of the twelfth century the enthusiasm which drew men to the religious life was moving into new channels. The friars, the followers of St Francis and St Dominic, belong to the high middle ages when the exuberant life of Europe was creating cities and universities, when nobles were growing richer and kings more flamboyant. They abandoned the isolation of the Cistercians and the elaborate organization of the Benedictines and chose to live and move among men. St Francis from his Italian birthplace preached repentance and a return to the simple holiness of early Christian days. He accepted, and expected his followers to accept, the absolute poverty of Christ and his disciples; to go out like them to preach to the people and to eat what men of their charity offered. St Francis himself was unlearned and a deacon and many of his followers were not in priest's orders. The simplicity and freshness of his teaching had an immediate appeal. St Francis, who from the first to the last insisted on poverty and simplicity, was the inspiration of both orders of friars. Dominic was a Spaniard who devoted himself to preaching the Catholic doctrine to the heretics of the south-west of France. He founded a Preaching order of friars who were dedicated to the maintenance of the strict dogma of the Church against both heretical and heathen perversions. Innocent III gave verbal blessing to the order of St Francis in 1210. At the end of his pontificate he instructed Dominic to choose a rule for his followers and present it for approval. Honorius III confirmed his provision in 1216.

The two orders initiated in very different circumstances were in a real sense complementary to each other. If it was the example of Francis which brought Dominic to found an order of friars rather than canons, it was the vision of Dominic which conceived the organization of a school in every Dominican house, with a larger school in the more important houses, and, in university cities, a school where work for a degree could be completed. Dominic chose Paris for the site of the first of these schools of university standing and it was set up there in 1228. It was not for another 35 years that a school of similar standing was established for the order in England at Oxford. Dominic from the first planned a student organization for his order and in time the Franciscans adopted, though hesitatingly, much of Dominic's idea. The Preaching friars came to England in 1221, travelling under the protection of that worldly and acute ecclesiastic, Peter des Roches, bishop of Winchester. He commended them to archbishop Stephen Langton, who, impressed by their sincerity and eloquence, gave them his patronage. The Franciscans came to England in 1224, a little company of nine men, transported across the Channel by the generosity of the monks of Fécamp, penniless, and dependent on the charity of those to whom they preached. Each little group knew exactly what its individual members must do when they reached England. Their plans had been thought out. Each group in turn made for Canterbury, London, and Oxford, and each in turn found eager converts, both learned and simple, so that by the middle of the century there were friaries in most important towns. In early days all that was needed to found a friary was a modest dwelling – not even a church was essential. Friaries were often built on poor sites outside the walls of towns, but land in towns was dear and scarce and the friars, who never meant to establish elaborate buildings, were not anxious for a favoured position.

It is no exaggeration to say that the eloquence and sincerity of the friars swept men of all classes under their influence. Preaching had never been a necessary accomplishment of the parish priest, monks taught by example not by exhortation, and the friars offered something most men had never experienced before, the exhilaration which can come from listening to a trained speaker preaching from both heart and head. Many of the famous teachers in the Paris schools had joined the friars. In 1229 many scholars from Paris, some of them Englishmen, came to Oxford when the university in Paris was temporarily dispersed. Some of these scholars were already friars and in 1230 the most famous of them, Alexander of Hales, joined the Franciscans. Robert Grosseteste, later as bishop of Lincoln to work strenuously for the betterment of English clergy, had been master of the schools at Oxford since 1214. He was a great teacher, the friend of many young scholars, like Adam Marsh, who had joined the Franciscans. Before 1229 Grosseteste was lecturing to the friars and the association between the University of Oxford and the Franciscan order was assured. Curiously enough the Dominicans were less active in the two English universities than the Franciscans, perhaps because their own organization of schools was more elaborate. But in 1256 a Dominican, William of Darlington, became a member of the king's council and his confessor. He was a successful diplomat, but did not live to enjoy the office of archbishop of Dublin to which he was appointed by the Pope. From Henry III's day for more than 100 years the king's confessor was a Dominican friar and in this, as in other matters, nobles often imitated the king. In 1273 a Dominican, Robert Kilwardby, became archbishop of Canterbury. He was succeeded by a Franciscan, John Pecham, in 1279.

Although the friars might seem to be sweeping all before them in the thirteenth century the older orders continued to draw recruits to fill their houses. Not all those who felt the religious vocation admired the friars' way of life. The black-monk houses with their ordered ritual and their days of peaceful work and the service of God satisfied the fundamental needs of many men. But the thirteenth century was a time when the older orders were bound to consider their position in the face of a challenge which they had to meet. Reform was enjoined on the Benedictine abbeys by direct decree of the Lateran Council of 1215 and papal legates drove home its demands. Thereafter something of the isolation of the individual black-monk houses was mitigated by the organization of chapters in which the heads of the individual houses could meet every three years to discuss matters concerning the welfare of the order. Even though attendance was not very regular in the early years, such meetings made the conduct of individual houses more uniform. More significant of changing times was the decision to cut short the elaborate liturgical chanting, to insist that simpler services should be recited slowly and devoutly. Time could thus be freed for more study. A college in Oxford was established for monks on part of the site where Worcester College now stands, but monks long settled in their routine had little desire to attempt a new and perhaps more arduous discipline. The Cistercians were moving in the same direction and in 1288 Rewley Abbey was founded in Oxford as a student house of that order.

The abbots of the older houses owed knight service like barons and like them were expected to take their place in the king's councils. The necessity of protecting the abbey's interests when, on the abbot's death, his lands were taken into the king's hands until the appointment of a successor, had forced the Benedictine houses to assign definite revenues to specific purposes. From the abbot's share the knight service due to the crown was paid, and the abbot maintained his own servants, and paid for a proportion of the abbey's hospitality. Heads of the various departments in the abbey were entrusted with the administration of definite estates for which they were wholly responsible. These officers, known as obedientiaries, were freed from much of the routine of services and could make journeys about the country to look after their property. Such arrangements as these existed in most houses by the middle of the twelfth century. Able men found absorbing interest in developing the resources of their lands, maintaining well-stocked farms, experimenting with manure and marl. They had learned that it was better to buy seed than sow their own, and they watched the markets, so that they could sell their corn when prices were high, even if they had to buy less good corn for home consumption. It is sometimes suggested that these monastic farmers led agricultural improvements, as the Cistercians are credited with a preponderating influence on the wool trade. It seems nearer the truth to believe that both Benedictines and Cistercians were knit into the general economic fabric of thirteenth-century society.

The Benedictine abbeys had behind them a long history which for centuries had been part of the history of the country. In discussing the religious life of this period it is easy to lay too much stress on the new movements which gave rise in the twelfth century to new orders like the Cistercians and in the thirteenth century to the great experiment of the Friars. The long-established houses of Black monks, like Abingdon or Malmesbury, Peterborough or St Albans, Bury St Edmunds or Glastonbury, Canterbury or Ramsey, Ely or Worcester, cannot have regarded the new orders as a serious challenge to their own supremacy. Such ancient houses as these pursued their ordered lives, raised great buildings, and entertained men of every condition. Peterborough cathedral stands today as proof that the abbots of the old Benedictine houses were no less princes of the Church than the bishops with whom they sat in the king's council. Of all medieval monastic historians, none surpassed William of Malmesbury in the twelfth century or Matthew Paris in the thirteenth. These venerable Benedictine monasteries were beset with cares which most houses of later foundation escaped – the management of large and complex estates, the maintenance of seemly relations with the king, their patron, the public and political responsibilities inherent in the possession of vast wealth. Institutions thus preoccupied, continuing an immemorial routine of service from age to age, cannot have the interest that belongs to communities unencumbered with great possessions, and by that very fact free to attempt new forms of devotion. For all this, in medieval England, as on the Continent, the Benedictine houses, like the founder of their order in the sixth century, represent the norm of the religious life.

CHAPTER VI

THE ARTS OF PEACE

At the beginning of the period covered by this book no one, not even the king, enjoyed a high degree of comfort. William I cannot have found any impressive palaces in the England of 1066. Edward the Confessor had a hall at Winchester with a chamber where his treasure was stored, and presumably he had a hall and chamber at Westminster, where he had begun to build the abbey. In royal manors about the country more modest accommodation for the king and his court enabled him to keep in touch with at least the southern shires and to consume produce near the place where it was grown. William I must have had halls large enough to entertain the great company of magnates and others who gathered to the three formal meetings of the council, by turns at Westminster, Winchester, and Gloucester. The new castles which in his reign were rising in every country town provided lodgings for the king. But most of these new castles were still in the making in his early years and wooden houses within the bailey, or outer defensive works of the castle, must have been the best that could be expected in William I's reign. The absence of glass for windows meant that no house or hall can ever have been properly lighted or very warm, for windows were as small as possible and the wooden shutters which protected the inhabitants from the worst weather cannot have eliminated draughts. Floor softened with a carpet of rushes and fires burning only wood without chimneys to carry off the smoke must have greeted the king in most of his castles.

The Norman and Angevin kings spent much of their time in forest country where they could enjoy the sport to which they were accustomed in Normandy. Some of the most important English castles lay adjacent to or within royal forests. Windsor, Northampton, Nottingham, and Marlborough are a few examples. Both at Windsor and at Winchester Henry II had the walls of his chamber decorated with paintings. The kings seem to have preferred their forest lodges, the secret places of which Richard fitz Nigel speaks. These they sometimes elaborated into palaces large enough for the court to be with the king. Henry I spent considerable sums on Brampton near Huntingdon. He was at Woodstock when the bishop of Lincoln, Robert Bloet, died. The king was riding in his deer park with the bishop of Salisbury riding on one side of him and the bishop of Lincoln on the other when the bishop of Lincoln fell off his horse saying 'Lord king, I faint.' The king dismounted and took the bishop in his arms. He had him borne to his lodgings but the bishop died in a little while. Many writs and charters of the Norman and Angevin kings were issued from Woodstock or Brampton, Gillingham or Clarendon. Henry I maintained a park of wild beasts at Woodstock, Henry II built a palace at Clarendon decorated with marble columns. Some of the most important councils of his reign were held there. Richard I saw very little of England, but in 1194, after he had taken Nottingham castle, held against him by rebels, he 'set out to see Clipstone and the forest of Sherwood which he had never seen before and they pleased him much'. He went back to spend Palm Sunday at Clipstone after he had held a great council at Nottingham.

The king might find his pleasure in his forests and his hunting lodges, but the problems of castle building must have been ever with him. All through this period cas es were becoming more elaborate and more expensive until the culminating point is reached with the massive Edwardian castles built to keep Wales quiescent after it had been conquered. The motte and bailey of the Conqueror's reign develops into the stone castle of the next generation. It seems probable that the outer walls along the bank which protected the bailey were built before the motte itself was fortified with stonework. The 'shell keep', which was in essence a mere wall round the edge of the motte, was the simplest way of strengthening the defensive heart of the castle. The familiar, solid, square keep was often built not on the motte but on fresh ground. Both at Rochester and Canterbury the original motte was abandoned in favour of a fresh site. To capture one of these strongly-built castles when properly supplied to stand a siege, it was necessary to have siege engines known as mangonels and petraries, large wooden erections which slung stone balls to batter down the walls. If these failed, sappers, protected by a defensive shield to hide their operations, were set to undermining the walls at a critical point. These tactics were adopted by Hubert de Burgh in 1224 when he laid siege to and took Bedford castle which was held against the Crown by one of the outstanding mercenary captains of the age.   424

Architecturally a square keep was a great advance on the wooden buildings which preceded it. A typical keep rose four stories high above an undercroft or cellar which stood on the ground floor. There was no entrance to this from the outside, and often, as at Appleby in Westmorland, this undercroft was a considerable height. It strengthened the building, kept it dry, and served as a repository for stores. The entrance was thus on the first floor, reached by an outside stair, removable in case of need. The defenders of the keep would live on this floor. The hall was a high, church-like room. Off the upper part of the hall, equivalent to the third floor, would be rooms or sometimes a continuous gallery. Small recesses in the thickness of the walls made little rooms, which might be larger on the floor above the hall. The stairs would be in an angle of the keep. But the narrow, unglazed windows, the chill stone stair and walls, the sense of being shut in high above the surrounding country meant that no one would live in a keep if he could help it. A hall and other necessary buildings in the bailey generally housed those who were obliged to inhabit a castle. To the keep they could resort in case of war. In England today the ruins of these castles remind every observer of the insecurity of daily life even in the twelfth and thirteenth centuries.

In the early middle ages social customs still showed the influence of early times when man was content with a single room with a fire on the hearth; when a single hall sufficed to house a great man and his household, who ate and slept together. All through this period the hall was the focus of the household's life. The lord and his family ate there with their servants. It was a genuine hall, like a church or an old barn. The ruins of the twelfth-century hall at Christchurch, Hampshire, illustrate this church-like appearance. Round the hall other rooms accreted as wealth increased and standards of comfort were raised. The first room to be added was the chamber for the lord and his wife to retire to for privacy in the day-time and to sleep at night. A room for the sons and another for the daughters of the house was also necessary. The kitchen was generally a separate building at the beginning of this period and it was not until late in the thirteenth century that chimneys became common in the ordinary house. In Henry II's reign Roald of Chelsfield leased a manorial property at Lenborough, Buckinghamshire, from Reading abbey at a rent of £3 a year in two annual payments. He agreed to hold the 'tenement' at the will of the abbot, to be restored to the abbey 'with the houses and tilled lands which they have handed to me, namely the hall and the chamber and the kitchen and two barns and the sheep-fold and the cow-byre, in good repair, and 12 acres of winter ploughing and 18 acres of spring ploughing'. This detailed description of a gentleman's modest estate in Buckinghamshire shows that in the latter part of the twelfth century the hall, the chamber, and the kitchen were still the only essential parts of a house.

None of the ancient brick and timber houses that can still be seen in the west country and East Anglia comes from a period so early as this, but here and there in country where stone was readily available in the twelfth century a fragment of an ancient house to which later generations have added survives to the present day. The stone hall at Appleton manor near Abingdon can be attributed to the twelfth century. But most of the lesser houses in this period must have been built of wood, the interstices of the walls filled in with wattle and daub, that is sticks and clay, and the roofs thatched with reeds or straw or wooden shingles. If such buildings survived the dangers of fire, a generation which needed more comfort would pull them down. Towns were constantly swept by fires, often started by a spark on thatch, or a charred beam. The first mayor of London, Henry fitz Ailwin, issued a set of building regulations for the city towards the end of the twelfth century. He ordered that 426 the walls should be of stone 3 feet thick and 16 feet high, from which the roof ran up to a point, the gable end being towards the street. Fitz Ailwin made no rules about roofing-materials and it was not until towards the end of this period that London citizens were enjoined to cover their houses with lead, tiles, or stone. At the end of the twelfth century London houses seem to have consisted of no more than two stories, the floor of the upper storey being about 8 feet above the ground. This upper room was the main room of the house, called by fitz Ailwin 'the house', but sometimes called the 'solar'. Mention has already been made of the fine stone house at Lincoln called the great hall of Peter of Legbourne by contemporary records, but known popularly as 'Aaron's house'. There, too, the upper room was the hall and the ground floor an undercroft.

The thirteenth century saw the gradual improvement of both the town house and the country manor house. Henry III was using glass for the windows of his palace at Westminster, but it is unlikely that it came into general use during the period of this book. The most striking development in house-construction that took place in the period was the appearance of the chimney. By the latter part of the 427 thirteenth century manor houses were being built with the material readiest to hand, with local and personal variations on the old theme of hall and chambers. Church Farm, Halloughton, Nottinghamshire, locally called 'an old friary', is in part a stone building with narrow lancets, the chambers branching off the central hall. Stokesay Castle in Shropshire is a larger version of the hall and chambers type.

Two windows in the principal chamber look into the hall, which has an open timber roof. Stokesay castle was built by a rich cloth merchant of Ludlow. It has more rooms than most country houses of the day would have had. In the years between the coming of the Normans and the death of Edward I builders and architects were applying all their ingenuity to strengthening castles and raising great cathedrals. They spent singularly little effort on elaborating the construction of the ordinary house.

The rich were content with little in the way of comfort. The ordinary villager, farming a peasant's holding, lived an even simpler life. The ordinary village house was a fragile erection which an evildoer could destroy single-handed if some of the stories told in the courts are to be believed. 'He cut the posts of that house through the middle so that that house fell down,' was said in court in 1202. The chattels of villagers set out in early pleas do not suggest that they possessed much beyond their farm stock and a few pots and pans. A certain Goda who lived at Alton, Hampshire, was buried without a report of her death being made to the coroner for him to hold his inquest. The consequent inquiry showed that she had a house with a chamber. Her chattels were 2 pigs, one cow, one leaden vessel, and many other utensils, which were locked up in her chamber because it was rumoured that she was a usurer. In 1202 the lord of a Lincolnshire manor admitted going to his villein's house and taking possession of his chattels, namely 5 thraves of barley, 13 sheaves of oats, and 25 hens. Nothing is said of any household goods at all; for the villein's poor pots and pans were left as furnishings for his wife. The chattels of a Cornish villein are set out in 1201 as 2 oxen, 1 cow, 1 mare, 2 pigs, 9 sheep, 11 goats. Into the houses of the poor animals could freely enter, and a man could be accused of keeping 2 stolen horses in his chamber for 8 days in return for 6 shillings.

The austerity of the twelfth-century house meant that men and women alike wore ample and warm garments. Contemporary drawings show men of position from the king downwards dressed in long full cloaks reaching to the feet, sometimes having short full sleeves, with undersleeves right to the wrist. When they were hunting or working they wore a gown ending at the knee and over it a short cloak of about the same length. Humble folk wore short garments reaching to about knee length, and girt about the waist. Most people of both sexes seem to have worn a variation of the simple gown with a rather low neck, sometimes decorated with embroidery, and drawn in at the waist. The sleeves were tight at the wrist, but might be exaggeratedly wide at the armhole. They look as though the sleeve and gown were cut in one piece. The cloak worn over this gown, both for men and women, generally had a hood and was fastened at the neck with a brooch. At the end of the century women were wearing tight sleeves with long hangings from the wrists. Belts and girdles were simple. Shoes or boots were slightly pointed, plain and without heels. Everyone not dressed in armour presented an untailored appearance with which jewels went well. King John habitually wore a string 433 of precious stones about his neck and men as well as women wore jewelled brooches. What was worn by way of under- 434 clothes it is impossible to say. It is probable that gentlefolk undressed for the night, but there is no evidence about their wearing of night clothes. King John had a furred cloak for use when he got up in the night. The fact that his accounts mention the purpose of the gown suggests that it was not usual to have a cloak specially made for a dressing gown. 435

It must have been possible to achieve a certain modest comfort and ease in a hall lit by candlelight, with the door shut and the windows covered, with the fire in the centre of the floor fanned to a blaze by the draughts so that most of the smoke was drawn up to the louvre open in the centre of the high roof. In 1214 Henry de Pomeroy, a magnate of great estate in Cornwall, told in court how when he and his friends were together in his house at Tregony and 'were making merry in the evening' one of his servants came and told him that he had seen a man lurking with a bow and arrows in the courtyard and that Henry had better take care.

A little later Henry called for a candle to light him to bed and as he was going to bed with his servant carrying the candle before him 'suddenly there came an arrow close by him, and it flew close to the hand of him who carried the 436 candle'. Whether the tale was true or not is irrelevant. It throws a vivid flash of light on an evening long ago – the merriment in the lighted hall and the danger from the skilled archer who could shoot through the unshuttered window at the passing candle. For people out all day the evenings must soon have ended in heavy sleep, the lord in his chamber on his bed with linen sheets and fur covers, his casual visitors making do on a mattress before the fire in the hall. The indoor game most popular in King John's court was 'tables', that is backgammon, but chess had won 437 favour in his grandson's generation.

The low standard of comfort in the ordinary house meant that the rigours of travel were hardly felt. This may have helped to encourage the large volume of traffic which passed over the English roads during this period. At the apex of society the king set the fashion, but it was less a fashion than a way of life. In places where the king and his court habitually stayed the great men had their accustomed lodgings to which they sent their servants on ahead to prepare for their coming. When Richard I was moving down the Northampton-Southampton road with a large company he spent the first night at his hunting lodge at Silverstone. The servants of the bishop of Durham rode on ahead to Brackley where a lodging had been assigned to the bishop by Henry II's marshal. Then the king of Scots' servants came up and tried to turn out the bishop's servants. They failed, but they bought food for the king and prepared it in a house in the same court. When the bishop arrived at Brackley and learned what had happened, he went into his lodging and ordered the tables to be laid for himself. The archbishop of Canterbury had been told about the affair, and while the bishop was eating, came and asked him to allow the king of Scots to have that lodging, offering his own lodging to the bishop. The bishop refused to move. When the king of Scots

THE ARTS OF PEACE

came late from hunting and all this was told him, he was angry, refused to eat the food his servants had prepared, and went back to complain to Richard I at Silverstone, more than six miles away: a sad ride on top of a day's hunting and on an empty stomach.

438

All ranks of society could be met on the roads of medieval England. The king and his court frequented most the forest-country, but that covered a very wide area. Magnates and barons of less exalted rank alike had estates in widely separated shires and moved their households from one to another as a matter of course. Those who were strong enough invariably travelled on horseback. They could easily cover the ground at an average of 30 miles a day. On urgent business and with relays of horses a considerably higher average might be reached. The ordinary business of shire and hundred courts produced a considerable volume of local traffic. The shire court met every four or five weeks and the court of each hundred or wapentake met at similar intervals, fixed by custom but varying from court to court. Each meeting brought together people of local position within the jurisdiction of the court. The course of justice was slow and litigants often found that they must make many journeys before their cases were concluded.

The medieval practice of going on pilgrimage to a near or distant shrine was the contemporary parallel to a modern holiday and pilgrims, like holiday-makers, used the same roads as other medieval travellers than whom they were certainly less numerous. The idea of special pilgrim ways is a modern fantasy. A great number of people must have moved about the country on foot or by careful stages on an inexpensive horse. Villeins, or more often their sons, who aimed at acquiring a living and freedom in a distant town, masons and carpenters who were expecting to be hired for work on a cathedral, a church, or a castle, must have added considerably to the volume of humble travellers of whom the records tell little. A case which came before the judges at Worcester in 1221 throws a little light on the circumstances of one of these itinerant masons. His name was

Robert of Hallow and he held three-quarters of a yardland freely. Before he left the county to follow his calling as a mason he entrusted the land and his two daughters to his brother, Peter. But Peter became a leper and entered a lazar house. Then Robert came home again and entrusted the land to his brother, Reginald, who tilled it for a time, but afterwards left it untilled so that the lord took it into his hand for default of service. Then the mason died and his children tried to get their inheritance, but the lord would not give it up. The case then came before the king's justices 439 who restored possession to the heirs. Such men as Robert of Hallow must have been counted in their thousands. Their work was seasonal and they must have moved backwards and forwards over all England, converging on great cathedrals like Lincoln or Salisbury, or hurrying to the urgent 440 work of castle building in Wales. The names of Geoffrey of Derby, Baldric of Sussex, John of south England, and William of Richmond have been preserved as workers on St Hugh's new fabric of Lincoln cathedral only because they fled for homicide.

The transport of heavy goods which could not be split up into packs was done in carts, sometimes described as 'long carts'. They moved slowly, particularly in winter. It took nine days in the winter of 1294 for 21 cartloads of treasure to be taken from London to Norwich for shipment over sea. The carters had managed to keep up an average of 12 miles a day by hiring extra help on several occasions because 'of the depth of the ways and the weakness of the horses'. Occasionally complaints about tolls exacted by individuals or towns from users of the roads came into the courts of justice. They reveal that despite all difficulties carts of produce which today would be regarded as perishable were slowly driven through the towns and villages of central England. The lord of Winwick in Northamptonshire was accused in 1202 of taking toll in kind from cartloads of eels, green fish, salmon, and herrings which passed through his land, whereas he ought to have taken toll only from cartloads of salt. Wherever the direction of the waterways made their use possible, heavy traffic was carried along them. The river Thames was used between London and Gravesend by those who were going to Canterbury or the ports on the coast of Kent. The inland waterway which was found most useful was probably that which connected Boston in the south of Lincolnshire with York. It depended for its central stage on the Roman Foss Dyke, which Henry I had recut in 1121 to connect the Witham at Lincoln with the Trent at Torksey. But the journey between Boston and York rarely took less than four full days by water. By road these places are little more than 100 miles apart. 441

From early times English kings had been interested to protect those who used the roads along which royal authority ran. Four roads in particular, Watling Street, the Fosse Way, the Icknield Way, and Ermine Street, were in the special peace of the king, so that those who committed crimes on them were at his mercy. This conception of the king's peace running on a high road had spread by the twelfth century to cover all the land, but high roads still retained some special flavour of majesty. They were 'royal ways' and are frequently so described. Custom had laid it 442 down that the highway should be so wide that two loaded carts could pass each other, that two rustics standing one on each side of the way could make their goads meet, that 16 knights fully armed could ride abreast. Encroachment on the king's highway must be reported to his judges when they visited the shire so that the land thus taken could be restored to the road. A medieval high road must have been 443 so wide that a horseman could generally find a good grass surface on which to ride at speed in safety. Such roads enabled drovers to take their flocks for great distances to stock manors or to sell in fairs, letting them graze as they passed through the countryside. A detailed account survives from 1322 of the cost of taking a miscellaneous herd of cows, a bull, and many sheep from Long Sutton in south Lincolnshire nearly 130 miles to Tadcaster in Yorkshire, where it was broken up for the stocking of various royal manors. Similar journeys must frequently have been accomplished at any time after a centralized monarchy had secured the king's peace along his roads.

There is little evidence that in this period the king felt it necessary to make any serious efforts to keep roads in repair, but occasionally military necessity compelled him to supplement the customary liability of each local authority for the condition of the roads which ran through its territory. The Welsh war in Edward I's reign caused him in 1278 to appoint Roger Mortimer to enlarge and widen the roads and passes in Wales and Denbighshire. In 1283 the king instructed Roger Lestrange and Bogo de Knoville to clear and widen the passes into Wales so that each pass should be 444 a bow-shot in width. The position in regard to bridges was different. From a very remote time the duty of bridge building had been regarded as a public duty from which no lands could obtain exemption. In this period the men of 445 Cambridgeshire maintained the great bridge of Cambridge. The Leen Bridge at Nottingham was repaired by the county. At Rochester the duty of maintaining the bridge 446 was shared among many estates in Kent. But increasing population and the interests of the king's hunting meant that many more bridges were needed as this period wore on. The Great Charter of 1215 expressed the general feeling of the countryside that 'no village or man shall be distrained to make bridges at river banks who ought not to do it by ancient custom and right'. In the reign of Henry III many general orders were issued to sheriffs that they should repair the bridges in their shires in readiness for the king's hunting. Occasionally the writ includes a clause limiting the work to the places which were customary in the time of king John. In forest country the king was very often willing to help those on whom the duty of bridge-making fell by providing 447 them with timber from his forests.

A bridge might well be turned to a source of profit for its builder. Complaint was made before the king's judges in 1221 that the abbot of Lilleshall, Shropshire, was taking a new custom of 1 penny from every loaded cart going over Atcham bridge. The abbot replied that in his predecessor's time there was no bridge over the river there and the abbot maintained 2 boatmen who ferried people across and paid the abbot 2 marks a year of what they took from travellers for their passage. 'Afterwards,' said the abbot, 'it was provided by the common counsel of William fitz Alan and the other magnates that the abbot should make a bridge and take from every loaded cart from Shrewsbury 1 penny and from others a halfpenny, and the bridge is now finished, except for one arch.' The jurors said that the abbot had been taking the toll for 20 years and had made no improvement to the bridge. Sometimes a hermit would settle beside 448 a bridge, taking alms from passers-by to help him keep the bridge in repair. All through the middle ages the problem 449 of keeping London Bridge in good repair was a heavy burden. Peter the chaplain of Colechurch began the building of the stone bridge in 1176. In 1202 on the advice of the 450 archbishop of Canterbury king John 'entreated, admonished, and urged' Isenbert the master of the schools of Saintes to come to London to build the stone bridge. In telling the 451 citizens of London of this arrangement the king said that he was moved to invite Isenbert in consideration of the short time he had taken to build the bridges of Saintes and Rochelle. The king declared that the profits of the buildings on the bridge should be applied to its maintenance. These must have been built of wood, for they were all burned in a great fire which swept through London in 1212, burning the bridge and buildings on each side of the river. In 1283 the 452 winter was so severe that 5 arches of London bridge and many other bridges were broken by the violence of the ice. 453

There survives in the Bodleian Library at Oxford a map drawn in the early fourteenth century as a guide to those who used English roads. The map is undated, but the names are written in a fourteenth-century hand and certain idiosyncrasies of the draughtsman suggest the earlier rather than the latter half of the century. The most interesting truth which this map reveals is the conservatism of English travellers. Apart from minor deviations the roads of this fourteenth-century map are the roads of the seventeenth century. No violent changes in the lines of English travel were made between the middle ages and our own days. Some parts of England were known to the map-maker better than others. He knew the north-western counties surprisingly well. He delineates five main lines of road radiating from London to the remotest parts, and he inserts a considerable number of secondary cross-country roads. Sometimes the modern main road takes a different course from that recommended in the fourteenth century. In such cases it generally appears that the change of direction has been taken in modern times. A notable feature of this medieval map is the care which its maker took to insert the number of miles between the places he marks. These mileages do not agree with those of modern measurement nor could it be expected that in the early fourteenth century the accurate estimate of mileage on so grand a scale would have been possible. These mileages represent the estimated distance between place and place and were near enough to the actual distance to guide the traveller. In the first great modern description of English roads made and published in 1675 in the *Britannia* of John Ogilby, each map is accompanied by a double list of distances, measured miles and what Ogilby calls 'computed' miles. In innumerable cases, these distances between place and place correspond exactly to the medieval estimate recorded on this fourteenth-century map. The living voice of tradition handed on these computations from a time which may run back to the 454 days when the sites of English towns were first determined.

Among many other problems, study of the map, whether a modern one or the map made in the fourteenth century, helps to explain the curious fact that Oxford became the first English university. In the late Saxon times Oxford was a large place and it suffered a grievous devastation at the Conquest. But no devastation could take from it its geographical advantage in the centre of England. Good roads met there from every direction to use the fords over the Thames and Cherwell beside which the town grew up. Apart from London, there was no English town in this period on which so many roads of general importance converged. Between 1016 and 1160 Oxford was repeatedly the meeting place of important national assemblies, ranging from the meeting when the English and Danes swore to observe king Edgar's law to that at which the magnates of England swore fealty to Henry II. Cambridge, too, is a town at a river crossing, but in the eleventh century it was little more than a local market town, the county town of a small shire, whereas Oxford was one of the chief towns in England. But the towns had a further common feature. Neither was the site of a dominant church or abbey. Cambridge drew in the thirteenth century, as it still largely does today, on the thickly populated eastern shires. Scholars were first gathering there in the decades when the agricultural prosperity of East Anglia was probably at its highest. The scholars who set their schools at Oxford may also have been conscious of the frequent presence of the court at Woodstock as well as at Oxford itself. But in the last resort it was the accessibility of a town which led to the gathering of scholars from which a university arose.   455

It is very easy to underestimate the amount of education that was being provided in the early middle ages. The common assumption that the knightly class was illiterate can be applied with too much rigidity. References to schools can be found for every period in English history from the Norman Conquest and before. If men of position were illiterate it was because they had made no effort to learn rather than that provision for their teaching was not available. When Lanfranc founded the first house of canons regular at Canterbury he provided that the song and grammar school to which the citizens and people from neighbouring hamlets had been sending their children should be in the charge of masters appointed by the priests of his new foundation. A boy who became one of the best- 456 known chroniclers of the twelfth century under the name Ordericus Vitalis was sent when five years old to a school in Shrewsbury of which the master bore an English name. There he learned reading, grammar, and the chants. He had

been there five years when his father decided that both he
457 and his son should enter religion. It would seem that his
education had begun long before it was determined that he
should be a monk. In the first half of the twelfth century the
Austin canons of Huntingdon complained to their bishop,
Robert I of Lincoln, that contrary to papal privilege
and episcopal confirmation certain people are presuming to
hold 'adulterine' schools in Huntingdon to the prejudice of
the canons' school. The bishop instructed his archdeacon to
impose silence on such schools by episcopal authority, so
that if they did not obey the archdeacon's command the
church in whose parish the schools were held should be
sequestrated. The archdeacon took action and in a curious
document restored to the canons their song school and
458 'offered it on the altar'.

The right to hold a school must have been profitable, for
parents then as now were ready to make sacrifices that their
children might rise in the world. Walter Map remarked that
education was often the way by which men rose to higher
station. In this period as throughout and beyond the middle
ages the right of licensing schools and teachers belonged to
the bishop of the diocese. The archbishop of York delegated
the authority of licensing schools in Nottinghamshire to the
chancellor of Southwell minster. St Paul's school in London
was in being at a very early date. In Stephen's reign Henry
bishop of Winchester, then papal legate, ordered the chapter
of St Paul's and the archdeacon of London to excommunicate all those who presumed to teach in London without the
licence of Henry, the master of all the city schools. The
bishop exempted from the sentence the masters of the
459 schools of St Mary le Bow and St Martin le Grand. This
Henry, 'master of all the city schools', was a canon of St
Paul's, to whom St Paul's school had been granted some few
years earlier. He was a pupil of Master Hugh, who had
460 succeeded Master Durand as head of the same school. In
his description of London William fitz Stephen said that the
three principal churches of the city, the churches of St Paul,
Holy Trinity, and St Martin, 'have famous schools by

privilege and in virtue of their ancient dignity, but through the special favour of one or more of those learned men who are known and eminent in the study of philosophy there are other schools licensed by special grace and permission'. 461

It is by their works and not their records that these early schools are known. By the death of Henry II the ability to express a legal transaction in clear and grammatical Latin was possessed by hundreds of individuals in every part of the land. Their number steadily grew as the years passed on, and in the thirteenth century there can have been few centres of habitation, even in the deepest country, without someone who could produce in accurate Latin a set of accounts, a survey, or a deed of gift. The handwriting of these records is highly stylized, but varies in accordance with the writer's personality, the age of the man who had taught him, and the rate at which new fashions in calligraphy had spread outwards to his part of the country. The Latin of these obscure clerks can easily be undervalued. It has no pretensions to classical elegance. Its aim, which is also its virtue, was simplicity. But it could not have been acquired without prolonged instruction during boyhood, and its prevalence is evidence of an educational activity which those who wrote general histories ignored.

In the twelfth century the Roman Empire and its successor, the Carolingian Empire, dominated men's conception of the past, and learned men looked back to the Latin culture of antiquity as the origin and source of their own studies. No vernacular language had yet become a language of the schools which could compete with Latin. Scholars were at home with one another from whatever land they came, for Latin was the common language of learning. All over the west boys who wanted to sit at the feet of scholars left home at fourteen or fifteen, and went to some town or city where famous teachers had settled with episcopal licence and under the protection of the Church, in the hope that their teaching would attract a group of students. The schools at Paris were the most famous of these congregations, but already before 1150 a number of learned men were living and teaching in Oxford. Theobald archbishop of Canterbury (1138–61) had come from Bec, a monastery with a tradition of learning going back to Lanfranc's day. He gathered around him in his household a number of young men of distinction and brought to England a learned lawyer named Vacarius to act as his legal adviser. Vacarius stayed on in England and lectured for a time at Oxford, where he founded a school of Civil Law. For the use of poor students he wrote a textbook on Civil Law, known as the 462 Book of the Poor, *Liber Pauperum*. When Henry II, in 1167, during his quarrel with archbishop Becket, forbade English scholars and students to go to Paris and summoned all English clerks home on pain of losing their benefices Oxford was the place to which the majority of these masters and students went. By the beginning of the thirteenth century it has been estimated that there were approximately 1,500 463 students there.

It was inevitable that disputes should break out between scholars and townsmen when large numbers of young men under no adequate supervision were left to find themselves lodgings and manage their lives in a town where they had no personal ties. When the Interdict was laid on England in 1208 because the king would not accept Stephen Langton as archbishop violence was shown to clerks in many places by the populace, who resented the pope's action. Late in that year a student at Oxford murdered an Oxford woman in his lodgings and fled the town. A mob of townsmen, mistrusting the justice meted out to clerks, seized two of his fellow-lodgers, and, though they had nothing to do with the crime, hanged them outside the city walls. The schools were closed at once and the scholars went to other towns, notably Reading and Stamford. The settlement of this quarrel was made a part of the reordering of the affairs of church and state 464 after the excommunication was lifted in 1214. In giving his judgement about the Oxford quarrel the pope's representative in England tried to provide a machinery for arranging the rents of lodgings. As the practice was in Paris rents charged to students were to be assessed by a committee

consisting of four masters of the university and four burgesses of the town.

The rapid increase in the number of students in the years
after 1214, despite the fact that a flourishing community of
scholars was also established at Cambridge, meant that the
king was obliged to intervene in the interest of both the
scholars and the town. The position was made more difficult
in the universities in 1229 when the temporary dispersal of
the university of Paris sent many scholars to England.
Henry III despatched a series of letters on 3 May 1231 to
the sheriffs of the shires of Oxford and Cambridge and to the
mayors and bailiffs of the two towns. Each sheriff was to
cooperate with the bishop of the diocese and the chancellor
of the university in repressing 'rebellious and incorrigible'
students, especially those malefactors among the student
body, who 'pretend to be clerks and are not'. The king
ordered the sheriffs to see that no student remained in the
university who was not under the tutorship of a Master of
the schools. At the same time the respective mayors and
bailiffs were warned that their exorbitant rents were likely
to drive students away. The king ordered them to allow
their lodgings to be assessed in regard to rents in the
customary fashion. 'It is clear to us,' said the king, 'that both
from this country and from overseas a multitude of scholars
has come to our town of Cambridge, which is very pleasing
and acceptable to us, since no little advantage to our
kingdom and honour to us accrues therefrom.' 465

These letters show that the two universities have become
established institutions. Their sons were already in high
places in the Church and were using their influence to see
that beneficed clergy studied in the schools before they took
up their cure of souls. When Henry III issued these letters
the archbishop of Canterbury was Richard le Grant, an
eminent scholar who had been chancellor of Lincoln. He
died in August 1231 and a successor was not enthroned until
1234. But in that year the man whom Sir Maurice Powicke
calls 'the first great teacher in the schools at Oxford' became
archbishop. Edmund Rich was a native of Abingdon and 466

was remarkable for his saintliness as for his learning. In 1235 Robert Grosseteste became bishop of Lincoln. He had been chancellor of the university of Oxford. It may have been a realization that the schools of Oxford and Cambridge had justified a privileged position which influenced the king in 1234 to prohibit the study of civil law in the schools of 467 London.

Despite the position of dignity and influence to which the schools at Oxford and at Cambridge had arrived it is difficult to over-stress the rudimentary character of university organization in this age. There were as yet no colleges and students had complete freedom to come and go as they wished. There were no vacations, no organized games, and no examinations. It was only in 1231, when the king made his strong directions to the sheriffs about university discipline that the universities themselves began the attempt to supervise students. Every student was thence-forward required to put his name on the roll of some Regent Master and attend daily at least one morning lecture given 468 by the Master with whom he was enrolled. The Masters were required to satisfy themselves that their students were of good character and to see that they were assiduous in their studies. But these directions failed to achieve their end. In the thirteenth century the university authorities did not show themselves very competent in the management either of their young students or of their financial affairs. In 1249 William of Durham bequeathed to the university of Oxford 310 marks to be invested for the support of Masters of Arts who were studying theology; but the money was lent with-469 out security and much of it was lost.

The first Oxford college was founded in stages between 1264 and 1274 by Walter of Merton, chancellor under both Henry III and his son. The statutes which Merton finally drew up for his foundation provided that such scholars as the revenues of the endowment could support should lead a common life as a corporate body under a warden. The virtue of this foundation appealed at once to both the universities. At Oxford the masters supported by William of

Durham's bequest were converted into University College. Balliol College was soon established on similar lines, while at Cambridge the statutes of Merton College at Oxford were taken as the model for the foundation of Peterhouse. Only the beginnings of college history fall into this period. When it ended the colleges were tiny institutions in which a few scholars who were already graduates enjoyed opportunities of further study.

Undergraduates lived in halls or in rooms. A hall was simply a house occupied exclusively by students under the charge of a Principal. He was generally a graduate, and he leased the house from its owner in order to let it out in rooms to students. He made his profit from letting the rooms and from teaching. The catering was undertaken by another officer, called a manciple, who provided the common meals of the hall and made his profit out of them. The university had no property in the halls, but it had been established that once a house was let as a hall for students it could not be converted to a private residence, unless the owner wished to live in it himself, so long as someone desired to rent it as an academic hall. The rents were fixed by assessors as had been prescribed in 1214 and their assessment was reconsidered every five years. Repairs must be done by the landlord, but if he did not do them when they had been asked for, the Principal, that is, the lessee of the hall, might have them done and deduct their cost from his rent. It was to these Principals that the university looked to aid them in keeping order among the students. The Oxford of 1307 was very different from the Oxford of today when all but one of the halls are gone and all but one of the colleges are overflowing with undergraduates, but in 1307 everything that was essential to the future development of the university had been secured.

*

Every cathedral and innumerable parish churches, the ruins 470 of abbeys and priories all over England, even its remotest parts, bear witness to the remarkable architectural achievements of the period between 1066 and 1307. The Normans in the generations immediately preceding the Conquest were in the forefront of those who were experimenting in the building of churches which could be protected from complete destruction by fire. It was not until the lifetime of the Conqueror himself, and very little before the invasion of England, that Norman builders succeeded in covering the main span of the church with a stone vault. The plan of a Norman church of the pre-Conquest period was simple. The choir, with two bays, ended in an apse. The transepts had in each arm a chapel with an apse, so that the east end of the church had the large central apse and a smaller one each side of it. A central tower was raised over the point where the transepts crossed between the choir and the nave, which was aisled and might or might not have twin towers at the west end. Very little decoration, and that crude and barbaric, distinguished the churches being built in the duchy before 1066.

The work of English builders of the age before the Conquest can be judged only from such parish churches as escaped destruction in the period of church building which began after William I's rule was secured in 1070. No Anglo-Saxon cathedral satisfied a Norman bishop. Canterbury cathedral itself was partially destroyed by fire in 1067 and archbishop Lanfranc began to build its successor soon after he was consecrated in 1070. His church was seven years in building, but it did not satisfy the pride of the monks of Canterbury. At the turn of the next century a larger choir was begun which was not completed until 1130. In the case of most cathedrals the ground plan of the Anglo-Saxon church is beyond recall. Of the ancient church which stood on the site of Southwell minster all that is left are two loose baluster shafts and a large carved stone showing Scandinavian motifs built into the north transept to serve as a lintel. All that can be seen of the Lincoln cathedral built by Remigius, the first bishop, is the west front with its two towers, all now set in later work. It includes a barbaric representation of Noah in the ark.

Anglo-Norman architects, while very generally preserving the ground-plan of the churches built in Normandy, quickly departed from the austerity of the early Norman models, both in decoration and in scale. But it was some time before they succeeded in dealing easily with problems of vaulting. In Blyth church, Nottinghamshire, built before 1090, the side aisles have a primitive form of vaulting. It seems doubtful whether any of the early Anglo-Norman cathedral churches were vaulted in stone across the nave. Lincoln cathedral was burned in 1141, after which bishop Alexander vaulted the nave in stone. The outstanding Anglo-Norman church is the cathedral at Durham begun by bishop William in 1093. Its builders had twenty years' experience in England to draw on, and both in plan and decoration it outstripped anything attempted at an earlier date. Its building continued all through Rannulf Flambard's episcopate and when he died in 1128 the nave had been carried up to the roof. It was finished in 1133. Within seventy years of the Conquest, with the building of a great cathedral having a complete system of ribbed vaulting, the Norman architects in England had surpassed the achievements of their European contemporaries.

By the reign of Henry I both architects and masons had achieved complete mastery of the particular form of architecture associated with the Normans. Much of the work of those generations has not survived, either because it fell down, like the central tower of Worcester in 1175, or because later generations wished to replace it by buildings in a different style. Old Sarum was deserted in the early part of the thirteenth century for the new town of Salisbury. Very little remains of the early Norman church built by bishop Gundulf (1077–1108) at Rochester. The central tower of the first Norman church at Winchester fell in 1107, but the crypt and transepts survive. The walls and piers of the nave are essentially those of the Norman church, although considerable renovation has been done. Nearly the whole of Norwich cathedral, begun by bishop Herbert Losinga in 1096 and completed under his successor before

1145, remains today. Ely cathedral preserves the greater part of a Norman church of the first class. St Albans shows large-scale Norman construction in Roman brick. There is no more perfect example of the best work of the early twelfth century than the nave of Southwell, begun between 1108 and 1114. It has none of the ostentation of the carved pillars and vaulted roof of Durham, but its solid majesty gives the impression of unshakable strength.

Between the building of Southwell minster and the beginning of Henry II's reign the simplicity of early Norman work has disappeared and ornament was inserted wherever opportunity offered. Capitals were richly carved and the mouldings of arches were decorated in a variety of forms, some of them certainly derived from local English inspiration, though their ultimate origin may be Scandinavian or Celtic. The space within an archway above a door was filled by carved stonework, often of figures barbarically executed. It was not until the latter part of the twelfth century that figure sculpture in England achieved a realistic appearance. Before the end of the century, partly under the influence of the Cistercians, who began their church building with a determination to return to primitive simplicity, English architects were moving towards the Early English forms. Between 1174 and 1184 the choir at Canterbury was extended under the direction of William of Sens, who planned a building with pointed arches with the vault supported on flying buttresses. St Hugh's new choir at Lincoln built in the early thirteenth century was purely 'Gothic' or 'Early English' in style. The Early English choir at Southwell can be closely dated, for archbishop Walter Grey issued an indulgence in 1235 for those who contributed 471 towards the work going on at Southwell. The Angel choir at Lincoln belongs to the latter part of the century and is contemporary with the chapter house at Southwell.

The Decorated chapter house of Southwell can be dated very nearly by a statute of archbishop John Romaine of 1292 ordering that certain money coming into the chapter 472 shall be applied to the fabric of the new chapter house. It is a smaller building than the chapter house of York but despite its elaborate decoration it gives an impression of chaste simplicity and perfect rightness. This effect is partly achieved by the symmetry and lightness of its construction and by the omission of a central pillar. The carvings of the capitals and of the wall arcadings were done by a master who knew the local hedgerows, where the plants that formed his models still grow today. He had achieved absolute mastery of the art of shaping recalcitrant stone into the similitude of growing leaves.

As in regard to architecture so in regard to letters the year 1066 marks a break. It would be wrong to say that in the early Norman period English speech, traditions, and culture were despised. The Normans knew well enough that English nobility was a real nobility resting on long history. English culture was respected among contemporary peoples. Such English nobles as weathered the first storms were accepted as equals by the newcomers. Earl Waltheof of Northampton was married to a niece of the Conqueror himself. But the majority of the English nobility had been killed and most of the rest had fled, so that soon the highest ranks of society had but little English leaven. The barons of Domesday Book were Frenchmen and regarded themselves as such. Under these circumstances it was inevitable that the English language should become unfashionable as the Normans came to dominate England in Church as well as state. Englishmen of the Norman age were sadly conscious that their native learning had fallen into disregard. Nevertheless 473 it was in English, and English which its modern editor can describe as 'magnificently alive', that the monks of Peterborough described the Conqueror himself and the miseries of Stephen's reign. Copies of Old English works were multi- 474 plied in the twelfth century. One of king Alfred's books is known only from a manuscript written in this age. Students of Old English literature owe some of their best material to the fact that at Exeter an English library, including a great treasury of Anglo-Saxon verse, was preserved by a Norman bishop who had known and revered Edward the Confessor. 475

The French nobility in England were dealing daily with an English tenantry. English land customs were protected and English courts of justice were preserved by the will of the Conqueror himself. English nurses and servants looked after the children born in England to the new lords. Although the second generation of Normans still regarded French as their national speech they were equally at home speaking English. Writing about 1170, Richard fitz Nigel said that 'nowadays when Normans and Englishmen live close together and marry each other it can scarcely be determined, that is in the case of free men, who is of English and who of Norman birth'. Before the end of the century the fact that Richard I's chancellor could not speak the native tongue was an additional reason for his unpopularity. But there is little evidence that in the twelfth century there was an audience for poems, stories, or treatises written in English. There was much in the twelfth century to encourage a European rather than a strictly national outlook. The main currents of English trade had shifted from Scandinavia to France, the Rhineland, and beyond it, to the Mediterranean. The Crusades drew men of all classes to the Holy Land, though it is true that quarrels between those of different nations often hindered the common effort. In Europe there was a constant stream of pilgrims as well as ordinary travellers on the roads leading to Rome. The Pope's headship of the church was maintained by constant intercourse between Rome and other lands. Latin was a true international language of the learned and those who wished to become scholars were rarely content to spend all their lives in the country of their birth without going to sit at the feet of masters in the schools of Paris or Bologna or Salerno.

The historical writers of the twelfth century wrote in Latin because it was the language of scholarship, not because they disdained to write in English or in French. Their writings show an increasing pride in England and its native traditions. The first of these writers is Ordric Vitalis, son of a Frenchman from Orleans, and born only nine years after the Conquest. At the age of 10 he was sent to become a monk in a Norman monastery, where his friends called him Vitalis the Englishman because they could not easily say his English name. He had been called Ordric after the priest who baptized him. Ordric wrote a history of Norman achievements, but he wrote and thought of himself as an Englishman in exile, though there is no evidence that any English blood flowed in his veins. Writing at the age of 67 the closing passages of his long history, he describes how as a child he had come over as an exile into Normandy, and had heard, like Joseph in Egypt, a tongue he did not know. William of Malmesbury, a most accom- 477 plished scholar of Anglo-Norman descent, who was proud of his English background, deliberately followed the example of Bede in writing history as distinct from bio- graphy or annals. 478

Henry I applied himself to uniting his Norman and his English subjects into a single nation. His own marriage to Maud of Scotland, who could represent through her mother the West Saxon royal house, was an assurance of his good- will towards Englishmen. In 1106 the king recovered Normandy from his elder brother, whom he defeated at Tenchebrai with an army composed partly at least of Englishmen. This victory did much to restore the national pride of the native English and to encourage a common feeling between all the king's subjects in England. This feeling is reflected in the imaginative writings of Geoffrey of Monmouth, bishop of St Asaph, who was born at about the beginning of the twelfth century. He wrote with exaggerated pride of the exploits of king Arthur. There was in the twelfth century a large Anglo-Norman audience for tales of the great doings of the former inhabitants of Britain.

William of Malmesbury and Ordericus Vitalis were early members of a succession of Latin historians through whose writings the leading actors on the contemporary stage stand out with singular clarity. These historians differed markedly from one another in education, experience, and natural ability, and their opportunities for acquiring information were by no means equal. Some of them were monks, like

Eadmer of Canterbury at the beginning of the twelfth century and Gervase of Canterbury at its end. In the thirteenth century St Albans produced both the ineffective and inaccurate Roger of Wendover and the brilliant – perhaps over-brilliant – Matthew Paris. Some of them were secular clergymen like Henry of Huntingdon, who served three successive bishops of Lincoln as an archdeacon, and Ralf de Diceto, who as Dean of St Paul's lived in the very heart of the national life. From the central years of Henry II until the early years of John the course of events in England and Normandy can be followed in minute and accurate detail in two chronicles which in their way are as remarkable illustrations of their age as Glanville's treatise on the Laws of England and Richard fitz Nigel's Dialogue about the Exchequer. One of them has long been known by the name of Benedict abbot of Peterborough. It has recently been established that both these works come from the pen of 479 Roger parson of Howden in south Yorkshire. These chronicles, in their precision of fact, the fullness of their political information, and their disinterested outlook, approach more nearly to the character of official narratives than any other medieval histories. There is no evidence that either of these works were written at the king's direction, but it is hard to believe that they lacked his approval.

French remained the language of the court and of aristocratic circles. Poems and stories were being written in French throughout this period. In Stephen's reign Gaimar was describing the remote past of England in French verse for the entertainment of Ralf fitz Gilbert and other south Lincolnshire barons. Contemporary events which stirred the imagination were frequently turned into French verse. The great rebellion of 1174, in the course of which William the Lion king of Scotland invaded England and was captured, produced a French poem by Jordan Fantosme, a secular clerk who in Richard of Anstey's story appears in attendance on bishop Henry of Winchester. The group of narratives inspired by the martyrdom of archbishop Thomas Becket includes a French poem, as accurate as any of them, which transmitted the story to an audience hardly to be reached by the devotional Latin of the Saint's other biographers. The story of Anglo-Norman adventure in Ireland is told in the French 'Song of Dermot and the Earl'. The most famous of these verse histories in French is a long account of the adventures of William the Marshal who married the heiress of the earl of Pembroke and was created earl himself by king John. The author was John of Earley, a tenant of the earl, who tried, like Fantosme and the author of the Song of Dermot, to tell a true story, but inevitably tended to exaggerate the importance of his hero. Stories about real people who for some reason had fallen into trouble with the king or the law were always popular, and strict adherence to the truth was neither expected nor desired. To this type of story belongs the French prose romance of Fulk fitz Warin, a lord in the Marches of Wales who caused considerable trouble there early in John's reign.

During the twelfth century there was formulated in France, arising out of the new romantic atmosphere, an artificial code of love and courtesy. It produced writers of *lays* or poems about the tournaments in which lovers and husbands take part. The most famous writer of these lays says of herself 'My name is Marie and I am of France.' She says, too, that she collected and translated her lays in honour of a noble king, that she translated Aesop's fables from English for love of 'count William', and that for the Lord's sake and the use of laymen she turned the Purgatory of St Patrick into French. Many suggestions have been made about the identity of Marie of France. That the noble king was Henry II and that 'count William' was his illegitimate son, William earl of Salisbury, is now generally accepted. The most likely suggestion about the identity of Marie herself seems to be that she is Mary abbess of Shaftesbury, an illegitimate daughter of Geoffrey count of Anjou, and therefore half-sister of Henry II. Although 480 Marie of France herself knew both Latin and English her translations imply that she hardly expected her audience to be able to appreciate the fables in their original English.

The poet Orm, who wrote in Yorkshire in Henry II's reign, was certainly not writing for the court. There is nothing to suggest that he wrote for anyone's pleasure but his own, and he must be regarded as a solitary portent. But at the end of the twelfth or early in the thirteenth century there appeared works in English intended for a popular audience, the so-called Proverbs of Alfred and Layamon's Brut, the last work consisting of tales of the British past. The work in English prose known as the Ancrene Riwle is more remarkable. It claims to be written for three ladies who had renounced the world to become anchoresses and aims at providing them with advice on the anchoress's way of life. Before long it was worked over and, as the Ancrene Wisse, was made to serve a community of men. Both versions were written in English for people of Norman or Anglo-Norman descent. No great quantity of literature in English has survived from the thirteenth century, but what is known shows an increasing versatility. The simple lyric known as 'The Cuckoo Song' was set in Reading to music of elaborate sophistication. The long satirical dialogue 'The Owl and the Nightingale', the English version of the romance 'Floriz and Blanchflur', and the story of 'The Vox and the Wolf' shows that an English audience existed for the same sort of literature as was being written in their own 481 tongue for contemporaries in other parts of Europe.

Throughout this period Latin was the language in which official records were kept, charters and writs were written, and diplomatic correspondence was conducted. It was the language of the law and of judicial records. Up to the middle of the thirteenth century no lawyer would have written a legal treatise in any other language than Latin. But in the latter half of the century French was gaining ground at the expense of Latin. The great treatise on the laws of England written in the middle of the century by Henry of Bracton is in Latin, but Britton recast Bracton's treatise and brought it up to date in French in Edward I's reign. In that reign, too, while the formal record of cases was enrolled in Latin, clerks were taking down in French the discussions between the judges and counsel about the cases which came before them. These judges and clerks very well knew that in substance it mattered not at all in what language they talked and wrote. The law that they administered was the national law of England, based on accepted custom, modified by statute and the practice in the courts.

The English people at the end of this period were still fully conscious of their Anglo-Norman origin and of the fact that their king still claimed to hold lands in France. But in whatever language they chose to speak or to write there was no doubt of their common loyalty to their own land and their realization of its identity. The men of London already [482] under John expressed a belief in their own right to control the narrow seas. In the middle of the century the baronage, in revolt against a king who leaned too strongly on foreign clerks and rewarded too richly his foreign kinsfolk, reiterated their determination that castles shall not be entrusted to the care of aliens and that English heiresses shall not be married where they are disparaged 'that is, to men not of the nation of the realm of England'. [483]

ANNOTATIONS

ANNOTATIONS

1. See F. M. Stenton, 'The Danes in England', *Proceedings of the British Academy*, vol. xiii, p. 241.
2. F. M. Stenton, 'The Scandinavian Colonies in England and Normandy', *Transactions of the Roy. Hist. Soc.*, 4th series, vol. xxvii, pp. 1–12.
3. Florence E. Harmer, *Anglo Saxon Writs*, Manchester, 1952.
4. Sir Frank Stenton, *The Bayeux Tapestry*, London, 1957.
5. Anglo-Saxon Chronicle *sub anno* 1100.
6. For the Latin text of Walter Map's *De Nugis Curialium*, see *Anecdota Oxoniensia*, ed. M. R. James, 1914. References here given are to the English translation by M. R. James published by the Honorable Society of Cymmrodorion, Record Series, No. ix, although the Latin text was used in writing, so that differences of wording may be noticed.
7. Map, p. 242.
8. Map, p. 259.
9. Map. pp. 242–3.
10. *Oderici Vitalis Historiae . . .*, ed. le Prevost, vol. iv, p. 164.
11. R. L. Poole, *The Exchequer in the Twelfth Century*, Oxford, 1912, Chapter III. Queen Edith's ability is attested by an encomiast:

> *De Regina Editha*
> *Nobilitas patrum te magnificauit Editha . . .*
> *Multa tibi spes fuit et sapientia multa .*
> *Sidera . mensuras . abachum monochordam et arte .*
> *discendique modos gramaticumque doces .*
> (Cott. Vit. A x ii, 131 b.)

12. *Magnus Rotulus Scaccarii . . . de anno tricesimo primo Regni Henrici primi*, ed. J. Hunter, 1833.
13. *Regesta Regum Anglo-Normannorum* vol. i, ed. H. W. C. Davis (Oxford), 1913, contains those of William I and William II; vol. ii, ed. Charles Johnson and H. A. Cronne, Oxford, 1956, contains those of Henry I. For an account of the development of the courts of Justice between 1066 and 1215 and their dependence on achievements of the Anglo-Saxon period see D. M. Stenton, *English Justice between the Norman Conquest and the Great Charter*, Philadelphia, 1964, and London, 1965.
14. *The Red Book of the Exchequer*, ed. H. Hall, Rolls Series, 1896, vol. iii, pp. 807–13. For a Latin text and translation see *Dialogus de Scaccario*, ed. C. Johnson, Nelson's Medieval Classics, 1950, pp. 129–35. Again the Latin text has been used in this book, but references are to the Nelson volume.
15. E.g. Pipe Rolls 4, 8, and 10 John, pp. respectively 93, 55, and 49.

The Pipe Rolls are, unless stated to the contrary, published by the Pipe Roll Society.

16. For the Chancellor of one of the king's greatest subjects, the earl of Chester, *see* F. M. Stenton, *The First Century of English Feudalism 1066–1166*, second ed., 1961, pp. 35 and 260.
17. *Sir Christopher Hatton's Book of Seals*, ed. L. C. Loyd and D. M. Stenton, 1950, No. 39, pl. 1.
18. *Complete Peerage*, 2nd ed., *sub* Oxford.
19. *Rotuli de . . . Misis . . .*, ed. T. D. Hardy, 1844. When the author wrote this book she was not, as she has since become, the owner of *Documents illustrative of English History in the Thirteenth and Fourteenth Centuries*, ed. H. Cole, 1844, in which more wardrobe accounts from John's fourteenth year are printed, pp. 231–69.
20. *Rotuli de . . . Misis*, p. 115.
21. *Ibid.*, p. 137.
22. *Ibid.*, p. 170. The King's baths were costing much the same four years later; 4½d. each at Odiham and Carlisle, Cole p. 237; 6d. at Havering, but only 3d. at Rochester, *ibid.*, p. 262.
23. *Rotuli de . . . Misis*, p. 159.
24. *Ibid.*, p. 120. Cole, p. 243.
25. Pipe Roll 22 Henry II, p. 122: 'pro xxxiiij libris zuccare . . . xxv solidos et vj denarios'.
26. Pipe Roll 8 John, p. 48: 'pro zucara et aliis speciebus'. Luxuries were beginning to come to the king's table in the latter part of John's reign. Almonds, dates, and figs are mentioned in the Pipe Roll of 13 John, pp. 108, 178; in the roll of 16 John almonds, figs, and rice, Pipe Roll, p. 79.
27. J. H. Round, *The King's Serjeants and Officers of State*, London, 1911. For 'money fiefs' see Bruce Lyon, 'The Money Fief under the English Kings', *Eng. Hist. Rev.*, vol. lxvi (1953), pp. 161–93.
28. *Ibid.*, pp. 143–4.
29. *Red Book*, vol. ii, pp. 755–60.
30. For these three serjeanties see Round, *King's Serjeants*, pp. 177–86.
31. Map, p. 266.
32. A robe for the messenger of the Sultan of Babylon cost 66 shillings in 1207, but 25 shillings was paid on the same account for a robe for William Revel, Pipe Roll 9 John, pp. 30–31. The price of robes varied greatly with their trimmings, see under *roba* in the Indexes to the Pipe Rolls.

   In January 1208 the king ordered for a chaplain a robe of virid or burnet with a hood of coney skin 'like our other chaplains', *Rotuli Litterarum Clausarum*, vol. i, p. 99b.
33. T. F. Tout, *Chapters in the Administrative History of Medieval England*, 1920–33, vol. ii, pp. 158–63.
34. T. F. Tout, *The Place of Edward II in English History*, 1914, pp. 270–314, for the text of the Ordinance of 1318, which refers to earlier household ordinances which have not survived.

35. Map, p. 262.
36. J. H. Round, *Peerage and Family History*, 1901, pp. 169–72.
37. Map, p. 261.
38. *Rolls of the Justices in Eyre for ... Warwickshire*, Selden Society, vol. lix, pp. 167–8.
39. Map. p. 265.
40. This important document is printed in full with a translation in *The Collected Works of Sir Francis Palgrave*, vol. vii, 'The Rise and Progress of the English Constitution', part 2, text, pp. 110–19, translation and notes, pp. 5–29. Dr P. M. Barnes has printed a new Latin text with a valuable introduction in *A Medieval Miscellany for D. M. Stenton*, Pipe Roll Soc., N.S., xxxvi, pp. 1–24.
41. Map, p. 277.
42. Map, p. 277.
43. *De Legibus et Consuetudinibus Regni Angliae*, ed. G. E. Woodbine, Yale, 1932. G. D. G. Hall's edition of Glanville with introduction, Latin text, translation, and notes will be published in Nelson's Medieval Classics in 1965.
44. *Dialogus de Scaccario* with Introduction, Latin text, translation, and notes, Nelson's Medieval Classics, 1950, ed. Charles Johnson.
45. L. Landon, *Itinerary of Richard I*, Pipe Roll Society, N.S., vol. xiii.
46. *William of Newburgh*, ed. H. C. Hamilton, English Historical Society, 1856, vol. ii, pp. 12–13.
47. Pipe Roll 10 Richard I, p. xxxiii.
48. *Foedera*, London, 1816, vol. i, part i, pp. 75–6, *Constitutio Regis de feodis magni sigilli*.
49. *A Description of the Patent Rolls to which is added an Itinerary of King John*, Record Commission, 1835.
50. See the introductions to successive Pipe Rolls for the reigns of Richard I and John, P.R.S.
51. D. M. Stenton, *English Justice*, 'King John and the courts of Justice', pp. 88 ff.
52. *Ibid.*, p. 94.
53. *Rot. Litt. Pat.*, p. 47b.
54. S. Smith, Pipe Roll 7 John, pp. xiii–xxi.
55. S. Smith, Pipe Roll 7 John, pp. xxvii–xxxii.
56. Pipe Roll 10 John, p. 46; *Rotuli Chartarum*, p. 171b; *Rot. Litt. Pat.*, p. 75b.
57. *Rot. Litt. Pat.*, p. 57.
58. *Ibid.*, p. 33.
59. *Rot. Litt. Claus.*, vol. i, p. 111.
60. See K. Norgate, *John Lackland*, Note II, pp. 289–93.
61. See Introductions to the Pipe Rolls of John's reign, particularly 10 John and afterwards.
62. A recent contribution to the literature of the Charter is an article by A. J. Collins, 'The Documents of the Great Charter of 1215', *Proceedings of the British Academy*, vol. xxxiv, pp. 233ff. He argues

that a single charter was prepared to be sealed before the barons and was entrusted by them to the archbishop. This is very likely, but it in no way detracts from the importance of the four surviving copies of the charter, each of which was sent out under the great seal and is therefore an 'original'. The year 1965 will be the 750th anniversary of the Great Charter and will see the publication of an important book by Professor Holt. In the United States a volume is being prepared by The Magna Carta Commission of the State of Virginia.

63. Roger of Wendover, Rolls Series, vol. ii, p. 198.
64. Pipe Roll 11 John, p. xiv.
65. Pipe Roll 12 John, p. xxxii.
66. Tout, *Chapters*, vol. i, pp. 67–9.
67. For a discussion of the earliest wardrobe accounts, see Tout, *Chapters*, vol. i, pp. 192–9.
68. Tout, *Chapters*, vol. i, pp. 206–13.
69. *Dialogus*, pp. 28–9.
70. Pipe Roll 11 John, pp. xxv and 16–17.
71. M. Mills, 'Experiments in Exchequer Procedure' and 'Reforms at the Exchequer' in *Transactions of the Roy. Hist. Soc.*, 4th series, vols. viii, 1925, and x, 1927.
72. *Close Rolls Henry III 1231–34*, pp. 64 and 392.
73. A. E. Stamp, 'The Court and Chancery of Henry III' in *Essays in Honour of James Tait*, pp. 305–11.
74. L. Landon, *Itinerary of Richard I*, pp. 181–2.
75. Stubbs, *Charters*, 9th ed., p. 383.
76. *Memoranda de Parliamento*, ed. F. W. Maitland, Rolls Series, pp. lvi–lvii. This seminal work began the modern treatment of the origin and purpose of Parliament.
77. Tout, *Edward II*, p. 313.
78. F. M. Stenton, *English Feudalism*, pp. 132–3
79. *Ibid.*, pp. 136–42, for the household knight.
80. See pictures in the *Bayeux Tapestry*.
81. Peterborough Chronicle, *sub anno* 1085.
82. *Dialogus*, p. 64.
83. *Ibid.*, loc. cit.
84. F. M. Stenton, *Anglo-Saxon England*, pp. 626–7.
85. W. Dugdale, *The Baronage of England*, London, 1675, vol. i, p. 257.
86. *Red Book*, vol. i, p. 338, where Curzun is spelt 'Curceini', *Historical Collections for Staffordshire*, vol. i, pp. 211–12, and *Records of the Templars in England in the Twelfth Century*, ed. B. A. Lees, pp. 191–2.
87. Stubbs, *Charters*, p. 126; *Leges Henrici Primi*, 55, i and i a.
88. *Book of Seals*, No. 301, plate V, and p. xxxvii.
89. *Red Book*, vol. i, pp. 336–40.
90. *English Feudalism*, pp. 51–4 and 263–4.
91. *Leges Henrici Primi*, 55, 3.
92. *Book of Seals*, No. 528, p. 366.

93. W. A. Morris, *English Historical Review*, vol. xxxvi, 1921, p. 45.
94. *English Feudalism*, p. 189.
95. *Danelaw Charters*, ed. F. M. Stenton (British Academy Record Series), London, 1920, pp. cxxxi and 390.
96. Printed in *Collectanea Topographica et Genealogica*, vol. ii, 1835, p. 163.
97. *English Feudalism*, pp. 172–7.
98. Stubbs, *Charters*, pp. 442–3.
99. *Rotuli de dominabus . . .*, Pipe Roll Society, 1st Series, vol. xxxv, p. 85.
100. Pipe Roll 6 Richard I, p. 163.
101. *Ancestor*, vol. xi, p. 153.
102. *Book of Seals*, pp. xxxvii–xxxviii, and No. 298, p. 205.
103. *Ibid.*, p. 279.
104. *English Feudalism*, pp. 158–9, see also p. 169.
105. *Ibid.*, pp. 164–8.
106. A. R. Wagner, *Historic Heraldry of Britain*, p. 40. See also J. H. Round, 'The Introduction of Armorial Bearings into England', *Archaeological Journal*, March 1894, pp. 43–8.
107. Pipe Roll 6 John, pp. xxxiv and 213.
108. *Ibid.*, p. 120.
109. Geoffrey of Monmouth, *Historiae Regum Britanniae*, Book i, chap. 1.
110. *Ibid.*, Book vii, chap. 1.
111. Benedict of Peterborough, Rolls Series, vol. i, p. 226.
112. Roger of Howden, Rolls Series, vol. iii, p. 202.
113. See the article by A. R. Wagner on 'Heralds and Heraldry' in *Chambers' Encyclopaedia*, 1950.
114. Geoffrey of Monmouth, Book ix, chap. 4.
115. *Chronicon Radulphi de Coggeshall*, ed. J. Stevenson, Rolls Series, p. 179.
116. William of Newburgh, Eng. Hist. Soc., vol. ii, pp. 127–8.
117. *Simeon of Durham* (continued by John of Hexham), vol. ii, p. 312.
118. N. Denholm-Young, in his valuable article, 'The Tournament in the Thirteenth Century', *Essays Presented to F. M. Powicke*, wrongly identifies Stamford with the place of that name in Suffolk between Thetford and Bury. He gives no reason, but suggests that it was an East Anglian tournament field. The present sandy waste south of Thetford may have been very different then. Nor have we any evidence that sandy country was suitable for the sport. East Anglians could easily get to the Great North Road.
119. Both writ and form of peace are printed *Foedera*, p. 65.
120. The only mention of tournament money in the Pipe Rolls is an incidental one, the payment of 100 marks from tournaments to the king by Geoffrey fitz Peter, Pipe Roll 10 Richard I, p. 64.
121. Benedict of Peterborough, vol. i, p. 350.
122. *D.N.B.*
123. *Rotuli de . . . Misis*, p. 123.
124. Roger of Wendover, vol. ii, pp. 137–8.

125. K. Major, *Acta Stephani Langton*, Oxford, 1950, p. 62. The tournament was at Staines.
126. Matthew Paris, *Chronica Majora*, ed. H. R. Luard, Rolls Series, vol. iii, p. 404. This tournament was held at Blyth, Notts, one of Richard's tournament grounds, and, moreover, on the borders of Northern and Midland England.
127. *Ibid.*, vol. iv, pp. 627–8.
128. *Ibid.*, p. 633.
129. *Ibid.*, p. 644.
130. *Ibid.*, p. 649.
131. *Ibid.*, vol. v, pp. 17–18.
132. *Ibid.*, pp. 54–5.
133. *Ibid.*, p. 83.
134. *Ibid.*, p. 265.
135. *Annales Monastici* (Tewkesbury), Rolls Series, vol. i, p. 151.
136. Matthew Paris, vol. v, p. 318.
137. *Book of Seals*, No. 64 and n., pp. 65–6.
138. *L'estoire de Guillaume le Maréchal*, ed. P. Meyer, Paris, 1901, vol. i, lines 2471–5094.
139. Stubbs, *Charters*, pp. 183–4.
140. M. G. Demay, *Le costume de guerre et d'apparat d'après les sceaux du moyen age*, Paris, 1875, pp. 8–9.
141. See note 90.
142. J. H. Round, *Feudal England*, pp. 270–2.
143. In 1184 the rate was a shilling a day in English money and 4 shillings in Angevin money, Pipe Roll 30 Henry II, p. xxviii and n.
144. *Rot. Litt. Pat.*, p. 55 (1205); Roger of Howden, vol. iv, p. 40 (1197–8).
145. Ralf de Diceto, ed. Stubbs, Rolls Series, vol. ii, p. lxxix.
146. Roger of Howden, vol. iv, p. 40.
147. Pipe Roll 6 John, pp. 36–7.
148. Pipe Roll 7 John, p. 129.
149. *Rot. Litt. Pat.*, p. 55.
150. S. Smith, Introduction to Pipe Roll 7 John, pp. xii–xviii.
151. D. M. Stenton, *English Justice*, chap. I.
152. Published respectively in the Lincoln Record Soc., vol. xxii, the Northamptonshire Record Soc., vol. v, and the Bedfordshire Historical Record Soc., vol. i. In the last volume only Beds cases are printed, but the omitted cases are printed in one or other of the two previous volumes.
153. Published by the Selden Soc., vol. liii.
154. Pipe Roll 10 John, p. 13.
155. Stubbs, *Charters*, p. 378.
156. *Ibid.*, *loc. cit.*
157. *Rolls of the Justices in Eyre for Lincolnshire*, Selden Soc., vol. liii, pp. lix–lx.

158. Close Rolls 1234–7, p. 156.
159. *Ibid.*, p. 38.
160. Quoted by N. Denholm-Young in his suggestive article, 'Feudal Society in the Thirteenth Century', *History*, 1944, pp. 107–19.
161. Roger of Wendover, vol. ii, p. 283.
162. Matthew Paris, vol. iv, pp. 85–6.
163. *Ibid.*, vol. v, pp. 267–9.
164. *Liber de Antiquibus Legibus*, ed. T. Stapleton, Camden Soc., 1846, p. 154.
165. *Annales Monastici*, vol. ii, p. 402.
166. *Dialogus*, pp. 59–60.
167. *Ibid.*, p. 60.
168. J. Manwood, *A Treatise of the Lawes of the Forest*, London, 1615, p. 18 and dorso.
169. *Ibid.*, p. 19 and d.
170. *Book of Seals*, No. 304, plate viii.
171. Pipe Roll 11 John, p. 76.
172. For a map of the area under forest law in the thirteenth century see *Transactions of the Roy. Hist. Soc.*, 4th series, vol. iv, 1921, p. 140. It illustrates a valuable article by Miss M. L. Bazeley on the extent of the forest in this period. She includes, at p. 160, a map of Northants, showing how much of the county was still forest as late as the thirteenth century.
173. *Early Yorkshire Charters*, vol. iv, ed. C. T. Clay, p. 25.
174. *Rotuli de . . . Misis*, p. 144.
175. See successive Pipe Rolls *sub* Worcestershire.
176. *Select Pleas of the Forest*, ed. G. J. Turner, Selden Soc., vol. xiii, pp. x–xii. The introduction to this book still remains the best account of the forest in the thirteenth century. The whole book, with its carefully selected cases and its valuable notes, has been used as the basis of this section.
177. *Registrum Antiquissimum of Lincoln Cathedral*, ed. C. W. Foster, vol. i, p. 34.
178. *Ibid.*, p. 68.
179. *Ibid.*, p. 69. A series of charters issued by Henry II, right of warren over their lands in Lincs and over Banbury and Thame in Oxon are printed, pp. 67–71. The king prohibits anyone else to hunt there without the bishop's permission.
180. Turner, *op. cit.*, cix–xv.
181. *Rot. Chart.*, p. 194. The date of the charter is 24 July, 1213.
182. *Book of Seals*, No. 7, p. 5.
183. Pipe Roll 9 John, p. 124.
184. Pipe Roll 9 John, p. 185.
185. *Book of Seals*, No. 101, p. 67.
186. F. M. Powicke, *Henry III and the Lord Edward*, p. 150 and n.
187. This is a much simplified statement of the effect of introducing by statute a writ of trespass against poachers, which gave damages to

the plaintiff, a fine to the king, and imprisonment to the defendant. T. F. T. Plucknett, *Concise History of the Common Law*, 5th ed., London, 1956, p. 457.

188. *Dialogus*, p. 61.

189. Pipe Roll 10 Richard I, p. 187.

190. *Dialogus*, p. 59 and n.

191. See successive Pipe Roll indexes under *Foresta*.

192. Cl. 5, for the charter see Stubbs, *Charters*, pp. 344–8.

193. Cl. 6.

194. Cl. 8.

195. Cl. 10.

196. Manwood, p. 3.

197. Pipe Roll 2 Richard I, p. 155.

198. Pipe Roll 6 John, p. 32.

199. *Ibid.*, p. 40.

200. *Ibid.*, p. 85.

201. Pipe Roll 9 John, p. 185.

202. Cl. 1.

203. Turner, *op. cit.*, pp. 38–9. Professor Bruce Dickens has suggested that the record of this foray may show that in what was once the Danish earldom of Northampton the inhabitants, even as late as the thirteenth century, retained some of the sinister habits of their heathen Danish past. Those in the saga world who wished to show contempt for others set a horse's head on a hazel pole and made it gape towards them. Runes written on the pole added to its effectiveness. Here are no runes recorded, but the head is made to gape towards the south, where the king lived. For a recorded instance of this practice, see *Egil's Saga*, ed. E. R. Eddison, pp. 130–31, and for notes on it pp. 249–50.

204. Turner, *op. cit.*, p. 44.

205. *Ibid.*, p. 90.

206. *Ibid.*, pp. 96–8.

207. *Ibid.*, p. 102.

208. Cl. 11.

209. Turner, *op. cit.*, p. 113.

210. *Ibid.*, p. 13 and p. 78.

211. *Red Book*, vol. ii, p. 101.

212. Turner, *op. cit.*, p. 101.

213. *Ibid.*, p. 77.

214. *Ibid.*, p. 78.

215. *Ibid.*, p. 13.

216. Cl. 7.

217. Turner, *op. cit.*, pp. xxiii–xxiv and cxxxix, for foresters in fee.

218. Cl. 14.

219. Turner, *op. cit.*, pp. 127–8.

220. MSS of the family of Wylde of Nettleworth *penes* F.M.S.

221. *Rolls of the Justices in Eyre for . . . Worcestershire*, Selden Soc., vol. liii, pp. 488–9.
222. *Earliest Northamptonshire Assize Rolls*, case 764, pp. 125–6.
223. *Pleas of the Justices in Eyre for . . . Worcestershire*, pp. lxvi–lxvii and 448–9.
224. *Ibid.*, pp. lxvii and 462.
225. *Pleas of the Justices in Eyre for . . . Warwickshire*, Selden Soc., vol. lix, p. 190.
226. *Rolls of the Justices in Eyre for Yorkshire 1218–19*, ed. D. M. Stenton, Selden Soc., vol. lvi, pp. 394–5
227. T. F. T. Plucknett, *The Legislation of Edward I*, pp. 85–6.
228. C. S. and C. S. Orwin, *The Open Fields*, Oxford, 1938.
229. This phrase is often used to describe also the straight ridge and furrow ploughing practised as late as the early part of the present century for the purpose of drainage. Even pasture land was occasionally so treated in the nineteenth century.
230. It is recorded in the Cornish eyre of 1201 that an eight-ox plough-team caused the ploughman's death. He was dragged by it. *Pleas before the King or his Justices 1198–1202*, ed. D. M. Stenton, Selden Soc., vol. lxviii, p. 57, case 273. It is interesting to see the eight-ox plough team in use in Cornwall. Since the oil field was begun at Eakring during the Second World War and the War Agricultural Committee intervened to stop the old arrangements in favour of larger production, the old lands in the open fields have suffered from tractor ploughing which has obliterated the ancient headlands.
231. *Danelaw Charters*, pp. lvii–lviii.
232. Ed. E. Lamond, London, 1890.
233. H. P. R. Finberg, *Tavistock Abbey*, Cambridge, 1951.
234. *Danelaw Charters*, p. 332.
235. *Ibid.*, pp. 394–5 and 397.
236. E. Power, *The Medieval English Wool Trade*, Oxford, 1941, is an account of the English wool trade and sheep-farming based on prolonged research.
237. *Danelaw Charters*, pp. xxxvii and references.
238. *Earliest Lincolnshire Assize Rolls*, p. 116.
239. Pipe Roll 10 Richard I, p. xiv and references.
240. *Red Book*, vol. i, p. 364.
241. *Lincolnshire Domesday*, ed. C. W. Foster and T. Longley, Lincoln Record Society, vol. xix, p. 93.
242. *Ibid.*, p. 203, see also pp. 57, 81, and 82.
243. *Ancient Charters*, ed. J. H. Round, Pipe Roll Soc., vol. x, pp. 39–40.
244. *Anglo-Saxon Charters*, ed. J. Robertson, Cambridge, 1939, p. 137: 'The king sent his seal to the meeting at Cuckhamsley (Scutchamore Knob) and greeted all the wise men assembled there.'
245. *The Antiquities of Nottinghamshire*, by Robert Thoroton, Doctor of Physic, London, 1677, p. 71.

246. *Bracton's Note-Book*, ed. F. W. Maitland, case 1730, vol. iii, pp. 565–7.
247. *Chronicon Petroburgense*, ed. T. Stapleton, Camden Soc., 1849.
248. *Ibid.*, pp. 161–2.
249. *Ibid.*, p. 159.
250. *Ibid.*, p. 159.
251. *Ibid.*, p. 164.
252. B.M. Harl. MS 61.
253. *Ibid.*, ff. 50 and 53.
254. *Curia Regis Rolls*, vol. vii, pp. 60–61.
255. B.M. Harl. MS 3688, f. 64.
256. B.M. Harl. MS 1708, f. 63.
257. *Rolls of the Justices in Eyre for . . . Worcestershire*, Selden Soc., vol. liii, pp. 56–7.
258. *Earliest Lincolnshire Assize Rolls*, cases 423 and 279.
259. *Earliest Northamptonshire Assize Rolls*, pp. 134–5.
260. *Rolls of the Justices in Eyre for Lincolnshire*, Selden Soc., liii, pp. 385–7.
261. *Earliest Northamptonshire Assize Rolls*, pp. 65–6.
262. *Rolls of the Justices in Eyre for . . . Shropshire*, Selden Soc., vol. lix, p. 533.
263. *Rolls of the Justices in Eyre for . . . Worcestershire*, Selden Soc., vol. liii, pp. 584–5.
264. *Ibid.*, p. 584.
265. *Ibid.*, 582.
266. Assize Roll 36, mem. 7.
267. *Facsimiles of Early Charters from Northamptonshire Collections*, ed. F. M. Stenton, Northants Record Soc., vol. iv, pp. 1–7 and frontispiece.
268. B.M. Canons Ashby Cartulary, Egerton 3033, f. 204.
269. F. M. Stenton, 'Early Manumissions at Staunton, Nottinghamshire,' *Eng. Hist. Rev.*, vol. xxvi, pp. 13–17.
270. *Glanville*, ed. Woodbine, pp. 86–7.
271. *Ibid.*, p. 87.
272. Bracton, f. 194b.
273. F. W. Maitland, *History of English Law*, vol. i, pp. 423–4.
274. B.M. Harl. MS 2110, f. 77.
275. B.M. Harl. MS 1708, f. 226b–230b.
276. For distraint in both its legal and personal aspects, see T. F. T. Plucknett, *The Legislation of Edward I*, Oxford, 1949, Index *sub voce* distress.
277. A very good example is the family of Galle of Saltfleetby, Lincs, whose fortunes can be traced through the latter part of the twelfth century and on to the middle of the thirteenth. By adding acre to acre from generation to generation the head of the family had become 'Sir Philip Galle'. The family fortunes can be traced in many charters surviving in the P.R.O.
278. See the Chapter ix, 'Personal Names in Place-Names', by F. M. Stenton, *English Place Name Society*, vol. i, part 1, Cambridge, 1924.

279. *Anglo-Saxon England*, p. 528. For the borough as a minting place in pre-Conquest days see pp. 527–30.

280. J. E. Jolliffe, 'The Chamber and Castle Treasures under King John', in *Essays Presented to F. M. Powicke*, Oxford, 1948, pp. 117–42.

281. Tout, *Chapters*, vol. i, p. 268, for the sending of money abroad to the king.

282. S. Smith, Introduction to Pipe Roll 7 John, pp. xxvii–xxxii.

283. *Catalogue of English Coins in the British Museum*, vols. i and ii. See also G. C. Brooke, *English Coins*, 2nd ed., Methuen, and articles in recent numbers of the *British Numismatic Journal*. See also 'Coinage', by R. H. M. Dolley, *Medieval England*, ed. A. L. Poole, Oxford, 1958, vol. i, pp. 264–86. But the only way to realize the importance of coins is to handle them.

284. P. Grierson 'Sterling', in *Anglo-Saxon Coins*, London, 1960.

285. F. Elmore Jones, 'Stephen Type VI', *British Numismatic Journal*, vol. xxviii, pp. 537–54.

286. For a series of discussions of the chief problems in the history of the origins of English boroughs, see J. Tait, *The Medieval English Borough*, Manchester, 1936.

287. E.g. 'soca Willelmi de Moiun', Pipe Roll 3 John, p. 261, and in other Pipe Rolls under London and Middlesex.

288. E.g. Stafford.

289. *Anglo-Saxon England*, p. 530.

290. *Visitations and Memorials of Southwell Minster*, Camden Series, 1891, p. 192.

291. *Facsimiles of Early Charters*, Northants Record Soc., vol. iv, pp. 128–9.

292. F. M. Stenton, *Norman London*, 3rd ed., in *Social Life in Early England*, ed. G. Barraclough, 1960, and *Anglo-Saxon England*, 531–3.

293. Pipe Roll 31 Henry I, ed. J. Hunter, p. 114.

294. *Ibid.*, p. 148.

295. For the attitude of Brian fitz Count to the political situation of the day, see his own letter to Henry of Blois, bishop of Winchester, printed with introduction by H. W. C. Davis, *Eng. Hist. Rev.*, vol. xxv, 1910, pp. 297–303.

296. Pipe Roll 2 Richard I, p. xxi.

297. 'Communa est tumor plebis, timor regni, tepor sacerdotii', Richard of Devizes, recording the establishment of the commune of London in 1191, *De rebus gestis Ricardi primi*, ed. J. Stevenson, Eng. Hist. Soc., 1838, p. 54.

298. For a map of twelfth-century London by M. Honeybourne see *Norman London*, by F. M. Stenton, Hist. Ass. Tracts, 2nd ed., 1934.

299. Tait, *op cit.*, p. 161.

300. Tait, *op. cit.*, pp. 176–7.

301. Sir Francis Hill, *Medieval Lincoln*, pp. 294–5.

302. Translated by H. E. Butler and printed, *Norman London*, 2nd ed.

303. *Anglo-Saxon England*, pp. 350–51, 519–20.

304. *Records of the Borough of Leicester*, ed. M. Bateson, Cambridge, 3 vols., 1899–1905. Only the first vol. concerns this period. See the account of the Merchant Gild in the Introduction, pp. xxvii–xxxviii and references.

305. *Pleas of the Justices in Eyre for … Worcestershire*, Selden Soc., vol. liii, pp. 567–9.

306. *Ibid., loc. cit.*

307. *Leicester Records*, vol. i, pp. xxviii–xxxix.

308. F. Consitt, *The London Weavers' Company*, Oxford, 1933, pp. 1–6.

309. Pipe Roll 26 Henry II, pp. 71–2.

310. *Ibid.*, pp. 95 and 93.

311. *Ibid.*, pp. 93–4.

312. *Ibid.*, p. 97.

313. *Ibid.*, p. 109.

314. *Ibid.*, p. 111.

315. *Ibid.*, p. 93.

316. *Ibid.*, pp. 153–4.

317. Pipe Roll 10 John, p. 166.

318. *Earliest Lincolnshire Assize Rolls*, p. 261, case 448. From the point of view of the development of the city government it is, as Sir Francis Hill implies (*Medieval Lincoln*, p. 294), even more interesting that a body of 24 citizens were associated with the mayor in making this sworn pact with the king's judges.

319. Pipe Roll 10 John, pp. 167–9.

320. Tait, *op. cit.*, pp. 154–5.

321. Tait, *op. cit.*, pp. 350–52.

322. Tait, *op. cit.*, pp. 197–201, where the references to the charters mentioned here will be found.

323. Tait, *op. cit.*, p. 352.

324. R. H. Gretton, *The Burford Records*, Oxford, 1920.

325. *Earliest Northamptonshire Assize Rolls*, pp. 3 *bis* and 9.

326. Roger of Howden, vol. iv, p. 172.

327. Tait, *op. cit.*, pp. 205–6 and 356–7.

328. M. McKisack, *The Parliamentary Representation of English Boroughs in the Middle Ages*, Oxford, 1932.

329. For Oxford markets, and the markets of neighbouring towns, see Salter, *Medieval Oxford*, 1936, pp. 77–8.

330. Salter, *op. cit.*, p. 82.

331. Michael Adler, *The Jews in Medieval England*, pp. 127 ff.

332. For William Cade of London see Hilary Jenkinson in *Eng. Hist. Rev.*, vol. xxviii, 1913, pp. 209–27, and in *Essays presented to R. L. Poole*, Oxford, 1927, pp. 190–210. For Gervase of Southampton see Pipe Roll 4 John, pp. xxi–xxii.

333. See above note 40.

334. Pipe Roll 31 Henry I, ed. J. Hunter, p. 149.

335. *The Life and Miracles of St William of Norwich*, ed. A. Jessup and M. R. James, Cambridge, 1896, with a valuable introduction.

336. Pipe Rolls 3 and 4 Richard I, p. xiv, 135, etc.

337. Pipe Roll 10 John, pp. xix, xx. *Rotuli de Oblatis et finibus*, pp. 420 and 436.

338. William of Newburgh, Eng. Hist. Soc., vol. ii. p. 18.

339. Roger of Howden, vol. iii, pp. 266–7.

340. Michael Adler, *op. cit.*, pp. 137–9.

341. For the facts quoted about Aaron of York see Michael Adler, *op. cit.*, pp. 127 ff.

342. *Select Cases of Procedure without Writ under Henry III*, ed. H. G. Richardson and G. O. Sayles, Selden Soc., vol. lx, p. 21.

343. Cecil Roth, 'The Intellectual Activities of the English Jewry', *British Academy, Supplementary Papers*, No. viii.

344. M. Adler, *op. cit.*, 'The Jewish Woman', pp. 23–4.

345. M. Adler, *op. cit.*, 'The History of the Domus Conversorum', pp. 279 ff.

346. Quoted by Sir Francis Hill, *op. cit.*, p. 177.

347. *Ibid.*, pp. 173–4.

348. *Ibid.*, p. 173.

349. Pipe Roll 6 John, pp. xliv–xlv.

350. *Ibid.*, p. 99.

351. J. H. Round, *King's Serjeants*, 'The Keeper of the Falcons', pp. 310–17.

352. *Rolls before the King and his Justices*, vol. iii; Selden Society, vol. lxxxiii, Case 2913. *Rolls of the Justices in Eyre for Lincolnshire*, Selden Soc., vol. liii, pp. lxxix and 264.

353. Pipe Roll 6 John, pp. xliii–xlv.

354. *Anglo-Saxon England*, pp. 148–9, 155–6.

355. The frequent association of church and mill in Domesday Book among the lord's valuable appurtenances to a manor well illustrates this attitude. It is expressed equally clearly in a charter granted by Robert de Caux to Thurgarton priory about 1150. He gave a mill on the Doverbeck, Notts, to be held by the brethren of Thurgarton 'until I shall give them a church or something else which would be more useful to them'. Southwell Minster, Thurgarton Cartulary, f. 54.

356. B.M. Lansdowne MS 207 A 304. The six parts are set out from this MS in *Danelaw Charters*, p. lxxv.

357. *Danelaw Charters*, pp. lxx–lxxi, 342.

358. *Rolls of the Justices in Eyre in Yorkshire*, Selden Soc., vol. lvi, p. lii, where the references to all these cases are set out.

359. B.M. Egerton MS 3031, f. 55.

360. F. M. Stenton, 'Acta Episcoporum, *Cambridge Hist. Journ.*, vol. iii, pp. 12–13.

361. Stubbs, *Charters*, p. 164.

362. *The Life of Wulfric of Haselbury by John Abbot of Ford*, ed. Dom Maurice Bell, Somerset Record Soc., 1933, vol. xlvii, with a valuable introduction and notes.

363. *Life*, pp. 30–31.
364. *Ibid.*, pp. 28–9.
365. *Ibid.*, p. 109.
366. *Ibid.*, pp. xxviii–xxxiii, where references to the appropriate chapters in the *Life* are given.
367. *Ibid.*, pp. 38, 105, 110.
368. *Ibid.*, pp. 44–5.
369. *Ibid.*, pp. 13–14.
370. *Ibid.*, p. 15.
371. *Ibid.*, pp. 22–3.
372. This boy, Walter of Glastonbury, was one of the chief sources of information about Wulfric's life, *ibid.*, pp. xxii–xxiii.
373. *Ibid.*, p. 56.
374. *Ibid.*, pp. 63–4.
375. *Ibid.*, p. 108.
376. *Earliest Northamptonshire Assize Rolls*, p. 70.
377. *Earliest Lincolnshire Assize Rolls*, p. 248.
378. *Ibid.*, p. 8.
379. For the ordinance of William I separating lay and ecclesiastical justice see *Registrum Antiquissimum of Lincoln Cathedral*, ed. C. W. Foster, vol. i, pp. 1–2, with note referring to the copy laid up at St Paul's.
380. *Anglo-Saxon England*, pp. 653–4.
381. Quoted from the Chronicle of Battle Abbey by M. D. Knowles, *The Monastic Order in England*, Cambridge, 1941, p. 598.
382. An early twelfth-century definition of tithe runs: 'in messe . et uitulis . in agnis . in porcis . in caseis . et in omnibus que decimari debent more catholico'. *Facsimiles of Charters in the B.M.*, ed. G. F. Warner and H. J. Ellis, 1903, pl. xii, No. 17.
383. Bishop Nicholas of Llandaff (1148–83) confirmed churches to Tewkesbury abbey on condition that when they fell vacant vicars with a reasonable income should be instituted. Quoted by M. D. Knowles, *op. cit.*, p. 600.
384. Alexander III had put out a similar canon in the third Lateran Council of 1179.
385. *Liber Antiquus Hugonis Wells*, ed. A. Gibbons, privately printed, Lincoln, 1888, pp. 1–2, and *Rotuli Hugonis de Welles*, Lincoln Record Soc., vol. iii, pp. 179–80.
386. *Rotuli Hugonis de Welles*, p. 252. Breedon Church belonged not to monks, but to the canons of Nostell priory, Yorks. They kept 5 canons at Breedon and a vicar.
387. *Ibid.*, p. 87.
388. *Ibid.*, p. 79.
389. *Ibid.*, p. 19.
390. *Ibid.*, p. 39.
391. *Ibid.*, p. 101.
392. *Ibid.*, p. 50.
393. *Ibid.*, p. 50.

394. Matthew Paris, vol. v, p. 300.

395. *Ibid.*, pp. 389 *et seq.*

396. Roger of Howden, vol. iv, pp. 130–31.

397. *Eynsham Cartulary*, ed. H. E. Salter, vol. i, Appendix II, on 'Pente-costals or Smoke-farthings', pp. 424–30.

398. *Eynsham Cartulary*, vol. i, p. 37, This was confirmed by the papal legate in 1138, p. 66.

399. *Ibid.*, pp. 39–40.

400. *Ibid.*, p. 38.

401. Quoted from the White Book of Southwell by A. F. Leach, *Visitations and Memorials of Southwell Minster*, Camden Series, 1891, p. xv,

402. B.M. Egerton MS 3031, f. 57b.

403. B.M. Additional Charter 19589.

404. B.M. Additional Charter 19598.

405. The list of indulgences granted to those who visited Reading on the feasts of St Philip or St James or both, or on the day of the dedication of the church, include the names of bishops from all parts of the British Isles and some from abroad as well, Harl. MS 1708, ff. 186b–187b.

406. Roger of Howden, vol. iv, p. 166, see also the great bull of 1199, *ibid.*, p. 111.

407. *Lincoln Cathedral Statutes*, ed. Bradshaw and Wordsworth, 3 vols., is a great quarry of material for other churches as well as Lincoln, but is not easy to use. The best account of cathedrals, collegiate churches, and chapters in the later middle ages is *The English Clergy* by H. Hamilton Thompson, chapter iii, pp. 72 ff.

408. *Registrum Antiquissimum of Lincoln Cathedral*, begun by C. W. Foster and continued by K. Major.

409. *Red Book*, vol. i, pp. 374–6.

410. *Registrum Antiquissimum*, vol. i, p. 34.

411. Sir Francis Hill, *Medieval Lincoln*, pp. 117–20.

412. *Ibid.*, pp. 120–21.

413. Roger of Howden, vol. iii, pp. 31–2.

414. *Pleas of the Justices in Eyre for . . . Worcestershire*, Selden Soc., vol. liii, pp. 274–5.

415. *Visitations and Memorials of Southwell Minster*, pp. xxx–xxxi.

416. Bradshaw and Wordsworth, vol. ii, where the 'Institutio Osmundi' is printed pp. 7–10.

417. *Henry of Huntingdon*, ed. T. Arnold, Rolls Series, pp. 302–3.

418. Bradshaw and Wordsworth, vol. ii, pp. 144–6.

419. *Visitations and Memorials of Southwell Minster*, p. xlv, where, having discussed non-residence at Southwell, the editor collects evidence from other churches.

420. For the subject matter of this section see M. D. Knowles, *The Monastic Order in England* and *The Religious Orders in England*.

421. For the charters of five of these Gilbertine houses in Lincolnshire,

see *Transcripts of Charters relating to Gilbertine Houses*, ed. F. M. Stenton, Lincoln Record Soc., vol. xviii, 1922.

422. Anglo-Saxon Chronicle *sub anno* 1123.

423. Roger of Howden, vol. iv, p. 240.

424. *Annales Monastici* (Dunstable), vol. iii, p. 88.

425. B.M. Harl. MS 1708, f. 91.

426. *Liber de Antiquis Legibus*, ed. Stapleton, Camden Series, 1846, pp. 206–11, and *Munimenta Gildhallae Londoniensis, Liber Albus*, ed. Riley, Rolls Series, vol. i, pp. xxx–xxxii and pp. 329–32.

427. *Liber Albus*, vol. i, p. xxxii.

428. *Earliest Lincolnshire Assize Rolls*, p. 108.

429. *Select Pleas of the Crown*, Selden Soc., vol. i, pp. 63–4.

430. *Earliest Lincolnshire Assize Rolls*, pp. 98–9.

431. *Pleas before the King or his Justices*, Selden Soc., vol. lxviii, pp. 60–61.

432. *Select Pleas of the Crown*, Selden Soc., vol. i, p. 121.

433. For a series of contemporary drawings illustrating English dress see 'Pictures of English Dress in the Thirteenth Century', *Ancestor*, vol. v, pp. 99–137. For the dress worn by great ladies their seals are the best evidence. Women's seals were vesica-shaped, so that the owner could be shown full length; sometimes she held a flower in one hand and a hawk on her other wrist; sometimes she held up shields of arms. The hangings from the wrists are thus shown. D. M. Stenton, *The English Woman in History*, London, 1957. Chapter II is illustrated by a plate of women's seals.

434. For king John's necklace see *Rotuli de Liberate etc.*, p. 23. John had lost his necklace of precious stones, which were, as he says, 'freely and faithfully' returned to him by the finder, a certain Bartholomew. The king instructed the Justiciar to see that Bartholomew was rewarded by an annual rent of 20 shillings in Berkhampstead where he was born.

435. *Rotuli de . . . Misis*, p. 151.

436. *Select Pleas of the Crown*, Selden Soc., vol. i, p. 92.

437. *Medieval England*, 'Recreations', by A. L. Poole, vol. ii, p. 613.

438. Roger of Howden, vol. iii, pp. 245–6.

439. *Rolls of the Justices in Eyre for . . . Worcestershire*, Selden Soc., vol. liii, pp. 484–5.

440. For the latter see J. Goronwy Edwards, 'Edward I's Castle-Building in Wales', *Proceedings of the British Academy*, vol. xxxii, 1946, pp. 15–81.

441. For all the references in this para., and some in the next, and a survey of English roads in this period, see F. M. Stenton 'The Road-system of Medieval England', *Economic Hist. Rev.*, vol. vii, pp. 1–21. See also *Medieval England*, ed. A. L. Poole, Oxford, 1958, vol. i, 'Communications'.

442. 'The royal way called Linnegat', *Book of Seats*, p. 229. 'The royal way called le Westrete', *ibid.*, p. 278.

443. For a good list of purprestures or encroachments presented to the

itinerant Justices, see *Pleas of the Justices in Eyre for ... Worcestershire*, Selden Soc., vol. liii, pp. 606–7.

444. *Public Works in Medieval Law*, vol. i, ed. C. T. Flower, Selden Soc., vol. xxxii, p. xxiii.

445. *Ibid.*, vol. ii, Selden Soc., vol. xl, p. xlv.

446. *Ibid.*, vol. i, Selden Soc., vol. xxxii, pp. 203–4.

447. For references see *ibid.*, p. xxv.

448. *Rolls of the Justices in Eyre for Gloucestershire etc.*, Selden Soc., vol. lix, pp. 562–3.

449. *Public Works*, vol. i, p. 262. A bridge between Lincoln and Brant Broughton was first made by a hermit after 'the first pestilence', who set a plank across a ford in the midst of the causey. *Ibid.*, vol. ii, p. 217: a bridge at Stoneleigh, Warwick, was first built by a hermit out of alms.

450. *Annales Monastici* (Waverley), vol. i, p. 240.

451. *Rot. Litt. Pat.*, p. 9.

452. *Annales Monastici* (Waverley), vol. i, p. 268.

453. *Annales Monastici* (Worcester), vol. iv, p. 483.

454. See F. M. Stenton's article on roads quoted in note 441. This map has now been reproduced in colour by the Bodleian Library.

455. For the University of Oxford in the middle ages see the chapter 'The University' in H. E. Salter's *Medieval Oxford*, Oxford, 1936. Mr Salter knew Oxford as only one who has spent a lifetime on its records can know a town, and in this book he sets out with simplicity and grace his garnered knowledge.

456. M. Bateson, 'The Huntingdon Song School and the School of St Gregory's, Canterbury', *Eng. Hist. Rev.*, vol. xviii, 1903, pp. 712–13.

457. *Orderici Vitalis Historiae*, ed. le Prevost, vol. ii, pp. 302 and 419–20, and vol. v, p. 134.

458. M. Bateson, *loc. cit.*

459. *Early Charter of St Paul's Cathedral*, ed. M. Gibbs, Camden Series, vol. lviii, p. 217.

460. *Ibid.*, pp. 215–16.

461. F. M. Stenton, *Norman London*, 3rd ed., p. 203.

462. *The Liber Pauperum of Vacarius*, ed. F. de Zulueta, Selden Soc., vol. xliv, pp. xiii–xxiii.

463. The number of students at Oxford had sunk to about 1000 by the middle of the fourteenth century, Salter, *op. cit.*, p. 110.

464. For the English universities in the middle ages, see *The Universities of Europe in the Middle Ages*, by the late Hastings Rashdall, new ed. by F. M. Powicke and A. B. Emden, vol. iii.

465. *Royal and other Historical Letters*, ed. W. W. Shirley, Rolls Series, 1862, vol. i, letters cccxxiv and cccxxvi.

466. *Henry III and the Lord Edward*, Oxford, 1947, vol. i, p. 134.

467. *Close Rolls 1234–1237*, p. 26.

468. *Royal Letters*, vol. i, No. cccxxv.

469. Salter, *op. cit.*, pp. 93–4.

470. For the flowering of English medieval architecture in this period, see A. W. Clapham, *English Romanesque Architecture*. Vol. ii deals with the post-Conquest period, Oxford, 1934.

471. *Visitations and Memorials of Southwell Minster*, p. xvi.

472. *Ibid., loc. cit.*

473. *Early Middle English Texts*, ed. B. Dickins and R. Wilson, p. 2, where is printed a Worcester fragment which recalls the great English scholars of the past and laments the present forgetfulness of their lore and the forlornness of the people.

474. *The Peterborough Chronicler 1070–1154*, ed. Cecily Clark; see particularly her section 'Literary Aspects', pp. lxvi–lxx.

475. *Anglo-Saxon England*, p. 669, note.

476. *Dialogus*, p. 53.

477. *Orderici Vitalis Historiae*, ed. le Prévost, vol. v, p. 135.

478. *De gestis Regum Anglorum Willelmi monachi Malmesbiriensis*, ed. Stubbs, Rolls Series, 1887, vol. i, *Prologus*, pp. 1–3.

479. D. M. Stenton, 'Roger of Howden and *Benedict*', *English Historical Review*, vol. lxviii, 1953, pp. 574–82.

480. See the articles by Sir John Fox, *Eng. Hist. Rev.*, vol. xxv, p. 303, and xxvi, p. 317.

481. For an account of and extracts from all these and other English writings see *Early Middle English Texts*, cited above.

482. *Norman London*, 3rd ed., p. 205.

483. Stubbs, *Charters*, p. 374, No. 6.

FURTHER READING

FURTHER READING

A COMPREHENSIVE survey of this period is given in three volumes of the Oxford History of England: *Anglo-Saxon England* by Sir Frank Stenton covers the period up to 1087, the death of William the Conqueror, 2nd ed., 1947. A. L. Poole's *From Domesday Book to Magna Carta*, 2nd ed., 1955, and F. M. Powicke's *The Thirteenth Century*, 1953, cover the rest of the period of this book. Each volume of the Oxford History contains a full bibliography. Miss Kate Norgate's books, although coming from a past generation, still retain much of their freshness today. *England under the Angevin Kings*, 2 volumes, 1887; *Richard the Lion Heart*, 1924; *John Lackland*, 1902; and *The Minority of Henry III*, 1912, are an impressive achievement. *Richard the Lion Heart* is the least good, for although its facts are generally reliable, it shows too great a sympathy with an irresponsible king. *Henry III and the Lord Edward*, Oxford, 1947, by F. M. Powicke gives a satisfying and leisurely picture of England in the thirteenth century seen through the mind of a great medieval scholar. Apart from their main subject matter Professor M. D. Knowles's two volumes, *The Monastic Order in England*, Cambridge, 1941, and *The Religious Orders in England*, Cambridge, 1948, form a great survey of a long stretch of history. Reference should also be made to H. M. Colvin's learned and penetrating study of the Premonstratensian order in England, *The White Canons in England*, Oxford, 1951.

The twelfth century has attracted much interest in recent generations. Stubbs's great editions of contemporary chronicles in the Rolls Series, Maitland's classic treatment of English law, F. Pollock and F. W. Maitland, *The History of English Law before the Time of Edward I*, 2nd ed., Cambridge, 1898, and J. H. Round's seminal essays on feudal genealogy, *Feudal England*, London, 1895; *Geoffrey de Mandeville*, London, 1892; *The Commune of London*, Westminster, 1899; *Studies in Peerage and Family History*, Westminster, 1901, set historians at work, and still inspire them today.

The First Century of English Feudalism, Oxford, 1932, 2nd ed., 1961, by Sir Frank Stenton is a reconstruction of feudal society from the evidence of contemporary charters. *Obligations of Society in the Twelfth and Thirteenth Centuries*, by A. L. Poole, Oxford, 1946, from the evidence of Pipe rolls, the rolls of the courts of justice, and other original documents discusses the burdens which fell on the tenants of land in this period. *The Exchequer in the Twelfth Century*, by R. L. Poole, Oxford, 1912, describes the origin and the working of that great institution. An English translation of the contemporary description of the Exchequer written by the Treasurer Richard fitz Nigel before 1179 can be read in *The Course of the Exchequer*, Nelson's Medieval Classics, 1950. The translator and editor is Charles Johnson, who has added also a translation and commentary on the description of the royal household written early in Stephen's reign.

F. M. Powicke's *Stephen Langton*, Oxford, 1928, is a penetrating study of the archbishop who was the cause of John's quarrel with the Pope. It contains also a chapter on Magna Carta which is indispensable for the understanding of that document. The first two volumes of Professor T. F. Tout's monumental work *Chapters in the Administrative History of Medieval England*, Manchester, 1920, deal with the period covered by this book. In *Seignorial Administration in England*, Oxford, 1937, Mr N. Denholm-Young shows how closely the administration of great estates corresponded to that of the kingdom. The development of the English common law and a permanent judiciary is traced in *English Justice 1066-1215* by D. M. Stenton, Philadelphia, 1964. Professor T. F. T. Plucknett's *Legislation of Edward I*, Oxford, 1949, throws a searchlight over a vast field by relating the formidable statutes of a great age of legislation to the life of the common man. *Rural England 1086-1135*, Oxford, 1959, by Reginald Lennard makes a detailed survey of rural conditions in the first generations after the Norman Conquest. In *The Royal Demesne in English Constitutional History 1066-1272*, Cornell, 1950, Professor R. S. Hoyt reviews the position of the men on land which belonged to the crown at the time of Domesday Book. Professor H. C. Darby has undertaken the heavy task of examining Domesday Book from the standpoint of the geographer. Four volumes of this work have appeared: *The Domesday Geography of Eastern England* by H. C. Darby, Cambridge, 1952, and *The Domesday Geography of Midland England* by H. C. Darby and I. B. Terrett, Cambridge, 1954, *The Domesday Geography of South-East England* by H. C. Darby and Eila N. J. Campbell, Cambridge, 1962, and *The Domesday Geography of Northern England* by H. C. Darby and I. S. Maxwell, Cambridge, 1962. V. H. Galbraith, *The Making of Domesday Book*, Clarendon Press, 1961, is the latest contribution to the perennial discussion of this subject. It is unlikely to be the last. Avrom Saltman, *Theobald Archbishop of Canterbury*, Athlone Press, 1956, illustrates the way in which the archbishop used his authority to protect the Church during the anarchy of Stephen's reign and the restoration of royal authority which followed. Two recent books on King John can be recommended: *The Reign of King John* by Sidney Painter, Johns Hopkins Press, Baltimore, 1949, and *King John* by W. L. Warren, London, 1961. J. C. Holt's *The Northerners*, Clarendon Press, Oxford, 1961, is a book of prime importance for the events leading to the issue of Magna

Carta in 1215. The same author's *Magna Carta*, Cambridge University Press, 1965, is a judicious account of the making and importance of the Charter. It will be the standard work for generations. The position of English women through the history of England down to 1869 is discussed in *The English Woman in History* by D. M. Stenton, London, 1957. The first three chapters concern the women of the Middle Ages.

Three King Penguins should be referred to: *Heraldry in England* by Anthony Wagner, *The Bayeux Tapestry* by Eric Maclagan, and *The Leaves of Southwell* by F. L. Attenborough. A definitive edition of the Bayeux Tapestry has been produced by the Phaidon Press, ed. Frank M. Stenton, 1957. For the literature of the period the best introduction is still W. P. Ker, *English Literature: Medieval*, Home University Library, and *Epic and Romance*, London, 1908. *Early Middle English Texts*, ed. Bruce Dickins and R. M. Wilson, Bowes and Bowes, Cambridge, 1950, gives 'the student and, indeed, the general reader . . . a good idea of the varied merits of the literature of an unduly neglected period'.

Medieval Lincoln by Sir Francis Hill, Cambridge, 1948, with illustrations, is the best history of a medieval English city. *Medieval Oxford* by H. E. Salter, Oxford, 1936, traces on equal terms the rise of the city and the University, see note 455 on page 297. *The Medieval English Borough* by James Tait, Manchester, 1936, is a definitive account of the early history of English towns. In *The Medieval Coroner*, Cambridge, 1961, R. F. Hunnisett has written an excellent account of the early history of an important office which still survives today.

No attempt has been made in this list of books for further reading to set out the many editions of documents and contemporary writings on which the history of the period is ultimately founded. Readers who are sufficiently interested will find references to many such works in the notes printed on pp. 281–98. One particularly valuable series which is often overlooked is the British Academy Records of Social and Economic History begun by Sir Paul Vinogradoff. Vol. v, *Danelaw Charters*, 1920, ed. F. M. Stenton, has been much used in writing this book. The Introduction reconstructs the rural society of the Danelaw in the twelfth century from the evidence of the many charters surviving from this period. A selection of sources can be consulted in translation in *English Historical Documents*, vol. ii, 1042–1189, ed. D. C. Douglas and G. W. Greenaway, London, 1953.

A SELECT LIST OF
ESSENTIAL DATES

A SELECT LIST OF ESSENTIAL DATES

1066, 14 October	Battle of Hastings
1066, Christmas Day	Coronation of William I
1069–70, Winter	Devastation of the North
1085, Christmas	Domesday Inquest ordered
1086	Domesday Inquest carried through
1086, 1 August	Oath of Salisbury
1087	Death of William I and accession of his son William II
1097	First Crusade
1100	Death of William II and accession of his brother Henry I
1102	Rebellion of Robert of Bellesme
1106	Battle of Tenchebrai
1110	Marriage of Maud daughter of Henry I to Henry V Emperor of Germany
1120	Death of William, heir of Henry I, in the wreck of the White Ship
1126	Return of the Empress (widowed 1125) to England
1127	Marriage of the Empress to Geoffrey count of Anjou
1130	Earliest surviving Pipe Roll
1135	Death of Henry I. Stephen, his nephew, succeeds him
1139	Maud the Empress comes to England and civil war begins
1153	Death of Eustace eldest son of Stephen
1154	Death of Stephen and accession of Henry II
1159	War in Toulouse
1164	Constitutions of Clarendon and flight of archbishop Thomas Becket
1166	Assize of Clarendon
1170	Inquest of sheriffs
1170, Christmas	Murder of archbishop Thomas Becket
1173–4	Rebellion of Henry II's sons
1176	Assize of Northampton
1180	Accession of Philip II to French throne
1181	Assize of Arms
1187	Fall of Jerusalem
1189	Death of Henry II and accession of Richard I
1190–91	Richard winters at Messina
1193, January	News of Richard's captivity

1194	Return of Richard to England and his departure to defend Normandy from French attack
1199	Death of Richard and accession of John, his brother
1204	Loss of Normandy
1205	Death of Hubert Walter, archbishop of Canterbury
1205	Issue of new coinage
1207	Consecration of Stephen Langton archbishop of Canterbury at Rome
1208	England placed under Interdict by the pope
1213	John receives Stephen Langton as archbishop of Canterbury and agrees to hold England and Ireland of the pope
1215, 15 June	Issue of the Great Charter
1216, May	Louis heir of France comes to England at the invitation of the rebellious barons
1216, 18 October	Death of king John
1216, 28 October	Coronation of Henry III
1216, 12 November	1st reissue of the Great Charter
1217, 12 September	Treaty of Kingston ends the war
1217, Sept.–Nov.	2nd reissue of the Great Charter
1217, 6 November	Issue of the Forest Charter
1219, 14 May	Death of William Marshal earl of Pembroke and regent for Henry III
1225, 11 February	3rd reissue of the Great Charter
1232	Fall of Hubert de Burgh earl of Kent and Justiciar
1234	Fall of the Poitevins
1236	Marriage of Henry III and Eleanor of Provence
1247	Issue of new coinage
1258	Provisions of Oxford and the beginning of the Barons' Revolt
1259	Provisions of Westminster
1264, 14 May	Battle of Lewes
1265	Simon de Montfort's Model Parliament
1265, 4 August	Battle of Evesham and death of Simon de Montfort
1266, 31 October	Fall of Kenilworth Castle
1267	Statute of Marlborough
1272	Death of Henry III and accession of Edward I
1275	First Statute of Westminster
1279	Household Ordinances and New Coinage
1285	Second Statute of Westminster
1290	Expulsion of the Jews
1295	Model Parliament
1307	Death of Edward I

INDEX